Catholicism:
Now
I Get It!

Catholicism: Now I Get It!

Claire Furia Smith

Our Sunday Visitor Publishing Division
Our Sunday Visitor, Inc.
Huntington, Indiana 46750

Nihil Obstat:
Rev. Msgr. Joseph J. Anderlonis, S.T.D., Censor Librorum

Imprimatur: ✠ Justin Cardinal Rigali
Archbishop of Philadelphia
October 19, 2005

The Scripture citations used in this work are taken from the *Catholic Edition of the Revised Standard Version of the Bible* (RSV), copyright © 1965 and 1966 by the Division of Christian Education of the National Council of the Churches of Christ in the United States of America. Used by permission. All rights reserved.

Catechism excerpts are from the English translation of the *Catechism of the Catholic Church, Second Edition,* for use in the United States of America, copyright © 1994 and 1997, United States Catholic Conference — Libreria Editrice Vaticana. Used by permission. All rights reserved.

Every reasonable effort has been made to determine copyright holders of excerpted materials and to secure permissions as needed. If any copyrighted materials have been inadvertently used in this work without proper credit being given in one form or another, please notify Our Sunday Visitor in writing so that future printings of this work may be corrected accordingly.

Our Sunday Visitor Publishing Division
Our Sunday Visitor, Inc.
200 Noll Plaza
Huntington, IN 46750

ISBN-13: 978-1-59276-152-4
ISBN-10: 1-59276-152-6 (Inventory No. T203)
LCCN: 2005926032

Cover design by Amanda Miller
Interior design by Sherri L. Hoffman
Back cover photography by Mark James

PRINTED IN THE UNITED STATES OF AMERICA

"You are Peter, and on this rock I will build my church, and the powers of death shall not prevail against it. I will give you the keys of the kingdom of Heaven, and whatever you bind on earth shall be bound in Heaven, and whatever you loose on earth shall be loosed in Heaven."

— Jesus

✝

The Catholic Church is the work of Divine Providence, achieved through the prophecies of the prophets, through the Incarnation and the teaching of Christ, through the journeys of the Apostles, through the suffering, the crosses, the blood and death of the martyrs, through the admirable lives of the saints. . . .When, then, we see so much help on God's part, so much progress and so much fruit, shall we hesitate to bury ourselves in the bosom of that Church? For starting from the apostolic chair down through successions of bishops, even unto the open confession of all mankind, it has possessed the crown of teaching authority.

— St. Augustine

✝

To be truly free means having the strength to choose the One for whom we were created and accepting his lordship over our lives. You perceive it in the depths of your heart: all that is good on earth, all professional success, even the human love that you dream of, can never fully satisfy your deepest and most intimate desires. Only an encounter with Jesus can give full meaning to your lives. . . .Do not let yourselves be distracted from this search. Persevere in it because it is your fulfillment and your joy that is at stake.

— Pope John Paul II

✝

*This book is dedicated to Caroline and David A. Poirier
and Anna, Oliver, Charlotte, and Daisy Jones.*

ACKNOWLEDGMENTS

✝

Many thanks to the Rev. Robert A. Pesarchick of St. Charles Borromeo Seminary in Wynnewood, PA, for reviewing my manuscript.

Thanks also to OSV project editor Janet W. Butler for her sharp eye and stores of wisdom; to Frederick A. Furia, Jr., for early editing on this project; and to author Michael Dubruiel for giving me this opportunity.

I am also obliged to the following individuals who generously offered helpful suggestions during the preparation of this book:

Eileen Witczak Watson, Joseph Martino,
Karen Poirier, Dann Furia, Ann Burrows,
Maria Minniti, Colleen T. Hoffman, Patty Hopkins,
Maryanne Furia, Maria Miele Boyd,
and the Dzwonczyk family.

Special thanks to Kevin Knight, the individual who I have learned was the driving force in getting the thousands of articles of the 1913 *Catholic Encyclopedia* (www.newadvent.org) published online.

Thanks to Grace Burrows for being my godmother.

Finally, thanks to my parents, Claire and Fred, for sending me to Catholic school.

I love you, Bill.

CONTENTS

✝

INTRODUCTION

✝

What you hold in your hands is the kind of book I wish I had received during my college days, or very soon thereafter. Although I sat through religion class for twelve years — despite having well-intentioned teachers, including many hardworking nuns — I just didn't "get it" until much later. Without nuns and priests in my social circle, a hodgepodge of unanswered questions floated around in my head for years. When objectors to my faith appeared left and right, I wasn't up to the challenge.

Had there been such a thing as the Catholic SAT, I fear my score would not have made the pope proud.

I did not grasp or digest the whole story about the Church, which I now love. And, although digging up the missing pearls of precious Catholic truth that I lacked took me almost a decade, with each pearl added, the beauty of the Church shone more brightly to me.

I began searching for information on Catholic teachings in my twenties. I was particularly deficient in knowledge of the origins of these teachings; I could have used a rundown of how the Church got started, and what it really taught. Armed with the facts and figures, I might have warded off some embarrassment. More importantly, I would have awakened each morning to a different set of goals. First priority? Daily attendance at Holy Mass, the most powerful prayer on earth.

The book that nobody gave me would have explained that the very Sacrifice of the Lord becomes present during the Mass, reaching right out to us from first-century Calvary through time. This all-powerful, one-time Sacrifice comes with a burst of grace for participants and the whole Church.

What else would I have done differently?

- I would have made it a point to stop in for Confession during my undergraduate years in New Haven, my graduate school stint in Manhattan, and my early single years outside Philadelphia — stages of my life where no teacher was looking over my shoulder — because I would have known that the sacraments were started by our Lord Jesus, rather than by flawed humans.

- Instead of walking around in a perpetual cloud of doctrinal and ethical confusion, I might have been able to differentiate between the snazzy new technologies benefiting humankind and the ones injuring human dignity. I would have had a better chance at conversing intelligently about captivating magazine articles discussing the potential to clone people or to freeze and discard human embryos. I would have reacted with horror instead of mild amusement when advertisements first started appearing, offering vast sums for eggs from female Ivy League students for the manufacture of Advanced Placement babies. What in the world was the Church's position on all this? And more importantly, what was the reasoning behind it? At the time, I was scarcely aware that such topics even fell within the radar of the Church. Had I been acquainted with natural law, which has remained constant since the first human being was put on earth, I might have seen things more clearly.

- With a bit of background, I would have appreciated the role of Catholic traditions, such as Lenten fasting and the Stations of the Cross, as valuable ways for drawing closer to Jesus while on earth. If I had known that the poor souls in Purgatory were suffering, I would have been praying for their relief. I would have been offering prayers and Masses for my deceased grandparents.

- If it had occurred to me that the *Catechism of the Catholic Church* featured vast sections of material that coincided remarkably with the missing Catholic files from my brain, I would have snapped up a copy. Certain chapters would have come in handy when various cross-examiners popped up to contest my beliefs. Instead, they walked away victorious, with the distinct and accurate impression that I didn't know what on earth they were talking about.

- A couple of briefings would have prevented my face from reddening when someone inquired in my college dining hall as to why I was a Catholic rather than a member of any of the other Christian denominations. I had no coherent explanation. I wasn't even aware of the Bible's admonition, "Always be prepared to make a defense to any one who calls you to account for the hope that is in you, yet do it with gentleness and reverence" (1 Pet. 3:15-16).

- With some extra factoids and Scripture verses up my sleeve, perhaps I could have prevented some former Catholic classmates from leaving the Church that Jesus left for us. I witnessed plenty of well-meaning Catholics switching to other churches, unaware that the Catholic Church was *the* Church of the Christians long before any these new churches had appeared on the scene, and unaware of the main doctrines offered by the Church to support the divine origin of the Catholic faith. My goodhearted acquaintances switched to "Bible-based" churches without realizing that the Catholic Church was responsible for determining the contents of the Bible in the first place. They left before discovering that the interpretations of Bible verses now being presented to them would have clashed with those of the early Church. They left before anyone told them that the same Church Fathers who testified to the authenticity of the 27 books of the New Testament *also* testified to the truth of Catholic doctrines such as the Real Presence in the Eucharist, a regenerative baptism, and the roles of Confession and doing penance. It did not occur to them that for the early Christians, Christianity *was* the Catholic faith.

Maybe things would have turned out differently for my friends had they seen the Bible verses where Jesus gave His Church His own power to govern on earth (Mt. 18:18), His own power to forgive sins (Jn. 20:23), and a promise to be with the Church always (Mt. 28:18). My friends may have been surprised to learn that Jesus promised the one Church "all the truth" in Jn. 16:13, that the Bible itself referred to the Church as the "the pillar and bulwark of the truth" (1 Tim.

3:15), and that Christ promised us His true Flesh and Blood (Jn. 6:35-71). The converts to these churches did not know any of these things. Neither did many of the people born into these churches. And I, for one, certainly could not have waxed poetic on the sermons of the Early Church Fathers, or on the process for determining the canon of the New Testament.

Instead, well-meaning, but mistaken, believers of other churches impressed commonly propagated myths about the Church upon these under-catechized souls. As these myths went unchallenged, they became ingrained, and then were spread to others.

Then there were the stubborn (albeit friendly) atheists, who proudly challenged the very existence of the One who created them. The gift of faith must be accepted, of course; still, it would have been nice if I could have referenced the salient arguments of brilliant thinkers such as Aristotle, Anselm of Canterbury, Thomas Aquinas, René Descartes, mathematician Blaise Pascal, calculus co-founder Gottfried Leibniz, and others who, through the ages, have provided a full panoply of proofs for the existence of God. Their arguments have only been bolstered by more recent scientific discovery pointing to an intelligent Creator with an intelligent design.

In the words of Antony Flew, a British scholar and octogenarian, modern DNA research "has shown, by the almost unbelievable complexity of the arrangements which are needed to produce (life), that intelligence must have been involved." (Flew was one of the world's leading advocates of atheism prior to his surprising reversal in late 2004.)

Although I never questioned God's existence myself, a weak faith can render a Christian susceptible to those passing sensations of emptiness that must haunt serious skeptics of the afterlife. I recall the hollow feeling that beset me upon hearing my astronomy professor deliver the disturbing news to us that our sun, like any ordinary G2 star, would eventually use up its fuel, swell into a red giant, then collapse into a white dwarf and die. *What? No more people?*

At the time, it would have been comforting to hear of the 1917 Miracle of the Sun in Fátima, Portugal (see Chapter 14). The nature-defying events that occurred in the sky during an apparition of the Blessed Mother are an assuring reminder that God is the Master of the universe, and not vice versa. Alternatively, I could have used the soothing news that when Jesus returns on the Last Day, the earth will indeed be intact, and human beings will be alive and well.

But neither faith nor the next life were ever the *topic du jour* in class, at my dinner table, or Friday nights at Toads Place or Naples Pizza, and I had "forgotten" to pack any religious materials in my suitcase for college. After all, as long as I got myself to church each Sunday and stayed away from the sins I had heard were mortal, what more was there to do? What more was there to learn?

Who would have guessed there was so *much* more?

This book I wished I'd had would have served as a starting point, a springboard for diving into the fountain of knowledge that soon swells into an ocean for those who reluctantly draw near. The sea of Catholic truth and grace is simply inexhaustible, because it is fed by Jesus Christ.

Fortunately, I was blessed with a lot of people who questioned me, challenged me, prayed for me, and, ultimately, helped me. Questions from new friends at nondenominational churches motivated me to dig deeper. The Christ-centered lives of the same friends reminded me to pray more and focus more on what was important. Some old and new Catholic friends — who were particularly devout — popped up, to further inspire my newfound appreciation for the faith. The new Catholic evangelists, who had begun churning out books and audiotapes defending the faith, were helpful in illuminating the origins of doctrines and the Biblical basis for our faith.

Like most Catholics desiring to understand my own faith more deeply, and how it differed from the theology of our Protestant brethren, I collected books or audiotapes from authors such as Alan Schreck, Karl Keating, Jimmy Akin, Patrick Madrid, Scott Hahn, Mark Shea, Tim Staples, and Dave Armstrong. I read transcripts of debates between top Catholic and evangelical Protestant apologists. I eventually studied the writings of the Church Fathers, including excerpts compiled in William A. Jurgens' *The Faith of the Early Fathers* as well as full-length documents, and saw how these first Christians interpreted the Bible and viewed Church authority.

Once you recognize the miraculous nature of the Church Jesus left for us — and once it hits you that the same living God who started it is truly present at whatever Catholic church is down the street, ready to be received by you in the Flesh — you go there more often.

Getting to Confession and daily Mass may require some extra effort and planning, some extra grace, some extra peer pressure, and maybe even a hardship or ailment to nudge you over at first, but all that really matters in the end is that you get there.

As a brown-robed friar on television once explained, we are not called to a natural existence while on earth; we are called to a super-natural existence fueled by divine help. Just as our bodies rely on food and water that are found on earth, our souls must be nourished by divine love called grace that is poured on us from heaven during real encounters with Christ in the sacraments. Without the benefit of God's grace, our souls cannot live . . . cannot be transformed to God's will . . . cannot enter into eternal life with the glorified Jesus.

A person with no eyes cannot fully understand the visual delight of a sunset or rose bush simply by hearing. A person with no taste buds cannot fully appreciate sweet flavors simply by seeing. A person who is not opening the heart to receive Jesus in the Eucharist cannot fully experience the power of Jesus that could be working in them.

Jesus First

This book opens with Jesus — because it is He who must come first in everything — and with the One, Holy, Catholic, and Apos-tolic Church that Jesus founded to guide us to heaven. Chapters 4 through 6 discuss Confession, the Eucharist, and Confirmation, sacraments that bring us right to the lake of grace won by Jesus. The grace that comes into us supernaturally helps us and steers us on our journey toward full union with God.

The degree to which we allow the living God to transform us dur-ing our earthly lives will directly influence our experience in the afterlife. Heaven, Purgatory, Judgment Day, and Hell are the subjects of Chapters 7 through 10.

Fortunately, we need not wait for the afterlife to know God's laws. Chapter 11 is a reflection on the laws of morality as divinely preserved and proclaimed by our Church, which we believe speaks with Christ's own voice (Lk. 10:16). Divine law is not always easy to live by, but it will forever transcend the most appealing ideologies that come and go. Even if we fail to honor the truth we are given, the door will always be open for our return. Once we are back, our tools for making amends include prayer and penance (Chapter 12). Our models for living are the saints (Chapters 13 and 14). Our sins have caused tragic divisions within Christianity (Chapter 15), but our hope lies with Jesus, whose Kingdom is of another world.

This book is not meant to be a soul-baring tale in the mold of *Swimming with Scapulars* nor a spiritual autobiography in the tradition of the classic *The Seven Storey Mountain.*[1] Nor am I a Trappist monk, but rather a happily married Catholic in Pennsylvania.

Rather than provide a meticulous account of my own spiritual journey or pour out my soul, I simply wrote the book that I wish someone had given me a long time ago, in hopes that others might be interested as well. I have attempted to carve out connecting pieces of the roadmap of knowledge and discovery that laid the groundwork for my journey so that others can take their own rides, presumably at higher speeds than my own.

Not an end in themselves, these chapters, I hope, will lead you to the good stuff — Scripture, the writings and meditations of the saints, and most of all, the sacraments, which allow Christ to come into us right now, with His infinite mercy, no matter where we are on the road. The goal of the trip is full union with Christ, the only thing that can bring a person everlasting happiness.

CHAPTER ONE

✝

Founded by Jesus:
Now I Get . . .
the Catholic Church's Claim

Once upon a time, the little girl in the maroon jumper, knee socks, and matching ribbon in her hair didn't know a lot about where the Church came from or how it all started. She wasn't familiar with the history of the Chair of Peter or what the first Christians believed. She didn't realize that the Apostles Peter and Paul had set up the Church of Rome, or that the Catholic Church had put together the Bible.

But she did have one question about her friend Joni's religion: Where did all the Presbyterian nuns live?

Sister Lisa, my first grade teacher, lived in a convent behind my Catholic elementary school. She shared quarters with principal Sister Elizabeth Ann Seton, music teacher Sister Cecilia, and all the other sisters at St. Louis School in Yeadon, Pennsylvania. All the other Catholic schools around my Philadelphia suburb also had convents on their properties.

But my friend Joni attended the public school down the street, and she went to the church on our own block. I was unable to find any convent-like buildings around her school or church, so one day, I just had to ask someone where Joni's nuns lived.

Of course, the reply I received was that her religion did not have nuns or priests. No reason was given why not, and I never asked. But privately, the information spoke to me.

Upon hearing the news, I was secretly grateful that my religion was the one with the nuns. It just seemed right to have Sister Lisa and these other joyful nuns running around, proudly declaring that they were married to Jesus.

As a five-year-old, I had only recently become aware that more than one religion existed. I found this disconcerting because it seemed to me that only one set of beliefs could be the truth. (Yes, this thought really occurred to me. Unfortunately, it would be at least two decades more before my next philosophical thought came to mind.) To allay my concern, a Catholic adult explained to me that our beliefs were virtually identical, except for some minor details about Mary. I felt better.

At school, Sister Lisa taught us about the Apostles, and how each of them left everything behind when Jesus called their names. We could see that our teachers had done the same. They had given up material possessions, trendy clothing, long hair, personal privacy, and the chance to marry and have a family — all for the same Lord. At the time, we had not yet learned that in the Bible, St. Paul described people consecrating themselves to the Lord and committing not to marry (1 Cor. 7:25-40) and Jesus praised those who remained celibate for the kingdom (Mt. 19:12). But we saw a sister dressed in a habit to be signaling the kind of relationship that would probably exist if Jesus were everything we were told He was.

One day, a nun told us that we were very lucky to be in the "true Church." I remember thinking to myself, "Sure, I bet all people think their church is the true one, or they would be somewhere else." Besides, I didn't think there was a way to confirm one over the other, since we couldn't pick up the phone and call Jesus.

Not that it mattered, as I was under the impression that the various Christian religions were pretty darn close in substance. Maybe one religion fasted on one day, and perhaps the next religion fasted on another, I conjectured, but I figured as long as a person loved God and obeyed whatever authority the person thought God had left here, God would understand.

On the other hand, a loving God would probably have seen to it that His children would possess some way to know, without doubt, the full truth about how God wanted people to live. If God existed — and indeed He did — it was highly plausible that there would be one spiritual authority on the planet that would have it completely right (I knew it could not be more than one, since all religions clashed on at least one point with every other one).

My gut feeling was that the prime candidate for this single source of truth was the Catholic Church. It seemed to possess a unique authority that ran deep. But where was the material proof? If such proof existed, I reasoned, then everyone would already belong to the same Church. At the time, I was not cognizant of the fact that in early centuries, all Christians were in the same Church.

Although our teachers diligently prepared us for the sacraments and taught us Bible stories and parables, none ever laid down the evidence that we were in the Church founded by Christ.

Perhaps each had assumed that our previous teachers had explained this. I also suspect that in our age of ecumenism, they were reluctant to say anything negative or unkind about our Protestant brothers and sisters. I am sincerely thankful for their Christian attitude, but unfortunately, that also meant I never learned the history of the Catholic Church or of any other segment of Christianity. I had no idea that the founders of Protestantism broke off from the Catholic Church during the sixteenth century, or that the term "Protestant" spoke to the "protest" of my Church.

Just when I began thinking that my lack of awareness of such core historical events must be a sad anomaly, I found myself at the Jersey Shore in my twenties, chatting with one of the smartest guys in my high school class. I'll just cut to the middle of it:

Friend: "He doesn't follow the pope?"
Me: "No, he's Protestant."
Friend: "Well, I knew he was Protestant. But you're saying he's not under the pope?"
Me: "No Protestants are under the pope."
Friend: "I didn't know that."

This guy, a devout Catholic who received his M.B.A. from one of the country's top business schools, didn't know any more than I did about the basics of our faith.

I was not alone in my confusion.

Over time, other Catholic acquaintances reinforced my hunch that we were all in the same boat of bewilderment when it came to a clear understanding of certain doctrines, morality teachings, and especially Christian history. St. Augustine? Bishop of What? Martin Luther? Was King his last name? St. Patrick? Was he a historical figure or more like the fictional Pied Piper? All Christians know they best avoid the act that makes babies until marriage, but what about cloning, the endless varieties of contraception, *in vitro* fertilization, tube-tying, divorce, annulments, surrogate mothers and euthanasia? Were there rules and theology related to each, and if so, was it permissible to disagree? Catholicism and Protestantism. Were there representatives of both in the Early Church?

Unlike our parents before us, some of us Catholics who graduated from U.S. Catholic high schools in the 1980s missed out on a few "little" facts.

I suppose I could offer up many excuses for my own ignorance — curriculum gaps at the time, "zoning out" during class and Mass, attending a non-Catholic secular college, and so on — but for whatever reason, my store of knowledge came up deficient.

Anyway, as it came to be, I was in my mid-twenties when suddenly, half my friends were part of a nondenominational Protestant church. On the one hand, these Christians had strong faith, shared my values, and were committed to living the Christian life; on the other hand, a surprising number of them seemed to be bursting with 101 grievances against everything Catholics did.

It was an eye-opening experience. Up to that point, I went through life assuming everybody respected the Catholic Church; in fact, thus far, I had never met even one Catholic critic in my life. Whenever I was among other churchgoing Christians, I had just assumed we shared this huge bond. We were the same. Almost like two people who meet and realize they both speak Portuguese, or both went to the same elementary school, or both share a passion for fly-fishing. But apparently, I hadn't heard the whole story.

Now, everywhere I turned there seemed to be people — nice people, I should add — with very strong opinions about my faith background. Some had been taught some mighty strange things about Catholic teaching. From what I could tell, they thought most of our doctrines were designed to disobey the Bible, and felt morally obliged to let the word out.

Wait a minute, I thought we were all Bible-believing Christians, weren't we?

In my own Catholic community, neither priests, nor teachers, nor friends had ever thought to mention the teachings of other religions, much less voice objections to them. I would have known if they had; I never missed Mass on Sunday. Yet here were a bunch of people at a church I had never heard of who seemed to have been in training their entire lives for the specific sport of debating Catholics.

In that same time period, I received many invitations to a distinguished Protestant church of a more formal character. The very first time I attended, the minister mentioned — that is, slammed — Catholics in his sermon. Did I just hear what I thought I did? No, impossible, I kept telling myself.

When some polite Jehovah's Witnesses came to my door years after the previous incidents, they, too, had some well-prepared quips to pull out about the Catholic Church.

Wow! All these other religions regarded the Catholic Church as the Big One — the one to beat. Flattering, yet sad. Sad because, even though I was an adult and supposedly mature in her faith, I wasn't prepared for the game. I hadn't a clue what led the Catholic Church to believe that it was the true faith — the one with God-given authority.

Apparently, even the nearest encyclopedia contained a better defense than I could come up with. *Britannica Online Encyclopedia* says that my Church "regards itself as the only legitimate inheritor of the ministry of Jesus, by virtue of an unbroken succession of leaders beginning with St. Peter the Apostle and continuing to the present day." It also designates my Church as the "largest single Christian denomination in the world, with some one billion members, or about 18% of the world's population."

My *faux pas* was ignorance of what Jesus said. I didn't know what Jesus had promised to St. Peter, the other Apostles, and the Church. But I did know that whatever Jesus said was the bottom line. No one could go wrong following His teaching, and I, for one, wanted to know what He had to say while He was here.

Did Jesus really hand over His authority to the Church? Did Jesus really say that whatever this Church did would be backed up in heaven? Did He really promise that not even the forces of Hell would topple this Church?

The answers to such questions were right in the Bible.

To Peter, the first pope, Jesus said:

> "Blessed are you, Simon Bar-Jona! For flesh and blood has not revealed this to you, but my Father who is in heaven. And I tell you, you are Peter, and on this rock I will build my church, and the powers of death shall not prevail against it. I will give you the keys of the kingdom of heaven, and whatever you bind on earth shall be bound in heaven, and whatever you loose on earth shall be loosed in heaven."   — MT. 16:18-19

Jesus promised to build His indestructible Church — on St. Peter. Two thousand years later, we look back and see that the Catholic Church, and only the Catholic Church, is still led by a direct successor of St. Peter himself. It's always been like that, from St. Peter all the way up to Pope Benedict XVI.

From the beginning, Christians knew that the Church that Jesus built would be divinely prevented from collapsing or disappearing. According to Jesus, the forces of Hell would be rendered powerless against this Church. St. Peter, the Rock on whom Christ would build the Church, would be entrusted with Christ's own authority, with the very power to bind and loose on earth. Whatever Peter ruled on in Christ's absence would be backed up by Christ in Heaven.

Jesus had been priming Peter for this special leadership role for some time. He had let Peter know that he was the one placed in charge of shepherding the flock.

> When they had finished breakfast, Jesus said to Simon Peter, "Simon, son of John, do you love me more than these?" He said to him, "Yes, Lord; you know that I love you." He said to him, "Feed my lambs." A second time he said to him, "Simon, son of John, do you love me?" He said to him, "Yes, Lord; you know that I love you." He said to him, "Tend my sheep." He said to him the third time, "Simon, son of John, do you love me?" Peter was grieved because he said to him the third time, "Do you love me?" And he said to him, "Lord, you know

everything; you know that I love you." Jesus said to him, "Feed my sheep."   — Jn. 21:15-17

Peter was the only Apostle to receive the special keys of ultimate authority. Peter, whose original named was Simon, was the only Apostle to be renamed "Rock" (*Petros* in Greek or *Cephas* in Aramaic) by Jesus[2]. He was the only Apostle instructed to "feed" Jesus' sheep.

Jesus mentions St. Peter's name in the Gospels more than any other Apostle's as well. Peter is referred to in the four Gospels — Matthew, Mark, Luke, and John — and the Acts of the Apostles (by St. Luke) 195 times. This compares to just 29 mentions of the name of the runner-up, St. John the Apostle.[3]

But Peter was not immortal. Jesus was wise enough to plan ahead for future generations of followers that would need shepherding. He promised that when it came to teaching the flock, He would be with His special teachers until the end of time.

> "Go therefore and make disciples of all nations, baptizing them in the name of the Father and of the Son and of the Holy Spirit, teaching them to observe all that I have commanded you; and lo, I am with you always, to the close of the age."
>   — Mt. 28: 19-20

What did guarding this teaching mission mean? It meant Jesus would leave us a surefire way to know true teaching from false teaching, and valid interpretations of Scripture from false ones; for when this Church spoke, it would be the voice of Christ Himself. Listening to the Church would be the equivalent of listening to Christ Himself. Rejecting the teaching of the Church would amount to rejecting the Lord, according to the Lord.

Jesus told the first leaders of His Church, "He who hears you hears me, and he who rejects you rejects me, and he who rejects me rejects him who sent me" (Lk. 10:16).

Keys to Heaven and Chairs to Be Filled

The keys of authority Peter received from Jesus have been passed down to Peter's successors. The Chair of Peter has been occupied by every pope throughout the ages. No other institution in history can make a comparable claim. The papacy is older than even the oldest government.[4]

A quick scan through the countries of the world — there are fewer than 200 — confirms this fact. The papacy of the Catholic Church has been in place for a longer period of time than any other legislature. Even the most ancient lands seem to have young governments. The People's Republic of China, for example, was founded only in 1949, and has gone through four constitutions since then.

The United States may be the oldest major government still functioning in the way in which it was designed; the 33-mile-long Isle of Man in the Irish Sea, on a smaller scale, may beat out even America for the old-government title; but no one comes close to the papacy.

Smart designs last a long time.

God's designs last forever.

The unending government designed by God came with a key and a chair. The idea of keys of authority and chairs of honor outliving their possessors was not new. In fact, in the Old Testament, one can find a parallel verse to the New Testament verses where Jesus granted his keys to Peter. The Old Testament figure Eliakim was given the key to the kingdom upon replacing Shebna. As the new palace administrator, Eliakim was assigned a throne of honor (Is. 22:23).

Just as comedian Jay Leno now sits in a recognized chair originally occupied by Steve Allen, the first host of *The Tonight Show,* modern popes sit in a chair once filled by St. Peter. Now, Leno may not sit in the exact four-legged piece of furniture warmed by the bodies of those in the line of succession, such as Jack Paar and Johnny Carson. However, TV viewers recognize that all of these men have sat in the same chair of honor, a chair revered and seriously coveted by many a comedian. (This chair, it has been announced, will be passed off to Conan O'Brien in 2009.)

How many years *The Tonight Show* chair will last is anybody's guess; the Chair of Peter will be with us until Christ's Second Coming.

But there's more.

Besides claiming the direct successor of St. Peter, the Catholic Church can also boast that all of its bishops around the world are direct successors of the original Twelve Apostles. Our present-day bishops all have a direct link back to the Apostolic Age. By virtue of their ordinations through the laying on of hands, our bishops form human chains stretching back to those first Church leaders, the Apostles, who were commissioned by Jesus Himself. We call this phenomenon Apostolic Succession.

In the early Church, St. Peter was first in authority, but his fellow Apostles were each given a piece of it when Jesus told them as a group, "Truly, I say to you, whatever you bind on earth shall be bound in heaven, and whatever you loose on earth shall be loosed in heaven" (Mt. 18:18).

In other words, the very Apostles tapped by Christ laid their hands on — thus ordaining — chosen men, who, in turn, laid their hands on other bishops, who in turn, going down the line, directly transferred Christ's authority and power to the modern-day bishop of your diocese.

How important was the idea of succession in the Early Church? It wasn't the Church without it.

With succession, Christians were ensured doctrines and moral truths that would forever be protected from error by the Holy Spirit. With succession, the awesome power of the holy priesthood would be passed down through the centuries. When priests forgive our sins or speak the words of Christ that change the bread and wine into the Body and Blood of our Savior, Jesus is there. Christ's own power is at work in our bishops and priests in a direct and physical way handed down from the first Apostles.

Apostolic succession, including the passing on of Peter's role in the Church, was in place even before the New Testament was put together. Even in the earliest Christian times, if your bishop was not a direct successor of Apostles, and if the head bishop was not a direct successor of St. Peter, you were outside the Church founded by Christ.

For example, early writings show St. Cyprian of Carthage spelling this out in no uncertain terms, about a man named Novatian:

> Novatian is not in the Church; nor can he be reckoned as a bishop, who, succeeding to no one, and despising the evangelical and apostolic tradition, sprang from himself. For he who has not been ordained in the Church can neither have nor hold to the Church in any way.
>
> — *Letters* 69[75]:3 (253 A.D.)

In 412 A.D., St. Augustine also proves that a Donatist bishop is not valid. (The Donatists were a schismatic group based in North Africa who seceded from the Catholic Church in the early fourth century. Separated from the Chair of Peter, the group possessed no legitimate authority.) The proof, again, is that he is not in the special lines of succession stemming from the Apostles. After naming all of St. Peter's successors up to Bishop Anastasius, who was the pope at the time, St. Augustine declares:

> In this order of succession a Donatist bishop is not to be found. [5]

St. Jerome understood the Chair of Peter, or office of pope, to be the rock on which Jesus built His Church. He wrote:

> I follow no leader but Christ and join in communion with none but your blessedness (Pope Damasus I), that is, with the chair of Peter. I know that this is the rock on which the Church has been built. Whoever eats the Lamb outside this house is profane. Anyone who is not in the ark of Noah will perish when the flood prevails.
>
> — *Letters* 15:2 (396 A.D.)

By virtue of its lines of succession, the Church had Christ's authority to say what was Scripture and what was not. By virtue of its lines of succession, the Church could give the final word on interpreting Scripture and preserving what was truly meant by its divine Author. By virtue of its lines of succession, the Church received power to validly administer the sacraments.

> No ancient Christian writer — not Tertullian, Origen or any other — ever denied the apostolic succession or the authority inherited by the bishops. That the Church had been established on the Apostles was a truth that no professing Christian would attempt to deny for at least another thousand years, when the mistaken idea that the faith of Christ could somehow be based on "Scripture Alone." [6]

Today, with its billion members, this same ancient Church continues to be led by successors of Apostles, including St. Peter, as it will be until the last day of earth. We call it the Catholic Church. The early Christians were calling it the Catholic Church as early as 107 A.D.

So how could any Christian even entertain the thought of breaking off from the apostolic succession that had continued to be a sacred mark of the Church since the first century? How could some Christians think it was all right to break off from the Catholic Church in the sixteenth century and form Protestant churches, despite the Bible's many warnings against schism?

Well, they saw Church members, including leaders, sinning. There were scandals and abuses related to indulgences and other doctrines. The Church's official doctrines had not changed, but many church leaders were obscuring sound teachings by promoting non-sanctioned practices.

Books could be written about these sins, and about more recent evils, but in the end, the sins of human beings have never been an excuse to break away from the Church Jesus promised to be with until the end of time. They do sound a bugle call for intense prayer and radical action and leadership by the laity; on the other hand, we just cannot afford to stay away from the household of God, the Mass, or the sacraments, through which Christ's own graces flow. Just as a cancer patient may be healed by surgery performed by a dishonest doctor, a Christian who shows up at Mass may be spiritually healed by the shower of graces Christ provides through the priest, regardless of the state of the priest's soul.

Even if a priest is headed to Hell, Jesus will not deprive His children of the gift of Himself in the Eucharist. The Apostles had Judas, who betrayed Jesus, and even Peter — the "rock" who denied knowing Jesus. St. Paul consented to the stoning of the first Christian martyr, St. Stephen. There have been sinners in the Church since Jesus founded it — in the first, second, and third centuries, and certainly in our day. Jesus compared it to a garden where wheat had been sown but also contained the weeds sown by an enemy! There will be sinners in the Church until the Last Day. But the truth remains with the Church.

Jesus said:

"When the Spirit of truth comes, he will guide you into all the truth; for he will not speak on his own authority, but whatever

he hears he will speak, and he will declare to you the things
that are to come."   — JN. 16:13

If Jesus promised "all truth," then we can expect a margin of error
of zero. The Church may continue to understand and clarify these
teachings as time goes on, but She will never reverse them.

When we say we are Catholic, we are saying that we trust in all
the Church's official teachings because we trust Jesus' words that the
Church will be divinely guided into all truth.

When we say we are Catholic, we are saying we trust the Bible's
words that the Church is the "pillar and bulwark of the truth" (1 Tim.
3:15). We are saying that we trust the guidance of the Church built
by Jesus more than we trust our own heartfelt personal opinions.

Therefore, if we find ourselves adhering to a belief that contradicts 2,000 years of Church teaching, we must realize this belief is not
coming from Christ. God loved us too much to have left us without
a sure way to know His plans for us to be with Him forever. He established an authority and promised its voice would be His voice (Lk.
10:16). Our official teachings on faith and morals are not mostly
truth, but all truth.

For me, following Jesus means respecting the fullness of Church
teaching. Either we trust in Christ's promises about the Church's
divine origins and divine nature, or we doubt them, and should join
a church that does not promise "all the truth" (Jn.16:13) and does not
claim to be the "pillar and bulwark of the truth" (1 Tim. 3:15).

Bishops on the Move

By the end of the first century, even before the Bible was put
together, the Apostles had appointed many bishops to serve as chief
shepherds of the Church. These bishops would go on to ordain
other bishops, who would ordain other bishops, all through the
Biblical laying of hands. Bishops were the highest-ranking ministers
appointed by Apostles and represented a distinct office by the late
first century.[7]

For example, in letters written around 107 A.D., St. Ignatius
recounts that the churches that he encounters during his travels oper-
ated on a three-tiered system of a bishop, priests, and deacons.[8]

He is so confident of this usage that he can say that without these three offices a local body cannot be called a church (*Trallians* 3:1-2). These facts show that the usage was already widespread at the dawn of the second century, so it must have first been established in the late first century, at the close of the apostolic age.

Christians were cautioned not to assemble in places outside the apostolic succession of bishops by St. Irenaeus of Lyons. St. Irenaeus was taught by the best. He saw and heard the preaching of Polycarp, a disciple of the Apostle St. John.

To prove that the glorious Church founded in Rome was the one blessed with the teachings of the Apostles, St. Irenaeus simply pulled out the succession proof. He was in awe of the Catholic Church, which he knew to have

> . . . [the] successions of bishops of the greatest and most ancient church known to all, founded and organized at Rome by the two most glorious Apostles, Peter and Paul, that church which has the tradition and the faith which comes down to us after having been announced to men by the Apostles. With that church, because of its superior origin, all the churches must agree, that is, all the faithful in the whole world, and it is in her that the faithful everywhere have maintained the apostolic tradition.
>
> — *Against Heresies* 3:3:2 (189 A.D.)

Then, to finish off his slam-dunk case for the Catholic Church, St. Irenaeus points out the Petrine succession of the Church, demonstrating that Peter's office was directly handed down to successors. He mentions the first four popes:

> The blessed Apostles [Peter and Paul], having founded and built up the church [of Rome], they handed over the office of the episcopate to Linus. Paul makes mention of this Linus in the letter to Timothy [2 Tim. 4:21]. To him succeeded Anacletus, and after him, in the third place from the Apostles, Clement was chosen for the episcopate. . . .
>
> — *Against Heresies* 3, 3:3 (189 A.D.)

From the beginning, the Church established in Rome held the "presidency" of the churches that formed the Catholic Church. All other churches must agree with it. The same is true today. From the Archdiocese of Buenos Aires to the Archdiocese of Tokyo, all bishops remain in communion with the blessed Church in Rome. St. Ignatius of Antioch, who walked the earth while Apostles were alive, referred to the Church in Rome this way:

> Ignatius . . . to the church also which holds the presidency, in the location of the country of the Romans, worthy of God, worthy of honor, worthy of blessing, worthy of praise, worthy of success, worthy of sanctification, and, because you hold the presidency in love, named after Christ and named after the Father.
>
> — *Letter to the Romans* 1:1 (110 A.D.)

St. Ignatius was in a position to know such things. He was a disciple of the Apostle St. John.

The necessity of the Chair of Peter to Christianity, and the one priesthood that stems from it, was also a theme of St. Cyprian of Carthage in the third century:

> There is one God and one Christ, and one Church, and one chair founded on Peter by the word of the Lord. It is not possible to set up another altar or for there to be another priesthood besides that one altar and that one priesthood. Whoever has gathered elsewhere is scattering.
>
> — *Letters* 43[40]:5 (253 A.D.)

As Bishop of Carthage, St. Cyprian was a direct successor of an Apostle. He spoke eloquently on the Sacrifice of the Mass, the Real Presence of Jesus in the Eucharist, and the importance of holding to the unity of the one Church if one wanted to be assured of Christ's teachings. St. Cyprian was a martyr for the Christian faith.

In later chapters, we'll see evidence that all the first Christian doctrines were Catholic doctrines. But for now, let's look at what St. Clement says about the greatest legacy of the Catholic Church: the Holy Sacrifice of the Mass. In the year 80 A.D., at which time the last Apostle was still alive, St. Clement attests to the Mass's sacrificial nature when he refers to the ordained members of the episcopate "who blamelessly and holily have offered its sacrifices. Blessed are those presbyters who have already finished their course, and who have obtained a fruitful and perfect release" (*Letter to the Corinthians* 44:4-5, 80 A.D.).

As the fourth bishop of Rome, St. Clement was a direct successor of St. Peter. It is believed that St. Peter ordained him.

Raising My Hand

Now, I don't recall reading the ancient writings of the Church Fathers back in school, but I do remember being in high school when a nun mentioned to us one time that Peter was the first pope, and that the popes went all the way up to John Paul II (and, of course, now Pope Benedict XVI). This sounded impressive. A bit too impressive, in fact. If we were the only church that had this, why on earth wouldn't everybody be in this church?

I wondered how other churches attempted to compete, and thought perhaps they had their own popes tracing back to a different Apostle — Philip? Bartholomew? Or, I ruminated, perhaps they had a whole different set of Apostles to begin with. The possibilities were endless.

I wasn't one for asking questions in class, always fearful that my question would be even dumber than I suspected, but I mustered up the courage to raise my hand on this rare occasion: "Sister, does each religion have its own pope?" (Obviously, I was a very confused child.) Sister answered no, but did not expound.

Of course, had I known then that the first Protestant church didn't start until the sixteenth century, I would have known not to ask that question in the first place. If I had known that the Reformation was not a synonym for the Renaissance, then I would have zipped my mouth. Prior to the sixteenth century, "Protestants" were actually Catholics. Luther was a Catholic monk, Henry VIII was a Catholic monarch. They were under the Catholic pope. They went to Mass. They honored the seven sacraments. They prayed for their dead. They asked the saints in heaven to pray for them.

The bell rang. The class ended, so it was time to push down the knee socks to the customary halfway point, sneak on the cool, non-regulation colorful sweater over the maroon jumper, and dart down Archbishop John Carroll's long hallway to the boys' side for more exciting classes like Calculus with Boys, History with Boys, and Biology with Boys. At my school, good grades were rewarded with admittance to the coveted co-ed honors classes.

Too bad all religion classes were single-sex; otherwise, perhaps, I would have been motivated to master my religion back then. Instead, my curiosity about the Church's history lapsed into hibernation for eight more years.

A cute fundamentalist Christian friend reawakened my curiosity when he told me that his church believed what the early Christians had believed. I quietly thought to myself, "Huh? I thought *my* religion did."

Clearly, the time had come for me to learn more.

CHAPTER TWO

†

Now I Get . . .
to the Bottom of Things

Well, the first few Catholic doctrines I researched turned out to be doctrines of the Early Church.

The next time I bumped into the fellow, I shared my findings. I expected to be pelted with lively objections and counterarguments. But I didn't hear anything of the sort. Instead he explained that the early Christians to whom he was referring had had to remain in hiding for fear of persecution. Therefore, there was no record of these Christians, the *true* Christians, of course.

So, apparently, I had gone on a wild goose chase. Whatever I could have possibly dug up about the early Christians would obviously not apply to the *real* Christians — because those courageous guys were hiding under rocks and bushes, and certainly weren't writing anything down.

Even before I could finish my investigation that would prove the Catholic Church was that single, original Church that Jesus founded, an atheist friend started challenging me as to whether Jesus was God in the first place. He wanted to know why Christ's own Father would send Him here to endure torture. Also, why didn't the Resurrected Jesus make Himself visible to every person on earth, so that we could all be sure?

I'm not so sure that firsthand knowledge of God would solve everything; as for myself, I know God is real, and I know well the punishment attached to sin, yet I still sin.

Nevertheless, I should have been able to provide Biblical, historical, and philosophical evidence for the existence of God. (Now, spending much time with my new evangelical friends, I could see how

I had long fallen flat in heeding Jesus' command to bring the Gospel to all and "make disciples of all nations"[Mt. 28:19].) Instead, I took the easy path, a path taken by many before me. I handed him the famous *Mere Christianity* by atheist-turned-Christian C.S. Lewis, whose own conversion was sparked by the writings of G.K. Chesterton. The C.S. Lewis book, I was told, had influenced the thinking of many converts and was the most widely read book in the Christian world, after the Bible.

To my delight, my friend converted!

To my frustration, he converted from atheist to agnostic.

While his doubts about the existence of a Creator and an afterlife would continue, he did admit that science could not explain everything. Science could not even answer fundamental questions such as: What is matter? Why do molecules behave like they do? Heck, it required faith even to accept the existence of atomic particles, as they did not behave according to the rules of the physical world, he mused. And, he added, science could hardly explain wave/particle duality of photons!

"Yes, Yes, Yes! Exactly what I was thinking!" I concurred.

After consulting my quantum electrodynamics files — known as "the Internet" — I found that what he was referring to was the fact that light sometimes behaved like particles, but at other times behaved like a wave, depending on the experiment. Physicists are forced to accept the phenomenon without understanding it.

Well, it was time to toss out some more arguments at the agnostic.

My friend Eileen advised him just to take Pascal's Wager. Its inventor, seventeenth-century French mathematician Blaise Pascal, reasoned that a betting person unsure about the existence of God would be wise to bet that there is a God. If the individual bets wrongly, he loses little. But if he bets correctly, the prize of Heaven greatly outweighs the pain of Hell. In the end, the stakes are just too high for anyone to live life as if there were no higher purpose, according to Pascal, who had undergone a profound conversion to Christianity; during his short life, he went from a marked worldly period to a desire to detach himself from the world and immerse himself in prayer and mortifications of the flesh. The brilliant scientific treatises and inventions generated by Pascal during his earlier years were pre-

empted by the theological and spiritual writings of his th₁
most famous work, *Pensées,* not quite completed when he
1662 at the age of thirty-nine, argues for the existence of G₁
defends the Christian faith.

But on to other arguments for atheists. The "Argument from
Design," which has increasingly grabbed headlines in recent years,
maintains that life as we know it could hardly have been made possible without an intelligent designer. Given the complex assembly of
the eyeball, the heart, the human brain, the ecosystem, and solar system, and given the fact that such things are meticulously arranged for
a purpose (the eye is exactly arranged so that we can see, the heart is
precisely arranged to pump, and everything is built to work together),
there must be a designer behind them. Neither the well-designed
human being nor the well-designed universe could have evolved by
random chance any more than could a pipe organ, an iPod, or the
Taj Mahal.

Imagine dumping a bag of computer components onto your
desk. What are the odds that the little pieces would eventually come
together, with no outside assistance, to form a functioning computer? What are the odds that if you placed two bags of components
on the desk, the pieces would start developing into two computers
that started kissing and popping out baby computers? In other words,
if the Big Bang explosion that put our universe into motion was not
directed by an intelligent force, then our surroundings should consist of massive piles of shattered glass and dirt whirling around with
no gravitational forces keeping them at bay.

Ultimately, my agnostic friend thought this argument had merit,
but was bothered by flaws in the designs for life. Couldn't human
bodies have been made to be more efficient, with more protection
from disease and disability? Probably; but that makes no difference
to the question of whether the design, in itself, has an intelligent
source. Even a flawed design is still a design, and *designs* are generated by *designers.*

Imagine walking into the workshop of Benjamin Franklin in
Philadelphia in the 1700s while the illustrious statesman was busy
over at a friend's house, helping to get those last typos out of the Declaration of Independence. Franklin's inventions and writings are lying

all over the place — some finished, some in progress, some with visible flaws. You see a prototype of his bifocals, his newly built iron furnace stove, his lightning rod, his medical catheter, his curious contraption for retrieving books on high shelves, his meticulous notes on the movement of the tides of the oceans, his plans for establishing America's first fire company, his freshly developed odometer and his sketches of routes that could speed up the U.S. postal delivery service, which he headed.

The visitor, upon noticing certain defects in his work, would surely not exclaim, "Aha! The flaws before us prove there was no mind or person behind any of this! These gadgets and theories must have randomly come together by accident with no intelligence or purposeful direction driving them!" Even if the visitor could prove that the perceived flaws were unintentional, serving no purpose, he or she would still have to acknowledge that thought was involved in the process leading to Franklin's inventions and developments.

Well, the thought process that went into Franklin's discoveries in electricity, meteorology, and other fields cannot compare to the ingenuity required to create the infinitely complex and skilled organism we call a human being.

The complexity of life is vaster than anyone had ever imagined — as increasingly evidenced by scientific observations of the building blocks of life, ever since James D. Watson and Francis Crick won the Nobel Prize for their landmark discovery of the double-stranded helix structure of DNA in 1953. In light of such discoveries over the last half of the twentieth century, many former atheist scientists and philosophers have abandoned their previous positions. A contrite Antony Flew, the prominent British scholar who had been one of the most renowned atheists of our time, withdrew his objections to theism in 2004.

Flew, the former atheist, who had spent much of his life promulgating his atheist views at universities and at lectures, was quoted offering this apology: "As people have certainly been influenced by me, I want to try and correct the enormous damage I may have done."

Flew has said that revelations in genetics have made it impossible to draw up an explanation for the molecular make-up and function of DNA without allowing that intelligence went into the design.

One of the extraordinary things about DNA, short for deoxyribonucleic acid, is that is possesses code. The codes contain information or instructions for how you and I should be built, from the color of our eyes to the shape of our internal organs. Even scientists who are tempted to claim that matter and energy originally came out of nowhere view the presence of information as something else altogether. Information and language indicate an intelligent source.

In his book *The Case for a Creator*, Lee Strobel recounts an interview he had with scientist Stephen Meyer, who compares DNA to a library that can be accessed by an organism for instructions on building molecules of protein.

Just to build a single protein, Meyer points out, 1,200 to 2,000 "letters" are needed.[9] The "letters" of DNA — A, G, C, and T — refer to the "bases" or building blocks they represent: adenine, guanine, cytosine, and thymine. The order of the bases determines sequences of amino acids, and, ultimately, specific hereditary traits.

By itself, a canvas not yet marked by an artist does not impress. But the canvas of DNA is imprinted with a language that spells out plans for new creations. The artist has been prolific, with billions of unique designs having been built to completion and brought to life.

In short, the human being is a masterpiece, incorporating a multitude of brilliant systems remarkably intertwined. Every person and creature that has ever walked the earth is the fruit of a design, the result of a plan.

One well-built machine within us is the human eye, equipped with stunningly advanced focusing and lighting functions that make a human-made camera look like child's play. The retina of the human eye performs millions of calculations per second.

And humans aren't the only ones who benefit from this kind of intelligence and design. Even rats are gifted with a brain structure that is truly mystifying.

Rat brains are built with "smart" little cells, able to communicate. In 2004, the University of Florida was host to experiments by biomedical engineering professor Thomas DeMarse, who isolated thousands of neurons from a rat brain and got them to control the motions of a simulated F-22 fighter jet. The neurons, having been cultured in a glass container, were connected to a computer while they learned to drive a plane. As for DeMarse, he was interested in studying the language the rat neurons were using to communicate with one another, with hopes that one day animal neurons could be used to pilot real unmanned flights for dangerous missions. Even as he watched, the rat neurons started to reconnect themselves and form a brain that functioned as a computational device.

If the calculator in our desk drawer works, we know it was programmed by an intelligent mind. If our Microsoft Word program works, we can assume it was programmed by an intelligent mind. If rat neurons start making calculations, we can assume that they, too, were programmed by an intelligent mind. I doubt it was the rat's.

DNA is not the only evidence of a designer's hand that science offers. Astrophysics, too, can be called to the witness stand.

Strobel points out that, both on earth and throughout the universe, the physics has been so precisely fine-tuned that if any one of the settings for a long list of parameters were tinkered with even slightly, that would be the end of life. Change the earth's gravity by a hair on the cosmological scale and we would not be able to stand up. Change it by two hairs and we'd go crashing downward into the planet's fiery core. Change the ratio of carbon to oxygen in the stars, and our ancestors would not have seen the light of day.

"Increase the mass of the neutron by about one part in seven hundred and nuclear fusion in starts would stop. There would be no energy source for life. And if the electromagnetic force were slightly stronger or weaker, life in the universe would be impossible," Strobel quotes physicist Robin Collins as saying.[10]

Thank heavens for the human race that the "cosmological constant" — which describes the energy density of empty space — is right on the mark as well.

In Strobel's book, Collins remarks that the cosmological constant baffles scientists; it was set so precisely that, were it simply happenstance, it would "be like successfully hitting a bull's eye that's one trillionth of a trillionth of an inch in diameter" with a dart tossed randomly toward earth from space.[11]

Scientific evidence indeed seems to indicate that if one wanted to believe that there was no Creator who had set all of this, one would need to believe in a pile of coincidences so high that a gambler who thinks he will win the million-dollar jackpot every day for the rest of his life would look conservative.

Science Aside, Consider History

But, science aside, the agnostic I mentioned surmised that his belief in God would likely come down to whether he could believe that Jesus was God, and this would depend on whether he could believe in the Resurrection. He is still deciding.

As Christians, we are commissioned to tell the world about Jesus. But as Christians in an unbelieving culture, we had better be able to offer some good reasons for believing in Him, His Divinity, and His saving work! The truth of Jesus' work on earth depends entirely upon reliable witnesses. If a greedy, womanizing scam operator tries to convince us of something, we doubt it; if our mother describes an incredible scene to us, however, we believe it.

Are the Apostles and disciples of Jesus as reliable as our mother? Are they as reliable as the witnesses of the signing of the Declaration of Independence in 1776, or the staging of the first Olympic Games in ancient Greece, or any other events we readily accept as true despite the absence of photographs and videotapes?

As we will see in a moment, the witnesses to the events of the first century are rock solid. They were honest, sincere, sane, and charitable. They were willing to die for the testimony because they knew firsthand of the prize that awaited them after death.

Even secular historians admit that something major happened in the early first century that caused so many people to radically change their lives. The Apostles, for example, had exhibited cowardly behavior prior to the Resurrection — recall St. Peter denying Christ three times, as prophesied by Jesus — but afterwards, these men were unwavering, unshakable, and unstoppable.

In fact, all the Apostles except for St. John were martyred for proclaiming what they saw. Even St. John was thrown into a cauldron of boiling oil. He miraculously emerged without a scratch, according to an account by Tertullian, an early Christian writer of the second and third centuries.[12]

As for St. Paul, this Apostle-come-lately rejected Jesus prior to the Resurrection. After the Resurrection, Paul (whose name was Saul before he was renamed by Jesus) was racing to Damascus to persecute Christians when he was stopped in his tracks, blinded by a light brighter than the sun, and brought to conversion by the booming voice of Christ himself saying, "Saul, Saul, why do you persecute me? . . . I am Jesus, whom you are persecuting" (Acts 9:4-5).

St. Paul is one of our many witnesses. According to this great Apostle, after Jesus was buried and rose

> . . . he appeared to Cephas, then to the twelve. Then he appeared to more than five hundred brethren at one time, most of whom are still alive, though some have fallen asleep.
> — 1 Cor. 15:5-6

Like Cephas (St. Peter), St. Paul went to his death for what he knew to be true.

So from this account, we know that altogether, at least 500 people saw or interacted with Jesus during the forty days after He rose. At the end of the forty days, about 150 people who were gathered at the Mount of Olives saw Christ rise and float up into the air, to be finally carried off on a cloud to the Father. Jesus had even predicted his Ascension during his Eucharistic discourse, when he chided the disciples who were having trouble believing His Flesh would become real food:

> "Do you take offense at this? Then what if you were to see the Son of man ascending where he was before?" — Jn. 6:61-62

Before they dispersed throughout the world to preach the Good News, the Apostles heeded Christ's instructions to stay in one place for the time being; for the Holy Spirit, who was the Spirit of truth, was about to come upon them. Sure enough, Mary and the Apostles were gathered together in a house when the floors and walls started shaking, and parted tongues of fire came down and landed on each one of them.

While skeptics may be able to visualize a twelve-way hallucination, it's much harder to envision a 150-person hallucination, let alone a 500-person hallucination. If these events did not occur, then, by process of elimination, everybody who claimed to have witnessed them must have been fibbing. That would be fine, if that were the end of it. But, as the field of psychology attests, fibbing people do not risk — or give up — their lives for something they made up.

If several different employees at separate firms contacted the F.B.I. to report an incident of fraud committed by their boss, the least believable one would be the employee who stood to get a promotion from the deed; the most believable story would come from an employee whose testimony would cause him to risk losing his job and lifelong career. The one who sticks to his story, at great personal cost, will always be trusted first.

The first Christians stuck to their personal accounts of what they saw, even when faced with the prospect of violence and death. That's because those Christians had first-hand knowledge that they would rise, just as Christ had.

"Men do not cling to mere fancies when facing lions, torture, and death," observed the late Rev. William G. Most, in his book *Catholic Apologetics Today*.[13]

Without miracles, Most continues, the uneducated Apostles would not have had a chance of convincing the sophisticated Greeks and Romans to accept such demanding Christian teachings.[14]

Christianity spread because people saw real miracles. They saw the living God walking the earth after rising from the dead. All around, people were dying for the things that they saw. Those who weren't called to die right away changed the course of their lives. Lives motivated by worldly ambitions were cast aside for austere, difficult existences that prepared Christians for paradise.

> From the very beginning, some Christians of both sexes embraced a way of life aiming at exact imitation of Jesus Christ: they kept virginity and continence, practiced prayer and Christian mortification, and engaged in works of mercy.[15]

What other wonders might we have witnessed if we had lived in the first century? The ground beneath us would have shaken, and the buried dead would have risen to proclaim the Good News. As the Bible records, Christ's death triggered an earthquake that split open tombstones and opened the graves of dead people, who then rose, walked into town, and preached about Christ. The quake caused the great veil at the Temple to be torn in half; what had been available only to the high priest in the Temple would now be available to all through Jesus. From the Gospel, we learn that:

> And behold, the curtain of the temple was torn in two, from top to bottom; and the earth shook, and the rocks were split; the tombs also were opened, and many bodies of the saints who had fallen asleep were raised, and coming out of the tombs after his resurrection they went into the holy city and appeared to many. When the centurion and those who were with him, keeping watch over Jesus, saw the earthquake and what took place, they were filled with awe, and said, "Truly this was the Son of God!"   — MT. 27: 51-54

According to one Gospel account, an earthquake struck when an angel descended from Heaven and rolled back the stone of Jesus' tomb. The guards were struck with terror upon the sight of this supernatural creature moving the heavy rock. The Roman authorities later paid the guards to say the body was stolen. But nobody could produce a body, and nothing could stop the news of the Resurrection as proclaimed by actual witnesses to the risen Jesus. Witnesses spoke with Jesus, shared a meal, and saw His wounds.

Even before His crucifixion and death, Jesus had raised people from the dead and had cured blindness, deafness, leprosy, and paralysis. He had walked on water. He had taken five loaves of bread and two fish and turned them into a meal for 5,000 people. At the moment of Jesus' baptism in the Jordan by St. John the Baptist, the Heavens opened up. A voice came down from a cloud, saying, "This is my beloved Son." On another occasion, Peter, James, and John saw Jesus transfigured before them. His face was shining like the sun, His clothes became white as light, and Moses and Elijah appeared and spoke to Jesus.

Jesus was truly the long-awaited Messiah, predicted by the Old Testament. According to the prophecies in Scripture, Christ would be a descendant of David (see Jer. 23:5 and Ps.132:11), conceived by a virgin (Is. 7:14). He would be betrayed by a friend and sold for thirty pieces of silver (See Ps. 41:9 and Zech. 11:12-13); He would suffer no broken bones (Ps. 31:20), but His hands and feet would be wounded (Ps. 22:1; Is. 53:12), and people would cast lots for His garments (Ps. 22:18). This suffering servant would lay down His life for sin, rise from the dead, and ascend into Heaven (Ps. 30:33, 68:18).

A prophecy found in Isaiah sums up the purpose of Christ's time on earth, and reminds us of the serious damage inflicted by human sin.

> But he was wounded for our transgressions, he was bruised for
> our iniquities; upon him was the chastisement that made us
> whole, and with his stripes we are healed.   — Is. 53:5

After Jesus ascended into Heaven, there were plenty of people left behind who were walking miracles, having been cured by His touch. The Apostles continued the miracles, with Christ working through his saints.

Even the shadow of St. Peter and facecloths that had touched St. Paul were able to cure people, according to the Acts of the Apostles (Acts 5:15-16, 19:11-12). In his classic of Christianity, *The City of God,* St. Augustine (354-430 A.D.) reports that in his day, miracle cures were still being worked through the sacraments, prayers, and relics. The Church Doctor testifies that in Carthage, he personally witnessed the cure of a devout man awaiting surgery to repair fistulas on his body. During a bout of intense prayer, the man was instantly cured. The arriving physicians were in awe at the sight of the healed wounds, and rejoicing commenced.

In a letter written in 388 A.D., St. Ambrose of Milan reports an incident in which a blind butcher named Severus instantly had his sight restored upon touching the robes of the bodies of two holy martyrs that were being transported to a basilica.

Healthy in Paris

Centuries later, an epidemic that had killed many in Paris — a violent illness known as the *mal des ardents* — was all but wiped out during a procession of the relics of St. Genevieve (c. 419-512 A.D.) through the French city in 1130 A.D. The French still celebrate the anniversary of that day, November 26, when so many were cured through the intercession of the holy virgin saint. During St. Genevieve's own lifetime, her prayer, fasting, and plea for the town to do penance had previously saved the city of Paris from a planned invasion by Attila the Hun and his troops in 455 A.D.

The thousands of miracles that have become part of our faith also include two instantaneous healings that occurred at the 1830 tomb opening of St. Margaret Mary Alacoque (1647-1690) in France. St. Margaret Mary was a saint to whom Jesus appeared frequently, conversing with her and giving her the mission to establish the devotion to His Sacred Heart. The holy virgin and saint is best known for the Twelve Promises made to her by Christ, including an assurance of salvation — the grace of final repentance — for all who worthily receive Jesus in Holy Communion the first Friday of nine consecutive months. Jesus keeps his promises.

Over at Lourdes, France — where Mary had appeared to St. Bernadette in 1958 — documentation for thousands of recorded on-site healings is available for public examination by physicians of any country or religion.

One famous but most skeptical visitor was Alexis Carrel, the renowned medical researcher who would later win the 1912 Nobel Prize for his blood-vessel research that led to advanced surgical techniques. The unbeliever came to town in 1902 wishing to prove and research his theory that unexplained rapid healings were prompted by psychological rather than supernatural factors. On the train from Lyons to Lourdes, Carrel was called upon to assist a young woman who was dying from tuberculosis peritonitis. It was this same woman, Marie Bailly, whose miraculous cure was witnessed by Carrel by the Grotto at Lourdes. The 23-year-old woman came to health after three pitchers of water from the spring at Lourdes were poured on her abdomen. What would this woman do with her life now? Carrel posed this question to the woman, who replied that she would join the Sisters of Charity and spend her life caring for the sick. That is what she did. As for Carrel (1873-1944), he wrote an account of the events in *The Voyage to Lourdes.* Official records and transcripts of doctors' depositions related to the Marie Bailly case are on file at the Archives of the Medical Bureau of Lourdes.

As long as you are a physician checking out the archives, do not miss the piles of X-rays, biopsy reports, and other reports documenting the miraculous cure of Vittorio Michelli, the young Italian soldier who, dying, was carried to Lourdes on a stretcher in 1963. Cancer had eaten away his hip and pelvic bone to the point that his leg was still connected to the rest of his body by only a piece of soft tissue . . . yet he was walking by the afternoon. His tumor had begun the process of shrinking down to nothing, a blessing that was followed by the most impossible event of all — his hipbone rebuilding itself.

According to a statement by the Vatican's Medical Commission, "A remarkable reconstruction of the iliac bone and cavity has taken place. The X-rays made in 1964, 1965, 1968, and 1969 confirm categorically and without doubt that an unforeseen and even overwhelming bone reconstruction has taken place of a type unknown in the annals of world medicine."

Ophthalmologists road-tripping to Lourdes' Medical Bureau will want to check out the documents on Madame Biré, whose blindness from atrophy of the papilla was replaced with sight at the precise moment that a procession of the Blessed Sacrament passed by her (1908). Most surreal for the examining doctors was that, at the moment, her nerve was still withered — which meant she should not have been able to see at all, yet she could read even the tiniest print with both eyes.

As long as you are going to Lourdes, France, stop over in the city of Nevers, where the incorrupt body of St. Bernadette Soubirous, the saint to whom Mary appeared at Lourdes, still lies stunningly preserved behind glass at the chapel of the Convent of St. Gildard. Her beautiful face has appeared peaceful and youthful ever since the day she died at the age of 35: April 16, 1879.

Alive Again

Besides incorruptibility, another phenomenon long a part of Christianity is the raising of people from the dead. In his book *Raised from the Dead,* Fr. Albert J. Hebert recounts the stories of 400 resurrection miracles that have occurred over the centuries, some involving the raising of deceased people whose bodies had already turned into skeletons, and many having been witnessed and recorded by the some of the greatest and most reliable figures in Christianity.

The long roster of saints mentioned in the book include St. Patrick (387-493), who raised 39 people from the dead; St. Vincent Ferrer (1350-1419), who raised 28 from the dead; St. Teresa of Ávila (1515-1582), who raised her six-year-old nephew; and St. Charbel

Makhlouf (1828-1898), the Lebanese hermit whose intercession was responsible for the raising of a drowned two-year-old.

Miracle in New York

Some of the Church's more striking miracles are mentioned in Chapters 13 and 14, but let me leave you now with an American miracle bestowed on Baby Peter J. Smith in Manhattan in 1921. Within hours of the birth of a healthy baby boy at a newly opened extension of Columbus Hospital in Manhattan[16], a usually competent nurse made the mistake of pouring a 50-percent solution of silver nitrate in the bright blue eyes of Baby Peter, instead of using the routine one-percent solution for cleansing newborns' eyes.

"The corneas were destroyed," Fr. John F. X. Smith, the brother of Peter, told me in a phone interview. "They were burnt out."

After destroying the eyes, the acid rolled down the now-blind baby's face, cutting trenches through his cheeks and then his chest. Fumes inhaled through his mouth and nose made their way into the lungs, leading to the onset of double pneumonia. A fever of 109 degrees ensued. Doctors said there was no hope of recovery.

The doctors "said he was blinded and dying," Fr. Smith added.

Soon after the accident, a medal of Mother Cabrini (1850-1917) was pinned onto the infant's clothing by the sisters of the hospital. Mother Cabrini (whose full name is St. Frances Xavier Cabrini) was the Italian-born missionary who was sent to the United States by Pope Leo XIII. She founded the Missionary Sisters of the Sacred Heart of Jesus to care for the poor by founding schools, hospitals, and orphanages all over the United States.

Immediately following the accident, the nuns at the New York hospital prayed all night in the chapel for the intercession of the holy nun, who had died four years earlier.

The following day, the baby's eyes were instantly and completely healed, without a trace of damage. However, it was observed that the baby still had a 109-degree fever and double pneumonia. One doctor noted that it would be a bit "strange" that Mother Cabrini would restore the baby's sight if he were going to die anyway. So, heeding the doctor's suggestion to pray for a second miracle, the nuns got back to work.

Within 72 hours of the accident, the baby had been healed of everything, appearing just as healthy as had upon emerging from his mother's womb three days earlier.

After an exhaustive investigation, the Church ruled the miracle to be worthy of belief. In fact, this miracle was one of four Church-approved miracles of Mother Cabrini that led the way to the saint's canonization.

One of the doctors on the case, Dr. Michael J. Horan, told *Time* Magazine (Nov. 8, 1937 issue), "The average man does not believe in miracles. I saw one."

Miracle baby Peter Smith (who grew up to become a priest) and a nun[17] (who received a later miraculous cure through Mother Cabrini's intercession) attended Mother Cabrini's canonization ceremony on Nov. 13, 1938, in Rome. In a Vatican Radio broadcast heard back in the United States, Smith, then seventeen, said, "I, for one, know the age of miracles has not passed."

Fr. Peter Smith died at the age of eighty in 2002 in Rhinebeck, N.Y.

Peter's younger brother John, a priest whose home parish is in Tuxedo, New York, has established a shrine to Mother Cabrini and three other holy people associated with the Hudson Valley: the Indian-Canadian Bl. Kateri Tekakwitha (1656-1680), French missionary priest St. Isaac Jogues (1607-1646), and Bohemian-native priest St. John Neumann (1811-1860), whose early missionary work in the United States was in New York state.

An approved miracle for Bl. Kateri Tekakwitha would pave the way for that virgin's canonization; the others on the list are full-fledged saints who, of course, already have Church-approved miracles.

CHAPTER THREE

†

Now I Get . . . Infallibility

Among the thousands of miracles Christians have witnessed over the past 2,000 years is the very existence of a miraculous government that Christ installed on earth. Thanks to the promises Christ made when He walked the earth, we know it is indestructible, and will be here on the Last Day. From His promises, we also know it is divinely guided from above, by the Spirit of Truth.

But how do we know that all of Church teaching is truth, and what is meant by infallibility?

Suppose for one moment that the Church could err in its teaching of the faith deposited here long ago by Christ. Well, this kind of Church would be no good at all, as no Christian would be sure of anything. Every single doctrine — from the Incarnation to the Ascension — would have the possibility of being wrong. Each doctrine would be subject to the personal judgment of the individual Christian, who would feel free to change his or her mind on any doctrine at any time.

Truth would be in the eye of the beholder. We would not have a Church but, rather, a movement marked by chaos and relativism. None would be held culpable for straying from even the most core tenets because the goal of achieving truth, much less having confidence in it, would be a futile pursuit. Truth would change like the weather, and people would feel free to conduct their lives in whatever manner suited them.

Fortunately, Jesus gave us an assurance that His Church would be guided into "all the truth" by the Holy Spirit (Jn. 16:13). From St. Paul, we know that the Church is "church of the living God, the pillar and bulwark of the truth" (1 Tim. 3:15).

If the Church is the foundation of truth, then by denying its teaching, we make ourselves higher than God Himself. If we believe

Christ is our Savior, then it follows that we believe His promise that he would provide our Church with divine guidance into truth.

The doctrine of infallibility means that official Church teaching on faith and morals is true. The Church is not even capable of erring when it officially and dogmatically defines matters of faith and morals, because it speaks with Christ's own voice. (See Lk.10:16.)

Does that mean our pope is immune from sin? Absolutely not.

Christ works through fallible instruments — popes and bishops who may sin — to infallibly teach us His truth and speak with His voice (see Lk. 10:16).

Each pope, starting with St. Peter in the first century, has sinned. In fact, the humble Pope John Paul II reportedly went to Confession several times per week, sometimes daily, although I have to wonder what his sins sounded like. Maybe he had a distracting moment during Morning Prayer, or maybe he got frustrated with his physical pain for a moment instead of joyfully offering it up to God.

The point is: our leaders are not perfect, but Christ makes sure our teaching is.

Does the doctrine of infallibility protect every utterance of our pope at the dinner table, of our bishop on the evening news, or of our priest in a homily?

Of course not. The doctrine of infallibility has never extended to the personal opinions or personal conduct of men, but rather only to universal teachings applicable to the whole Church.

Now, you may be asking what vehicle or mechanism is in place for preserving the purity of teaching.

Presently, the Catholic Church counts more than a billion members, and I am one of them. As a full-fledged member of this Church, could I personally sit down and start defining infallible truths if I should desire?

Of course not. Jesus provided a divinely protected organ that would carry on His teaching mission until the end. It was an organ to be composed of fallible men through whom infallible teaching would come. This organ has always been the Apostolic College and its successors. Among these successors, the pope (successor of St. Peter) has always sat in the highest place of authority.

From the beginning, whenever bishops (successors of Apostles) from around the world would assemble for a council, morally binding decisions could be made. Their decisions, where approval by the pope was granted, became official.

The Early Church had such confidence in the truth of its decisions at ecumenical councils, that bishops would not hesitate to excommunicate or exile those who opposed its binding pronouncements.

Take the Council of Nicaea in 325 A.D., for example. This Council had been called to combat the Arian heresy, which claimed that the Son was not of the same substance as the Father. After the Council, the Church banished two of the 318 bishops present because they refused to sign the creed issued by the Council. The Church also banished Arius — the churchman who promoted the heresy — and burned his books.

And so it has been with the Church's 21 Ecumenical Councils, the last of which was the Second Vatican Council (1962 to 1965).

As we have seen, the bishops as a body, when in union with the pope, can serve as one avenue of infallibility when defining tenets of faith or morals applicable to the universal church. Because of the special promises made by Christ to St. Peter, we also know that our pope, when acting by himself, also has the ability to infallibly define doctrine.

As we saw in Chapter 1, it was St. Peter on whom Christ said he would build His Church and to whom the power to bind and loose on earth was given first. Later, the power was extended to the rest of the Apostles. We also saw how Christ promised to protect the teaching mission of the Church and send it divine guidance until the end of time (see Mt. 28:19-20 and Jn. 14:16). We saw how St. Peter was given the keys to the kingdom (Mt. 16:19) and was told to shepherd Christ's sheep (Jn. 21:17). St. Peter even led the first Church council in Jerusalem (Acts 15:7).

When a pope speaks *ex cathedra,* or from the official Chair of St. Peter, he is divinely granted the special assistance promised to St. Peter.

The First Vatican Council explained it this way:

> The Roman pontiff when he speaks *ex cathedra,* that is, when he, in the exercise of his office of his supreme apostolic author-

ity, decides that a doctrine concerning faith or morals is to be held by the entire Church, he possesses, in consequence of the divine aid promised him in St. Peter, that infallibility which the Divine Savior wished to have His Church furnished for the definition of doctrines concerning faith or morals.

As the Church grew from thousands to millions over the centuries, the Church has more clearly defined and understood the role of the pope, as well as doctrines ranging from the Trinity to predestination.

But the awareness that the successor of St. Peter was the final arbiter of truth in matters of faith was always present in the Early Church. St. Augustine remarked, "All doubt has been removed by the letter of Pope Innocent of blessed memory" (*C. Duas Epp. Pelag.,* II, iii, 5).[18] In 451 A.D., we see the Fathers of Chalcedon asserting that "Peter has spoken through Leo," and, later, from the Third Council of Constantinople (680-681), we hear that "Peter has spoken through Agatho."

Even without a specific pronouncement, the early Christians knew that if something was part of the faith, then it had come to them from the Apostles, and thus from Christ.

According to St. Augustine, writing in 400 A.D.:

What the universal Church holds, not as instituted by councils, but as something always held, is most correctly believed to have been handed down by apostolic authority.

— *Baptism,* 4:24:31

The Bible Reveals; the Church Receives and Interprets

Infallibility can be applied to the Church as well as the Bible, but in very different manners. Scripture reveals the Word of God; the Church teaches and interprets it.

The writers of the Bible, though not perfect people, were divinely prevented from introducing error into the Scripture they penned, just as the Apostolic College and its successors were and are prevented from introducing error into official pronouncements of the faith.

One should note there is a difference between the infallible teaching of Scripture and of our Church authority. Sacred Scripture has as its author God, who chose human authors to pen His living Word. He inspired and employed these human writers to commit to writing the very content, not more, that He wanted our canonical Scriptures to contain.[19] While the Church does have the ability to interpret Christ's teaching (which was deposited in full by Christ through the Church during the Apostolic Age), it does not today generate fresh Revelation from God, nor does it claim to write divinely inspired documents about the Word of God.

Although its official teaching is correct, the Church is not immune from clumsily or even deficiently explaining the reasons for a teaching. But the teaching itself will always be true. Things like the Incarnation, the Trinity, the Resurrection, the Ascension, the Assumption of Mary into heaven, the Sacrifice of the Mass, the evil of abortion, and the permanent nature of Christian marriages are all part of the faith that was deposited in the first century by Christ. We have a divine assurance they are true.

Back in college, one professor would assign us plays by Lope de Vega, Pedro Calderón de la Barca, and other Catholic dramatists of the golden age of Spanish literature. Students would turn in essays on their opinions of the themes, messages, and symbolism of these works. As would be expected, different students would understand the same authors to be expressing contrasting ideas. If Lope and Pedro had been alive, they could have told us which students came closest to the mark. Then they could have explained their true intentions, point by point.

Christ is not visibly present here on earth to explain His true intentions, but he did entrust others with His own teaching. We were not left here to guess about what He meant when he taught about the way to salvation. He established a living authority through which He would speak.

Fallible human beings like me have enough trouble trying to keep God's commands; how much more difficult would it be if we first had to figure out which were God's commands to begin with?

Many Interpretations, Some Wrong

The fact that individual Christians can err in their reading of the Bible becomes obvious if we just survey several Bible readers selected from a sampling of churches. Asked to examine a particularly controversial verse of Scripture, participants would surely pose contradicting interpretations. According to the rules of logic, at least one of two conflicting interpretations would be false. Without an authoritative Church, a Christian could only wonder if the Holy Spirit was leading him or her more so than the next Christian.

Christians can gain much from personal readings of Scripture. The Catholic Church not only permits but encourages us to interpret for ourselves. As long as we are not reading anything into Scripture that defies the original deposit of faith, as protected by the Church through the Holy Spirit, then we may contemplate and interpret the Word of God as our soul pleases.

The problem arises when a Christian draws a "creative" conclusion from Scripture that clashes with Church tradition. For example, look at the third chapter of the Gospel of John, at a verse traditionally said to teach that baptism was a condition for entering Heaven:

> Jesus answered, "Truly, truly, I say to you, unless one is born
> of water and the Spirit, he cannot enter the kingdom of God."
>
> — JN. 3:5

For 2,000 years, the Catholic Church has taught that the "water" that Jesus speaks of is the real water of Baptism. On the other hand, certain churches that have emerged since the sixteenth-century claim that He refers to symbolic water. Both interpretations could not be correct simultaneously. Dare we hedge our bets on the meaning of something of such import for entrance into Heaven?

The fact is, the Early Church knew full well that "being born of water and the Spirit" was the literal definition of being baptized. St. John even reinforces his point by mentioning right afterwards that Jesus and his Apostles begin baptizing in Jn. 3:22 and the Apostles alone in Jn. 4:2! The Bible has always taught that Baptism is linked to our salvation.

St. Peter also taught the saving role of Baptism in a letter to Christians. Referring to the story of Noah's ark during the Great Flood, St. Peter writes: ". . . eight persons were saved through water. Baptism, which corresponds to this, now saves you" (1 Pet. 3:20-21).

Unfortunately, a saving Baptism[20] is not the only example of a doctrine once taught as a universal Christian truth, then subsequently discarded by some denominations. The literal nature of Christ's words at the Last Supper is another instance where the original intent of the Word of God has seemed to lose something in individual interpretation.

During the Last Supper, Jesus held up the bread and wine and said, "This is My Body" and "This is my Blood." For 2,000 years, the Catholic Church has interpreted these lines literally. Likewise, the Orthodox churches have also upheld the literal nature of these statements. Still, some Christian churches that have taken root since the sixteenth century — although not all of them — have decided to opt for a symbolic interpretation of Christ's words.

What's the difference? Considerable, since these teachings are attached to the promise of eternal life:

> Jesus said to them, "Truly, truly, I say to you, unless you eat the flesh of the Son of man and drink his blood, you have no life in you; he who eats my flesh and drinks my blood has eternal life, and I will raise him up at the last day."
>
> — Jn. 6:53-54

If we consider the fact that God's designs cannot change from society to society or century to century, then the Church founded by Jesus, by definition, must be promulgating the same doctrines and morals it taught in the earliest centuries. The Church may understand doctrines more clearly as it goes along, but it never reverses them or contradicts them. Unsurprisingly, the Catholic Church is the only Christian Church that can claim the kind of consistency that would be expected of a Church instituted by Christ himself.

Some churches have done away with the priesthood. Some have declared that penance is no longer necessary after personal sin. Others have lifted their ban on contraception, something considered immoral by all Christians as recently as the twentieth century. Several denominations have eliminated the ban on female clergy. Many have done away with the Sacrifice of the Mass and the sacraments of Confession, Confirmation, and the Anointing of the Sick. Such is the nature of what can happen when "creative" interpretation of Scripture is taken too far.

Ironically enough, many denominations with these differing practices all claim to be based on Scripture — even though the Holy Bible itself is one of the things originating from the Catholic Church. We can know that our Bible contains the correct books only if we first understand that the Catholic Church, which chose the books, is protected from error. When a teaching is handed down to us by the One, Holy, Catholic, and Apostolic Church, we can be assured that the Holy Spirit is responsible for it. And this is a darned good thing, because there were many writings from which to choose.

In the late fourth century, it was the Catholic Church that decided, without error, which 27 books would become bound together to make up our New Testament.[21] There were other writings, now commonly known as the "Gnostic gospels" or "apocrypha," that some claimed to be authored by Apostles and other holy men. It was the Catholic Church that was ultimately able to distinguish the Word of God from the word of men. This was not a task God would expect each individual Christian to tackle personally. Nor would God have expected individual Christians to each spend their lives developing doctrines such as the Trinity or the process of justification. Instead, Jesus gave us a teacher and called it His Church.

The Church, and only the Church, has possessed the gift for determining which writings were Scripture and for preventing Scripture's teachings from being falsely interpreted.

"Where Holy Scripture is disjoined from the living voice of the Church, it falls prey to the disputes of experts," Pope Benedict XVI has said.

The canon of the New Testament, composed of 27 books, has been held universally by the Church since the fourth century.[22] The Church Fathers trusted that they had received the correct contents of the Bible because they trusted in the divine origin of the Catholic Church. As St. Augustine once ruminated:

> Indeed, I would not believe in the Gospel myself if the authority of the Catholic Church did not influence me to do so.
> — *Against the Letter of Mani Called "The Foundation,"*
> 1581 (397 A.D.)

The fact that the bishops of the Church were successors of apostles meant Christians could be confident their Bible's table of contents was divinely determined. This is how and why St. Augustine chided Faustus:

> The authority of our books, which is confirmed by the agreement of so many nations, supported by a succession of apostles, bishops, and councils, is against you.
> — St. Augustine, *Reply to Faustus the Manichean*,
> 13:5 (400 A.D.)

Without access to personal Bibles, early Christians became accustomed to learning the Word of God at Mass. It wasn't until the mid-1400s that a Catholic inventor named Johann Gutenberg[23] would introduce the printing press. Prior to that, it was almost exclusively our Catholic monks who preserved Holy Scripture, spending their days devoted to the laborious task of copying Scripture by hand.

Often, Protestants will graciously recognize and credit the Catholic Church for giving them the Bible. They will even acknowledge the infallibility of the Bible. But rarely does it occur to them that, in doing so, they are simultaneously accepting the infallibility of the work of the Catholic Church in producing this Bible.

If the Catholic Church could be infallible in the fourth century — centuries after the last Apostle died — then it becomes incumbent upon the Protestant to explain when and how the Church subsequently lost its divine nature, or how it lost the guidance of the Holy Spirit into "all truth," part of Jesus' promise to be with the Church until the end of time. Without the Church having lost either of those things, it's hard to explain the logic of accepting the full text of our New Testament — as these Protestants do — while at the same time rejecting the rationale our Church Fathers had for admitting each of the books into the Bible.

For example, the Church Fathers never would have admitted any book into the Bible that denied the possibility of a person losing saving grace after receiving it. Yet, some Christian denominations that use our same Bible — including Presbyterian and non-denominational churches — hold to the "once saved, always saved" formula. In other words, they believe that once a person has received justifying grace, he or she can never lose it. They don't seem to mind that the first 1,500 years of Scripture scholars disagree with this interpretation.

Those scholars include St. Augustine, whose book, *The Gift of Perseverance,* specifically ponders the question as to why some Christians persevere in their justifying grace, while others lose it before dying:

> [Of] two pious men, why to the one should be given perseverance unto the end, and to the other it should not be given . . .

The Catholic Church admitted into our Bible only the writings that it knew clearly proclaimed early Christian teachings such as the literal Flesh and Blood of Jesus in the Eucharist, the power of a priest to forgive sins, and the necessity of Baptism. So, it is remarkable to see Christians among us who can read these same texts that were regarded by brilliant bishops of the Early Church to uphold the set of core Catholic doctrines, now saying that these Catholic teachings are denied by the precise texts that were chosen to proclaim them.

Although our Church leaders may sin, the official Church teachings are trustworthy to the core. Not even the so-called "bad popes" who have sat in the Chair of Peter have succeeded in reversing or eliminating a single doctrine. In fact, the Catholic Church is the only Church that has preserved all Christian morals and doctrines, reversing none of them.

The Church founded by Jesus still represents Jesus. The sacraments that He instituted, the Sacrifice of the Mass, and the sanctity of the male priesthood are just a few of the teachings that will forever be protected. Even if every other church in the world begins allowing female priests or ministers, and even if sincere protesters picket for the rest of their lives, the Catholic Church will be prevented by the Heavens from conforming. For, on the last day of the world, our Church will still be adhering to God's designs.

In the words of St. Augustine:

> The Catholic Church is the work of Divine Providence, achieved through the prophecies of the prophets, through the Incarnation and the teaching of Christ, through the journeys

of the Apostles, through the suffering, the crosses, the blood and death of the martyrs, through the admirable lives of the saints. . . . When, then, we see so much help on God's part, so much progress and so much fruit, shall we hesitate to bury ourselves in the bosom of that Church? For starting from the apostolic chair down through successions of bishops, even unto the open confession of all mankind, it has possessed the crown of teaching authority.

— *The Advantage of Believing*, 35 (392 A.D.)

Okay, let's start from the top.

How do we know the Bible is infallible? We know this because the Catholic Church infallibly tells us so. How do we know our Church is infallible? We have the word of Jesus, who is God. Jesus promised the Church He built on Peter would be guided into "all truth" by the Holy Spirit, and that that the gates of Hell would never triumph against it. In the New Testament, the Church is called "the pillar and bulwark of truth" and "the Church of the living God." Jesus said the Holy Spirit would be with His Church "always." Jesus told the Apostles to start teaching, and promised to be with them "always, until the close of the age."

In hindsight, we can see that the Catholic Church has lasted two millennia, never once contradicting ancient teachings. This, in it itself, is a miracle. But it was an expected miracle, for the Catholic Church was built on the Rock of Peter, the first bishop of Rome, to whom the keys to Heaven were granted.

Practices Are Practical

In addition to preserving Christ's doctrines and morals, which are unchangeable, the Church is also responsible for establishing practical ways for the faithful to best live out the Christian faith and honor its doctrines. These are called practices or disciplines. These practices are changeable — thus, not in the category of infallible pronouncements. But although practices may change, we are still obliged to obey them, for Christ Himself gave to His Church the power to legislate in His absence. Thus our Church not only has the power to bind and loose on earth (Mt. 18:18) in pronouncing matters of divine law, but also has the authority to specify how divine law can be applied to the faithful.

Therefore, if the Church obliges the faithful to attend Mass on Ascension Thursday or on All Saints' Day, God expects us to listen.

One practice regulated by the Church is penance, particularly Lenten fasting. The Church has said that our minimum obligation is to abstain from meat on Ash Wednesday as well as the Fridays of Lent; also, on Ash Wednesday and Good Friday, we must limit ourselves to one regular sized meal, and two light meals, with no snacking during the day. Of course, serious Catholics do much more: they may give up sweets for Lent; they attend daily Mass; they do charity work; they donate extra money to the poor; and some able bodies commit themselves to full 24-hour fasts. But to refuse to do the minimum, assuming one's health allows for it, would be sinful.

To uphold the unchangeable doctrine that Jesus gave to his representatives His own power to forgive sins, the Church hands us guidelines concerning the sacrament of Confession. We are obliged to confess mortal sins to a priest and are encouraged (but not required) to confess venial sins. We are given the option of seeing the priest face-to-face, or anonymously, but the validity of telephoned or e-mailed confessions is rejected.

If we listen to the Church, we cannot go wrong, according to Jesus:

> "But the Counselor, the Holy Spirit, whom the Father will send in my name, he will teach you all things, and bring to your remembrance all that I have said to you."
>
> — Jn. 14:26

Our official teaching comes from the only government on earth that rules with God's eternal truths. Not everyone is a member, but every human being is called to be.

CHAPTER FOUR

✝

Now I Get . . . Confession

During the weeks leading up to a momentous occasion in the life of every sinning child — an event known as First Confession — Sister Carol instructed our third-grade class at St. Louis School to start examining our consciences for things that may have offended the Lord. The list of things that popped into my head began to accumulate: "Fought with brother, made a fresh comment to Grandma, snuck cookies and gave my brother a haircut while my parents were asleep . . ."

As the big day approached, I realized I had a problem. What if I drew a blank after entering the confessional? I didn't want to forget anything, but how was I supposed to remember a lifetime of sins on cue?

Then, a light bulb went off in my head. I could bring my sin list into the confessional to use as a cheat-sheet . . . if that was allowed.

"Sure, why not?" my mother said, encouragingly.

With that pressing question answered, I felt comforted and relieved — that is, until someone mentioned that the confession booths at this church might be dark.

Oh, no. I wouldn't be able to read my notes! Now what was I going to do?

I think it was my mother, who, while trying to keep a straight face, suggested a novel solution to this age-old predicament: a flashlight. Looking back on it now, I can't believe that I actually decided to take her up on that idea, but I did. I showed up at the church with a crumpled piece of paper, folded ten times lest any all-too-curious classmate try to catch a peek at my oh-so-private sins.

And a flashlight.

And an outfit with large pockets to help camouflage it all.

After practicing my lines in the pew, which included a recitation of the Act of Contrition, I took my turn in the confessional. The priest must have wondered what in the world was going on with the blinding flashes of light emanating from my side of the booth, not to mention the loud crumpling paper commotion. I was delighted the priest did not admit to noticing any of this.

I pretty much forgot about the whole ordeal until the following year, when a friend from the incoming third grade, preparing for First Confession, informed me that her teacher announced to the class, "And . . . you don't have to bring a flashlight like Claire did last year."

Boy, was I embarrassed! I hadn't even realized anybody had taken note of my quasi-covert operation, much less that that my *modus operandi* had been discussed and remembered a whole year later.

Anyway, I continued going to Confession for years with religion class, but I eventually began avoiding it. I convinced myself it wasn't something I needed. I wasn't getting a grade for it. It wasn't fun. I just didn't realize how important it was.

I avoided the reality that it was something Christ created for us — not just a superfluous sacrament that benefited only some people, but, rather, the precise way that our own Savior provided for us to restore grace to our souls and reconcile with the God we have hurt.

I am too ashamed to admit how long I avoided Confession, but, finally, in my mid-twenties, I returned to the sacrament, also known as Penance or Reconciliation.

With all the sins I had collected over the years, my heart was fluttering, but I got through it. I knew Christ had directly forgiven my sins through the priest, for I had read the words of Jesus in the Bible where He gave His representatives the authority to forgive people in His own name.

> Jesus said to them again, "Peace be with you. As the Father has sent me, even so I send you." And when he had said this, he breathed on them, and said to them, "Receive the Holy Spirit. If you forgive the sins of any, they are forgiven; if you retain the sins of any, they are retained."   — Jn. 20:21-23

Not only had Jesus given His Church the authority to administer His forgiveness, but also the authority to withhold forgiveness if necessary. Of course, the withholding of forgiveness is reserved for sinners with no intention of changing their ways.

Since the beginning, the Church has understood itself to be entrusted with the ministry of reconciliation. Early Church Fathers warned Christians not to fool themselves into thinking that it would suffice to go only to God with sins, in a secret, private manner. They warned Christians that the authority given to the Church in Christ's ministry of forgiveness was not to be taken lightly.

St. Augustine, perhaps the greatest Doctor of the Church, cautioned:

> Let no one say I do penance secretly; I perform it in the sight of God, and He who is to pardon me knows that in my heart I repent. . . . Was it then said to no purpose, "What you shall loose upon earth shall be loosed in Heaven?" Was it for nothing that the keys were given to the Church?
> — *Sermo cccxcii*, n. 3, in P.L., XXXIX, 1711

Attempting to go straight to God for serious sins is not much wiser than deciding to go straight to God for the treatment of a heart disorder or a brain infection. Although God is the source of both physical and spiritual healing, He has entrusted certain shepherds to care for us in these regards.

St. John Chrysostom (347-407 A.D.), an Antioch-born Doctor of the Church, once mused, "No one says: Because I have an ulcer, I will not go near a physician or take medicine. . . . We (priests) know well how to pardon, because we ourselves are liable to sin"(Homily, "On Frequent Assembly," in *P.G.*, LXIII, 463).

The Old Testament precursor to Confession was Yom Kippur, or the Day of Atonement. Once a year, the people of Israel would fast and offer sacrifices to atone for the sins of all the people of the nation. The day involved confessing sins (Lev. 16:21) and called for a high priest (Lev. 16:32) to sacrifice a goat.

Christ, the Lamb who was sacrificed for our sins, gave the power to forgive sins — something not even granted to the Old Testament priests — to priests of the New Covenant. The power was bestowed on Christ's special disciples when He breathed the Holy Spirit on them. Those disciples have handed down that power and authority over the centuries to the modern-day priests of the Catholic Church. In fact, each Catholic priest has been ordained by a bishop who is in a straight chain of succession leading back to an Apostle.

St. Paul recognized that the "ministry of reconciliation" of the New Covenant was entrusted not to all Christians, but to himself and to others serving as ambassadors of Christ. Rather than saying it is fine to go straight to God for forgiveness, St. Paul stresses that God makes his appeal "through" his ambassadors.

> Therefore, if any one is in Christ, he is a new creation; the old has passed away, behold, the new has come. All this is from God, who through Christ reconciled us to himself and gave us the ministry of reconciliation; that is, in Christ God was reconciling the world to himself, not counting their trespasses against them, and entrusting to us the message of reconciliation. So we are ambassadors for Christ, God making his appeal through us. We beseech you on behalf of Christ, be reconciled to God.   — 2 COR. 5:17-20

As mentioned in the first chapter, the Church had been given the full authority to exercise its ministries in whatever way it saw fit.

Jesus had told Peter, "Whatever you bind on earth shall be bound in Heaven, and whatever you loose on earth shall be loosed in Heaven" (Mt. 16:19). Later, Jesus repeated those instructions to the Apostles as a group (Mt. 18:18). Therefore, Christ acts through the Church during the sacrament. What the priests are dispensing is Christ's own forgiveness.

St. John Chrysostom marveled at this incredible power of forgiveness granted to priests by Christ. He wrote that priests "can bind with a bond which pertains to the soul itself and transcends the very Heavens. Did [God] not give them all the powers of Heaven?" (*The Priesthood* 3:5).

When is the best time to confess? Now.

Around 250 A.D., St. Cyprian of Carthage warned that after death, sinners will not have a second chance to "confess their sins to the priests of God."

> I beseech you, brethren, let everyone who has sinned confess his sin while he is still in this world, while his confession is still admissible, while the satisfaction and remission made through the priest are still pleasing before the Lord.
>
> — *The Lapsed,* 28

When we are forgiven, Christ's graces are instantly showered on us. Our souls shine more brightly and beautifully, as anyone wearing soul goggles can plainly see.

Few Sins Are Original

The first time our soul is alive with Christ's grace is at Baptism, whereby we are incorporated into the Church, which is the Body of Christ.

The water of Baptism easily wipes away the original sin we have inherited from Adam and Eve, as well as any personal sin we may have accumulated (if we were not baptized as a baby). But most importantly, in Baptism, we die with Christ and we rise with Christ; we are new creations now worthy of the perfect and eternal joy God intended us for at the beginning of the world.

In his letter to the Romans, the Apostle St. Paul proclaimed:

> We were buried therefore with him by baptism into death, so that as Christ was raised from the dead by the glory of the Father, we too might walk in newness of life.   — ROM. 6:4

To the Galatians, St. Paul delivers another astonishing message:

> I have been crucified with Christ; it is no longer I who live, but Christ who lives in me.   — GAL. 2:20

Christ truly lives within us right here and right now, not just in heaven far away. He continues to transform us, feeding us life-giving grace through the sacraments. As long as we do not decline His spiritual gifts (by choosing our own will instead of His), we keep receiving. But if we do sin after the one-time sacrament of Baptism, Jesus will generously restore the Baptismal grace we have lost through the sacrament of Confession if we repent of our sin and turn back to Him.

HOT TIPS FOR SMOOTH CONFESSING

a.   When you arrive, you may choose between the anonymous confession booth and the one where you face the priest.

b.   The priest is not allowed to repeat anything you say. If he directly violates this rule, there is a little penalty involved: he is excommunicated and only the Pope can forgive him.

c.   Sincere Catholics try to confess at least monthly. Great saints have been known to go weekly or even daily! All Catholics are required to go at least once a year if they have committed a serious sin.

d.   Whatever you are confessing, take comfort in the fact that the priest has heard much worse in his lifetime. Plus, he is a sinner himself.

e.   We must confess ALL mortal sins on our souls that we haven't previously confessed, even if they are from 20 years ago. There is no need to delve into gory details — simply name the types of sins and the number of times each was committed. If one slips our mind, we can always confess it next time.

f.   Do not confess the sins of your boyfriend, cousin, or neighbor. Do not speak so quietly that the priest cannot hear you. Do not speak in a rambling, confusing manner so that the priest thinks you confessed cheating at Scrabble when, actually, you committed an ax murder.

g.   If you have a mortal sin on your soul, you may still attend Mass, but refrain from Holy Communion until you have confessed. Receiving the glorified Christ unworthily is a serious offense. For the Bible says: "Whoever, therefore, eats the bread or drinks the cup of the Lord in an unworthy manner will be guilty of profaning the body and blood of the Lord" (1 Cor.11:27).

The *Didache,* an important Christian document written between 70 and 80 A.D., warned the faithful to confess sins before the Sacrifice of the Mass.

> Confess your sins in church, and do not go up to your prayer with an evil conscience. This is the way of life. . . . On the Lord's Day gather together, break bread, and give thanks, after confessing your transgressions so that your sacrifice may be pure.
> — *Didache* 4:14, 14:1 (70 A.D.)

h. Prior to Confession, conduct a thorough examination of conscience. Once you enter the confessional, you can begin by saying, "Bless me, Father, for I have sinned. It's been one month (or 30 years) since my last Confession, and these are my sins. . . ."

   The priest will then ask you to recite an act of contrition stating that you are sorry and that you have the firm intention of sinning no more. The important thing is that you sincerely desire and aim to avoid all future temptation. If you forget the Act of Contrition, look for copies of the prayer around the confessional booth, or ask to repeat after the priest. Finally, you will be assigned penance for your sin.

i. The penances being handed out nowadays are considerably lighter than those from the old days. Compare "ten years of penance" — a common sentence to sinners of yesteryear — to this recent penance assigned to a local sinner: "Spend ten minutes thanking God for all the blessings in your life."

j. No matter how terrible your sins are, every trace of them will be erased from your soul before you leave the confessional. That's what we can expect from an awesome, merciful God.

k. Once you come out of the ordeal alive, you should demand that your friends send you a "Congratulations! You were brave enough to go to Confession!" greeting card. You deserve it.

According to the catechism, the Fathers of the Church present the sacrament of Confession as "the second plank [of salvation] after the shipwreck which is the loss of grace." The shipwreck of sin brings instant and sometimes lasting damage into our lives and the lives of others. It is a disease that we spread to others.

Long ago, I gave a present to someone on my annual exchange list. She opened it and said she would not be interested in that type of gift in the future. So, the next time I gave her a present, I opted for a completely different gift category. She thanked me but said never to get that type of gift, either.

At that point, I decided that in the future I would ax her name from my shopping list. I happened to mention my secret plan to someone older, who, fortunately, advised me to do no such thing. Petty revenge would only deteriorate the situation further, and the guilt would then fall on me. The simple solution, this wise person told me, was to grin and bear it and stuff some cash in a greeting card. That worked perfectly, and past tensions were healed. But I can think of plenty of other past situations where my actions or words could have permanently planted seeds of ill will in people, wherever they now may be.

Sins can have permanent consequences, spiritually or physically. Thankfully, God's mercy is bigger than even the biggest sin, and can wipe our souls clean the moment we confess with true repentance. Often, even after forgiveness, we will still have to deal with the punitive consequences of whatever damage we have unleashed into our worlds.

I can think of acquaintances who bear ongoing, heavy crosses directly created by their own personal sins from one or more decades ago — sins committed in less than a day's work. But these sins brought pain, physical and emotional, that may be with them until they die.

Sin ruins everything; it ruins the infinite good that God planned for us.

We simply cannot survive without God, whose grace keeps our soul alive, any more than we can live without food. By sinning, we place ourselves at peril, hopping onto a path to nowhere, a path to death. Only God can give us life.

While all sins cause a shipwreck in the relationship of an individual and God, for whom each of us was created, the Bible does make the distinction between regular sins and deadly (mortal) ones.

> If any one sees his brother committing what is not a mortal sin, he will ask, and God will give him life for those whose sin is not mortal. There is sin which is mortal; I do not say that one is to pray for that. All wrongdoing is sin, but there is sin which is not mortal.   — 1 JN. 5:16-17

St. Augustine also warned against these deadly sins, which make our souls incompatible for heaven should we die in them.

> For light sins, without which we cannot live, prayer was instituted.... But do not commit those sins on account of which you would have to be separated from the body of Christ. Perish the thought!
> — St. Augustine, *Sermon to Catechumens on the Creed* 7:15; 8:16

Through the Church, though, even the most horrid and unthinkable sins can be forgiven. St. Augustine wrote:

> Let us not listen to those who deny that the Church of God has power to *forgive all sins.*
> — *De agon. Christ.,* iii

According to the catechism:

> ... regular confessing of our venial sins helps us form our conscience, fight against evil tendencies, let ourselves be healed by Christ and progress in the life of the Spirit. By receiving more frequently through this sacrament the gift of the Father's mercy, we are spurred to be merciful as he is merciful (cf. Lk. 6:36).
> — *CCC,* 1458

No matter the type, each and every sin has sobering consequences, and must be dealt with. For, sin is the only thing that can separate us from God.

> If we say we have no sin, we deceive ourselves, and the truth
> is not in us. If we confess our sins, he is faithful and just, and
> will forgive our sins and cleanse us from all unrighteousness.
>
> — 1 JN. 1:8-9

So, perish the thought of committing a mortal sin, but be advised
that even the worst mortal sin is no match for Christ's mercy. Only
a heretic would deny this, according to St. Augustine:

> There have been those who would say that no penance is
> available for certain sins; and they have been excluded from the
> Church and have been made heretics. Holy Mother Church
> is not rendered powerless by any kind of sin.
>
> — St. Augustine, *Sermons* 352, 9

Well, at this point, you probably want to take a break to check
out neighborhood Confession times in the weekend entertainment
section of your local newspaper. If that fails, Confession schedules for
most U.S. churches are listed at *www.masstimes.org*. You might also
peruse your church bulletin or call your parish rectory.

It may not be fun to confess our sins. But for those desiring eternal life, it is a non-negotiable. Just ask St. Basil the Great, a Doctor
of the Church, who wrote:

> It is necessary to confess our sins to those to whom the dis-
> pensation of God's mysteries is entrusted. Those doing
> penance of old are found to have done it before the saints. It
> is written in the Gospel that they confessed their sins to John
> the Baptist [Matt. 3:6], but in Acts [19:18] they confessed to
> the apostles.
>
> — *Rules Briefly Treated*, 288 (374 A.D.)

CHAPTER FIVE

✝

Now I Get . . . the Real Presence

Once our sins are confessed with a repentant heart, we are ready to receive Jesus. Nothing else on earth can compare to this privilege. By receiving the immortal Jesus, we, too, become immortal.

St. Ignatius of Antioch, in the year 100 A.D., called the Eucharist "the medicine of immortality and the antidote, so that we do not die, but live forever in Jesus Christ."

St. Irenaeus, a Church Father who was born in the first half of the second century, said that it was precisely this supernatural nourishment that gave us the hope of rising.

> For just as the bread which comes from the earth, having received the invocation of God, is no longer ordinary bread, but the Eucharist, consisting of two realities, earthly and Heavenly, so our bodies, having received the Eucharist are no longer corruptible, because they have the hope of the resurrection.
>
> — *Against The Heresies* 4, 18:4-5

Still, our faith must be strong to believe the words of Jesus: "This is my Body" (Mt. 26:26). St. Ambrose, Bishop of Milan, assured the early Christians in 390 A.D. that they should believe Jesus' words over their own sensibilities:

> Perhaps you may be saying, "I see something else; how can you assure me that I am receiving the body of Christ?" It but remains for us to prove it. And how many are the examples we might use! . . . Christ is in that sacrament, because it is the body of Christ.
>
> — *The Mysteries* 9:50, 58 (390 A.D.)

Earlier, in 150 A.D., St. Justin Martyr testified that the bread and wine is "made into the Eucharist by the Eucharistic prayer set down by him, and by the change of which our blood and flesh is nourished, is both the Flesh and Blood of that incarnated Jesus" (*First Apology* 66, 20).

Overall, in the Early Church, the receiving of Christ's real Flesh and Blood defined a Christian, whereas the rejection of the doctrine defined a heretic.

Heretics "abstain from Eucharist and from prayer because they do not confess that the Eucharist is the Flesh of our Savior Jesus of our Savior Jesus Christ," wrote St. Ignatius of Antioch, not too long after the turn of the first century (*Letter to Smyrnaeans* 6:2 [110 A.D.]).

My Catholic school nuns and lay teachers were every bit as clear as these guys were on the Real Presence of Christ's Body and Blood, so it surprises me when I catch reports of Gallup and other national polls showing that a large percentage of the Catholic population in America, especially the youngest Catholics, are confused about whether we receive a symbol or our Savior.

Even though I had grasped the doctrine from an early age, it wasn't until later that I appreciated it or learned its Biblical or historical basis.

Why do we believe that Christ is truly present under the appearance of bread and wine? Because . . .

- The teaching is one of the clearest in the Bible.
- The teaching is one of the clearest from the mouth of Jesus.
- The gift of Christ's Real Presence is the most precious and ancient treasure of the Church. The lives of the early Christians revolved around the breaking of the bread, the true sacrifice of the real Jesus.
- The Early Church Fathers were unanimous in holding to the doctrine of the Real Presence in the Eucharist, which was instituted at the Last Supper.

Need more assurance? Find a friend who has received the risen Lord in the Eucharist daily for many years, and that person will surely testify to changes of heart that could not be of human origin.

It is no coincidence that the greatest saints throughout history have been those with the greatest faith in the Real Presence. When it comes to extraordinary devotion to the Sacrament, count in St. Thomas Aquinas, St. Teresa of Ávila, St. Thérèse of Lisieux, St. Francis of Assisi, St. Clare of Assisi, St. John Neumann, St. Catherine of Siena, St. Thomas More, St. Bernard of Clairvaux, St. John Chrystostom, and Mother Teresa.

Mother Teresa said it was the long hours of adoring Jesus in the Eucharist that enabled her and the other Missionary Sisters of Charity to accomplish the work for the poor in Calcutta. Writing to a parish church in Illinois, the late nun described how the Blessed Sacrament transforms Christians into His personal instruments:

> Each one of us is a co-worker of Christ — we must labour [sic] hard to carry Him to the hearts where He has not yet been known and loved. But, unless we have Jesus, we cannot give Him; that is why we need the Eucharist. Spend as much time as possible in front of the Blessed Sacrament and He will fill you with His strength and His power. Tell Him, "Come to our hearts Lord and stay with us." Then you will become the instruments of His love, peace and joy.
> — The Real Presence Association, Chicago, IL

St. Augustine, one of the greatest Church Fathers, wrote:

> Christ was carried in his own hands when, referring to his own body, he said, "This is my body" (Mt. 26:26). For he carried that body in his hands.
> — *Explanations of the Psalms 33:1:10* (405 A.D.)

In his book Early Christian Doctrines, renowned early Church historian J.N.D. Kelly (a Protestant) agrees, stating that early Church fathers regarded the consecrated bread and wine as, literally, "the Savior's body and blood." Kelly wrote:

> Eucharistic teaching, it should be understood at the outset, was in general unquestioningly realist, i.e. the consecrated bread and wine were taken to be, and were treated and designated as, the Savior's body and blood.[24]

For the Eucharist to be valid, it must be celebrated by a direct successor of the Apostles (a bishop) or one appointed by the bishop (priest). Since both the Catholic Church and the Eastern Orthodox Churches are led by successors of Apostles, the Sacrifice of the Mass is valid for each.

St. Ignatius of Antioch cautioned that the Eucharist was valid only if administered by a valid bishop or priest of the Catholic Church.

> Let that be considered a valid Eucharist which is celebrated by the bishop, or by one whom he appoints. Wherever the bishop appears, let the people be there; just as wherever Jesus Christ is, there is the Catholic Church.
>
> — *Epistle to the Smyrnaeans*

The Words of Jesus

In the sixth chapter of the Gospel of John, Jesus tells us over and over again that His flesh is true food and His blood is true drink. When the Apostles don't understand, he takes care to repeat Himself. He makes it clear that He is not speaking symbolically.

In the end, many disciples leave Jesus because they cannot accept this hard teaching. Their faith has reached its breaking point, and Jesus knows who these unbelievers are. He has known from the beginning the ones who would not believe, and the one who would betray him.

> And he said, "For this reason I have told you that no one can come to me unless it is granted him by my Father." As a result of this, many (of) his disciples returned to their former way of life and no longer accompanied him. Jesus then said to the Twelve, "Do you also want to leave?" Simon Peter answered him, "Master, to whom shall we go? You have the words of eternal life."   — JN. 5:64-68

The Apostles believe Jesus about His flesh being true food, and they stay with Him, for Jesus had told them:

> "I am the living bread which came down from Heaven; if any one eats of this bread, he will live for ever; and the bread

which I shall give for the life of the world is my flesh." The
Jews then disputed among themselves, saying, "How can this
man give us his flesh to eat?" So Jesus said to them, "Truly,
truly, I say to you, unless you eat the flesh of the Son of man
and drink his blood, you have no life in you; he who eats my
flesh and drinks my blood has eternal life, and I will raise him
up at the last day. For my flesh is food indeed, and my blood
is drink indeed. He who eats my flesh and drinks my blood
abides in me, and I in him."   — JN. 6:51-56

The Apostles trusted Jesus and remained with Him. But they
were probably wondering how in the world His promise to give His
flesh and blood as food and drink would be accomplished. What
occurred at the Last Supper on Holy Thursday answered all their
questions.

That is where the promise was fulfilled. Jesus held up the bread
and said, "This is my body." He held up the wine and said, "This is
my blood," thus instituting the sacrament of the Eucharist. What
appeared to be bread and wine was now something completely different. Jesus gave his Apostles the authority to do what He did. Jesus
said, "This is my body which is for you. Do this in remembrance of
me" (1 Cor. 11:24).

Now the Apostles understood exactly how Jesus planned to give
Christians His flesh and blood to eat and drink after He was gone.

From the very beginning, the Apostles took Jesus' words literally and passed the literal teaching down through the succession of
bishops. The Catholic Church never stopped teaching it. The Real
Presence of Jesus in the Sacrifice of the Mass will be ours until the
Second Coming of Christ.

When the Mass is celebrated, Jesus' once-and-for-all Sacrifice on
Calvary becomes present to us, uniting us to His Cross and saving
mission until He comes again.

"For as often as you eat this bread and drink the cup, you proclaim the Lord's death until he comes" (1 Cor. 11:26).

To prepare our hearts for His entrance, we must fast for an hour
before receiving. If we receive Holy Communion unworthily, with
our soul stained by mortal sin, we are guilty of sinning against the

actual Body and Blood of Christ. According to the Bible, this is so serious that it could bring death to our soul. When we receive, we must discern the great price paid by the Flesh and Blood received.

> Whoever, therefore, eats the bread or drinks the cup of the Lord in an unworthy manner will be guilty of profaning the body and blood of the Lord. Let a man examine himself, and so eat of the bread and drink of the cup. For any one who eats and drinks without discerning the body eats and drinks judgment upon himself. That is why many of you are weak and ill, and some have died. But if we judged ourselves truly, we should not be judged.   — 1 COR. 11:27-31

We might as well be kneeling before the risen Jesus on the Mount of Olives as He prepared to ascend into Heaven, because His Body, Blood, Soul, and Divinity are just as present to us when we receive Holy Communion as they were to his first-century friends.

When we receive Jesus, we are made part of the One Bread, which is the One Body. We not only become connected to Jesus, but to every other person who receives the same Jesus under the appearance of bread and wine, and to all the souls in whom He lives in Heaven.

Different parishes around the world may start out with different bread, but before the end of the Mass, it is all the same. It is Jesus. The one Bread is the one Body. We become part of Jesus' very Body. We become part of Jesus. It is mind-blowing. It is truth.

St. Augustine brought home this point when he wrote: "If you have received worthily, you are what you have received" (*Sermons*, 227).

Receiving Communion foreshadows the way things will be in Heaven, when Jesus will be within us all the time. By our participation in the Sacrifice of the Mass, we unite ourselves to Christ's cross and death. Christ's sacrifice will be offered up to the Father eternally for our sins.

According to the catechism:

> Every time this mystery is celebrated, "the work of our redemption is carried on" and we "break the one bread that

provides the medicine of immortality, the antidote for death, and the food that makes us live forever in Jesus Christ (*LG3;* St. Ignatius of Antioch, *Ad. Eph.* 20, 2: SCh10, 76)."

— *CCC*, 1405

Upon examining the lives of so many saints who were propelled to such great holiness and love by their radical devotion to the Eucharist, it is not so hard to believe it is truly Jesus.

The Critics

It wasn't until the sixteenth century that some Christian denominations reversed themselves on this historically Christian doctrine. Christian denominations that broke off the Church prior to the sixteenth century — whether it was the Armenians, Copts, or Nestorians in the fifth century or the Orthodox Christians in the eleventh century — all kept the ancient Christian doctrine of the Real Presence:

> Suppose for a minute that the Catholic doctrine of the Real Presence is false. Jesus must have foreseen that the whole Church would embrace this false doctrine and fall into idolatry. He would have known that the very words he spoke in John 6 and at the Last Supper led them to do so. Why would he have deliberately used language that he knew Christians would misinterpret? Why would Jesus have allowed his followers to be so horribly mistaken when he could have prevented it with a simple word of explanation? It is simply impossible that the Divine Teacher was so clumsy in proclaiming his doctrines that he led all his students into error.[25]

No, the Church that Jesus had promised would be guided into "all truth" (Jn. 16:13) was not wrong for 1,500 years about its most sacred doctrine. The first 1,500 years worth of priests and bishops of the Church did not operate under a mere delusion whereby they thought they were doing something that they weren't.

". . . The Mass was, after all, the act that defined them as Christians," according to Mike Aquilina in his book, *The Mass of the Early Christians* (see pp. 21-22).

Jesus' gift of Himself in the Eucharist is a surprising one, but it is no harder to believe than His Resurrection or the fact that Jesus could be man and God at the same time. The Apostles had been prepared to accept such wonders after experiencing the multiplication of the loaves of bread and fish to feed the crowd, and the walking-on-water incident. Jesus can and does provide for us supernaturally. He can and does control the laws of nature.

With so much evidence that the Eucharist is our Lord, how can anybody not believe in the Real Presence?

The vast majority of Christians on the planet do profess it. The world's billion Catholics — who, alone, make up half of all Christians — are joined by Orthodox Christians, Anglicans, and many Lutherans in the belief that the Body and Blood are truly present with the appearance of bread and wine. Catholics, Orthodox Christians, and most Anglicans hold to transubstantiation (after the consecration, there is not one crumb of bread or drop of wine. It is Jesus and only Jesus). Using their preferred terminology, Lutherans would say the Body and Blood of Christ are "in, with, and under" the bread and wine.

The truth of the Real Presence is hard to dispute, either Biblically or historically. Nothing can change the fact that Jesus testified that His "Flesh is true food" and His "Blood is true drink."

I remember a Sunday service at a nondenominational church, which held to a symbolic presence. The pastor held up the bread before the prayerful congregation, saying, "This represents my Body." He held up the chalice and said, "This represents my Blood."

Clearly, he was trying to communicate his belief that what Jesus had wanted to say was "represents." Yet that's not what Jesus said. The pastor did not get those words from the Bible. If Jesus had wanted to say "represents," he had many Greek and Aramaic words to choose from. He chose the word "is."

The pastor then distributed grape juice to the congregation instead of the Biblical wine. But Jesus' instructions were not "Do something like this;" they were "Do this."

Catholics believe that the Mass is not only a remembrance, but also a sacrifice where Christ truly becomes present. Some Christian denominations regard the Eucharist as a remembrance and nothing more. Other denominations, such as Presbyterian, believe Jesus becomes spiritually present but will deny the literal nature of Jesus' words "This is my body" and "unless you eat the flesh of the Son of man and drink his blood, you have no life in you." The church where "is" was replaced with the word "represents" was a church that adhered to faith-alone theology. Ironically, the founder of this theology, Martin Luther, vehemently defended the literal interpretation of "is" in "This is my Body."

Notice how St. Clement of Rome, the third successor of St. Peter (fourth pope), mentions the offering of sacrifices at a time when the Apostle St. John was still walking the earth:

> Our sin will not be small if we eject from the episcopate those who blamelessly and holily have offered its sacrifices. Blessed are those presbyters who have already finished their course, and who have obtained a fruitful and perfect release.
>
> — St. Clement of Rome,
> *Letter to the Corinthians* 44:4-5 (80 A.D.)

The imperfect sacraments of the Old Testament have passed away. They have been replaced by the perpetual and perfect sacrifice of Jesus Christ, which is the forever sacrifice of the New Covenant, in which Jesus is both priest and victim: "You are a priest forever according to the order of Melchizedek" (Ps. 110:4).

Even after this world passes away, Jesus the Lamb will forever continue to offer "in Heaven this same victim that he once offered on the Cross for the glory of God and for the salvation of mankind," according to St. Alphonsus Liguori.[26]

The Sacrifice of the Mass is a fulfillment of the Old Testament prophecy by Malachi:

> "For from the rising of the sun, even to its setting, my name is great among the nations; And everywhere they bring sacrifice to my name, and a pure offering; For great is my name among the nations, says the LORD of hosts."   — MAL. 1:11

This same once-and-for-all sacrifice will continue to serve as a perpetual fountain of grace for God's children. Author Jason Evert explains:

Jesus is eternally a priest, and a priest's very nature is to offer sacrifice. In the case of Christ, the eternal sacrifice that he offers is himself. This is why he appears in the book of Revelation as a lamb, standing as though he had been slain (Rev. 5:6). He appears in Heaven in the state of a victim not because he still needs to suffer but because for all eternity he re-presents himself to God appealing to the work of the cross, interceding for us (Rom. 8:34), and bringing the graces of Calvary to us.[27]

In Old Testament times, the Paschal lamb was slaughtered and then eaten. Jesus has been slaughtered. Today we eat the actual Lamb of God, who was slaughtered for us. We do not eat a symbol of the Lamb sacrificed for us any more than the Old Testament Jews ate a symbol of their sacrificed lambs.

St. Paul affirms that what happens at Mass is nothing less than a participation in the Blood and Body of Christ.

> The cup of blessing which we bless, is it not a participation in the blood of Christ? The bread which we break, is it not a participation in the body of Christ? Because there is one bread, we who are many are one body, for we all partake of the one bread.   — 1 COR. 10:16-17

Still, other opponents of the Real Presence will say the doctrine is impossible for the reason that Jesus cannot be digested nor subjected to decay. We respond that we agree: it's impossible for Jesus to decay or be digested. In fact, as soon as the Eucharistic elements are metabolized or broken down into its base components, we no longer have that special presence of Jesus. It is only under the species of bread and wine that we are promised His Heavenly presence. Similarly, when God appeared as the burning bush, His subsequent disappearance did not involve decay or damage in any way.

According to Catholic apologist Dr. Scott Hahn, a former evangelical pastor, the Mass is the only way we can logically interpret the Book of Revelation. Describing his first visits to Mass as an evangelical Protestant visitor, Hahn recalls what he experienced as the priest raised the host and chalice, saying, "This is my Body" and "This is My Blood."

In less than a minute, the phrase "Lamb of God" had rung out four times. From long years of studying the Bible, I immediately knew where I was. I was in the Book of Revelation, where Jesus is called the Lamb no less than 28 times in 22 chapters. I was at the marriage feast that John describes at the end of that very last book of the Bible. I was before the throne of Heaven, where Jesus is hailed forever as the Lamb. I wasn't ready for this, though — I was at Mass![28]

With renewed interest in early Christianity, Hahn recounts how he dove into the writings of the first bishops and Church Fathers, only to learn that they had already unlocked the connections between the events of the Book of Revelation and the Mass, which "turned out to be the event that sealed God's covenant. . . . "[29]

Even the Church Fathers who mention the memorial aspect of the Eucharist simultaneously teach the Real Presence. This includes St. Augustine.

Referring to St. Augustine's belief in the Catholic teaching of the Real Presence of Christ's Sacred Body and Blood, the Protestant historian J.N.D. Kelly wrote: "There can be no doubt that [St. Augustine] shared the realism held by almost all his contemporaries and predecessors."[30]

Critics of the Mass as a sacrifice will sometimes point to early writings that refer to the Eucharist as a memorial. Unfortunately for them, the memorial aspect of the Eucharist hardly takes away from the fact the Flesh and Blood of Christ become present. In fact, searching the works of the Early Church Fathers, critics would be hard pressed to find any sort of protest against the literal interpretation of Christ's "flesh" and "blood" in the sixth chapter of St. John's Gospel, or against the literal interpretation of "my body" during the Last Supper. Mike Aquilina, author of *The Mass of the Early Christians,* explains:

> The first Christians, like today's Christians, experienced the Mass as a sacrament, a sacrifice, the new Passover, the re-presentation of the Paschal Mystery, the communion of God with man, the revelation of Heavenly worship, and the source and summit of the Church's life and unity.[31]

A Miracle for a Doubting Priest

In the year 700 A.D., back when all Christians believed in Christ's Real Presence in the Eucharist and the God-given power of priests to consecrate the host, a monk of the order of St. Basil in Lanciano, Italy, was having great trouble accepting the truth of the teaching. One day during Mass, when he said the words of the consecration, a real circle of flesh appeared around the outer part of the host. The wine turned into visible blood. Everyone in the church saw and was amazed. With tears of joy, the priest praised God for revealing Himself. The awestruck congregation rushed forward to see it up close, then spread word of the miracle through the town, prompting others to come running over to see for themselves.

"Behold the flesh and blood of our Beloved Christ," declared the newly believing priest.

Soon after, the blood in the chalice coagulated into five small pellets of different sizes and shapes. The flesh remained intact.

The Archbishop ordered that a scale be fetched. To everyone's surprise, the monks found that the weight of any individual pellet equaled the weight of a few pellets put together, or even all five pellets together! This completely harmonizes with Catholic teaching that even if there is just one crumb of Holy Communion left in our mouths, Jesus is fully present. His Body cannot be divided.

The Flesh and dried Blood from the miracle of Lanciano are preserved today at the Church of St. Francis, constructed on the same grounds as the basilica where the miracle took place. The Flesh is on display in a shiny monstrance, while the Blood is exhibited in an ancient crystal chalice thought to be the same chalice used by the unbelieving monk in the year 700 A.D.

Over the centuries, many doctors and scientists studied the Flesh and Blood, repeatedly finding the same miracle of the equal weights. The miracle of the weights continued for at least 874 years. The last time the phenomenon was officially noted was in 1574, at which time, Monsignor Rodrigues weighed the pellets in the presence of reputable witnesses. The results were the same, with each pellet individually weighing the same as any other pellet, or any group of pellets.

Today, the weights of the aging pellets may differ, but modern science has uncovered even greater wonders.

A thorough scientific analysis of the Flesh and Blood was conducted from 1970 to 1971 with the permission of Pope Paul VI. The study was overseen by Dr. Odoardo Linoli, head physician at the hospital of Arezzo, and a university professor of anatomy and pathological histology, chemistry, and clinical microscopy. The results were independently verified by an assistant, Dr. Ruggero Bertelli, Professor Emeritus of human anatomy at the University of Siena. In 1981, Dr. Linoli did further testing, using more advanced technology, which confirmed the findings from a decade earlier — and provided some new information.

Here are the findings:

- It truly was flesh and blood, not bread and wine. The Flesh and Blood were human, not animal. No trace of preservatives was found.
- The Flesh consists of muscular tissue of the heart. In fact, the structure of a complete human heart was present in the circle of flesh, including myocardium, endocardium, the vagus nerve and the heart's left ventricle, as if it were expertly cut.
- In the blood were proteins in proportions resembling the normal make-up of fresh human blood. Despite the fact that the specimens were more than 1,200 years old, the blood and heart tissue appeared to be from a living person.
- The Blood and the Flesh appeared to come from the same person. Both were found to have blood type AB. Blood found on the Holy Shroud of Turin years later also turned out to be of the type AB. Many believe the Shroud is the clean linen in which Christ's body was wrapped before it was laid in the tomb. Another relic, the Sudarium of Oviedo, Spain, also revealed blood of type AB. The Sudarium is thought to be the face cloth of Jesus, used to wipe His face after the Crucifixion.

Interesting.

As you may recall, highly publicized results of carbon-14 dating tests on the Shroud in 1988 cast doubt on the authenticity of the revered 14-foot-long linen cloth by suggesting that the cloth only dated back to the Middle Ages. But, in more recent years, evidence has surfaced that showed that the carbon dating results were not reliable for dating the Shroud. Scientists have learned that cloth added by nuns to the original Shroud in the sixteenth century, to mend it after a fire, may have caused the discrepancy in the carbon dating.

In fact, had sixteenth-century material been mixed with first-century material at a 60/40 ratio for the carbon-14 dating, the results would have supported a thirteenth-century dating of the Shroud; this, according to the prestigious Miami-based Beta Analytic, one of the world's largest radiocarbon-dating firms.

Scientists and chemists have several other reasons to doubt the carbon dating results.

In 2002, Dr. Mechtild Flury-Lemberg, a textile restoration expert who headed a Shroud restoration project, found clues during her examination of weaving methods and other properties of the fabric that caused her to place the Shroud's origin between 40 B.C. and 73 A.D.

If the Shroud and the Sudarium turn out to be authentic, as only time will tell, they will be two added jewels that shine on the glory of Jesus and His Church. The Miracle of Lanciano is already one of the hundreds of confirmed Eucharistic miracles illuminating the vast reservoirs of precious Catholic truth.

CHAPTER SIX

✝

Now I Get . . . Confirmation

As if it were not enough to personally receive the living Jesus of the Eucharist, we also get to receive the Holy Spirit at Confirmation. Once the Holy Spirit enters us in the Sacrament of Confirmation, we are perfectly equipped to be mature Christians.

Lisa, Sharon, Jackie, and Christine were the girls who I deemed the prettiest or coolest in our eighth-grade class. Coincidentally, Lisa, Sharon, Jackie, and Christine were the exact names I came up with when our teacher told us to start thinking about selecting our new middle name that we would acquire at Confirmation before the bishop.

We were encouraged to consider the name of a devout saint who could help serve as models for our lives. So, after checking things out, I was delighted to learn that there did indeed exist a saint named "Christina," another form of the name "Christine," the name on my list that seemed to flow best with the rest of my name.

In my defense, I wasn't particularly familiar with any female saints, other than the one who already accounted for my first name. But it all goes to show I was sorely in need of this sacrament!

The Holy Spirit was poured out on each of my classmates and me as Philadelphia's late John Cardinal Krol placed his hands on us and anointed our foreheads with oil called chrism. The one-time sacrament perfected and completed the graces we received in Baptism.

We received an indelible mark on our souls, which we will continue to sport even in the afterlife, whether that be in Heaven or Hell. We became more empowered, and more obliged, to give witness to the truth of the Cross through our words and deeds.

The Holy Spirit now resides in, and speaks through, those of us who have been confirmed. Who is this third person of the Trinity? He is God. He is a distinct person from the Father and Son, yet He is in perfect harmony with them.

Like all Catholic bishops, the bishop who sealed us with the Holy Spirit was a direct successor of the Apostles. In other words, he was ordained by the laying on of hands by one bishop in a long chain of bishops, going straight back to an Apostle 20 centuries ago.

Therefore, in a real way this bishop received the gifts of the Holy Spirit from an Apostle filled with the Holy Spirit on Pentecost, an event that occurred 50 days after Christ's Resurrection. On that day the Twelve Apostles, along with Mary, were gathered in an upper room when the house shook and tongues of fire (the Holy Spirit) came down and settled upon their heads.

In the first four centuries, Confirmation was referred to as the "disposition of the hands," "unction," "chrism," or "sealing."

Often in the early Church, Baptism and Confirmation would be received on the same occasion, although they were separate rites (Acts 8:14-17, 19:1-6). Similarly, adult converts to the faith today receive Baptism, Confirmation, and the Eucharist on the same day.

To be eligible for Confirmation, candidates should have been baptized previously and should receive the sacrament of Penance to cleanse their souls for the sacred entrance of the Holy Spirit. But the effects of Confirmation are so important to the formation of our souls that even young children, if in danger of dying, are allowed to receive it immediately.

In the sacrament, we become more closely bonded with Christ and more deeply rooted in our divine Sonship with God as our Father. The catechism instructs:

> Confirmation perfects Baptismal grace; it is the sacrament which gives the Holy Spirit in order to root us more deeply in the divine filiation, incorporate us more firmly into Christ, strengthen our bond with the Church, associate us more closely with her mission, and help us bear witness to the Christian faith in words accompanied by deeds.
>
> — *CCC*, 1316

The catechism also notes:

> By the sacrament of Confirmation, [the baptized] are more perfectly bound to the Church and are enriched with a special strength of the Holy Spirit. Hence they are, as true witnesses of Christ, more strictly obliged to spread and defend the faith by word and deed (*LG* 11; cf. *OC,* Introduction 2).
>
> — *CCC,* 1285

The Church teaches that after Confirmation, we are equipped to defend our faith fearlessly, even in the face of obstacles or danger. Pope John Paul II gave young people a nudge when he told them:

> "Do not be afraid to go out on the streets and into public places, like the first Apostles who preached Christ and the Good News of Salvation in the squares of cities, towns and villages. This is no time to be ashamed of the Gospel. It is the time to preach it from the rooftops."[32]

In confirmation, we receive the seven gifts of the Holy Spirit: the spirit of [1] wisdom and [2] understanding, the spirit of [3] right judgment and [4] courage, the spirit of [5] knowledge and [6] reverence, and the spirit of [7] wonder and awe in His presence.

You say you forgot to write the Holy Spirit a thank-you note for all the gifts? No problem. The third Person of the Trinity will accept various alternative tokens of your gratitude: start a Bible study, rent a spiritual movie, head to the Catholic bookstore for reading materials and Christian music, volunteer with a homeless program, form a dance troupe to perform at nursing homes, or make a generous donation to a charity that assists the poverty-stricken in Third World countries.

For Catholics who somehow missed out on Confirmation altogether, due to moving or switching schools, Theophilus of Antioch urges you to step up to the plate.

> Are you unwilling to be anointed with the oil of God? It is on this account that we are called Christians: because we are anointed with the oil of God.
>
> — *To Autolycus* 1:12 (181 A.D.)

St. Cyprian of Carthage warns that this is not something optional, like say, a plasma television or video camera phone.

> It is necessary for him that has been baptized also to be anointed, so that by his having received chrism, that is, the anointing, he can be the anointed of God and have in him the grace of Christ.
>
> — *Letters* 7:2 (253 A.D.)

Cyprian adds that, contrary to our senses, what occurs at Confirmation is not natural but supernatural.

> For just as the bread of the Eucharist after the invocation of the Holy Spirit is simple bread no longer, but the body of Christ, so also this ointment is no longer plain ointment, nor, so to speak, common, after the invocation.
>
> — *Catechetical Lectures,* 21:1, 3-4 (350 A.D.)

Interestingly, St. Patrick (387-493 A.D.) the great Catholic bishop credited with converting Ireland to Christianity, wrote in his work *Confession* that he was the first to administer Confirmation, or chrism, in Ireland.[33]

The catechism tells us that oil signifies abundance and joy. It is a sign of healing and cleansing. Christians who are anointed in Confirmation "share more completely in the mission of Jesus Christ and the fullness of the Holy Spirit with which he is filled, so that their lives may give off 'the aroma of Christ' (2 Cor. 2:15)" (*CCC,* 1294).

Just as soldiers were marked with the seals of their leaders, we are marked with the seal of the Holy Spirit, which testifies to the fact that we belong to Christ forever. We are in His service. In the sacrament, an installment of Christ's promise of redemption is applied to our souls.

CHAPTER SEVEN

✝

Now I Get . . . Heaven

After being made spiritually alive by the Eucharist and Confirmation, we are ready for Heaven. Because Christ is in Heaven, we have literally been taking little steps into Heaven every time we have received Communion. The only problem is: we cannot see where we're going! Not only can we not see Heaven; we cannot imagine it. We simply do not have the capacity in our current states.

In the Bible, St. Paul tells us: "What no eye has seen, nor ear heard, nor the heart of man conceived, what God has prepared for those who love him" (1 Cor. 2:9).

Neither breathtaking sunsets nor glistening seas can compare to the supernatural riches that will abound in Heaven. But the scenery will not serve as Heaven's main attraction. Rather, the true prize of Heaven is a personal relationship.

According to the late Pope John Paul II, Heaven

> . . . is neither an abstraction nor a physical place in the clouds, but a living, personal relationship with the Holy Trinity. It is our meeting with the Father which takes place in the risen Christ through the communion of the Holy Spirit.[34]

Not even the husband or wife of one's dreams could come close to measuring up to what God will be to us. He is the most lovable, most irresistible thing in the universe, as well as the creator of all lovable things. He will be united to us more intensely than a spouse could be on earth. Not an iota of stress, worry, disappointment, embarrassment, or hurt will ever come between us. Instead, we will experience the joy of an eternal wedding feast.

Just as the sight of a stunning snow-capped mountain might provide a tiny glimpse into the majesty and glory of our God in Heaven, the permanent matrimonial bond between a man and woman gives us a hint as to the pure and giving relationship between Christ and His Church. Because the image of God is reflected by the male and female made one, theologians say that the moment of bodily union — when the husband and wife are "one flesh" — actually foreshadows the divine mystery of the bond between Christ and the Church that we will fully experience in Heaven.

Just check out the work of Pope John Paul II. Starting in the 1970s, the late Pontiff had been doing groundbreaking Scriptural analyses on the "theology of the body," offering insights into what the human body, conjugal union, and procreation reveal about God. His insights into the spousal relationship of Christ to His Church are surely historic — and they must be interesting as well, because people have been filling up lectures by Christopher West, an expert in the field and author of the books *Theology of the Body for Beginners* and *Good News About Sex and Marriage*, to hear more.

Of course, the pope and other theologians would be quick to add that although males and females will retain their separate male and female identities in Heaven, there is no indication that there is sex in Heaven. God's children in Heaven will be so completely fulfilled that they will yearn for nothing. Our stomachs will not feel empty; our mouths will not feel dry.

So in light of all this, the question is, "How do we get to Heaven in the first place?"

We simply accept the free graces showered on us by Christ every day. We use these graces to love God and others, which is what we were created for. It is that simple.

If our soul has grace when we die, we go to Heaven. If not, we know where we go. It's not that God wants to be cruel. It's just that, without grace, we would be no more suitable for union with the holy, living God than a person with no oxygen or spacesuit would be compatible with living on the Saturnian moon Titan.

We can be confident that the gift of saving grace is ours, as long as we don't trash it by sinning mortally. Judas did just that. He rejected the grace and love showered on him by Christ, then refused to repent, instead killing himself.

Grace may be invisible, but it is as real as the sound waves that transport the sound of Christian music from your boom box to your ear.

The sacraments are the ordinary means created by God for receiving grace.

The Catholic Church teaches that we first receive grace in the sacrament of Baptism, which turns us into a new creation. For the Bible says we cannot enter the kingdom of God unless we are baptized, which means being spiritually reborn through water and Spirit.

Jesus answered, "Truly, truly, I say to you, unless one is born of water and the Spirit, he cannot enter the kingdom of God" (Jn. 3:5).

After Baptism, we are spiritually alive and fit for Heaven, no longer marked with the original sin of Adam and Eve.

Graces are also poured onto us in the one-time sacrament of Confirmation, and for the rest of our lives in the sacraments of Confession and the Eucharist. We receive grace through the Anointing of the Sick when our health is in danger.

The graces we receive in the sacraments continually recharge our souls and empower us to say no to the things that take us off course — namely, attachments to worldly things, which are incompatible with God's kingdom. It is grace that fashions our soul into the finished piece of artwork that we will be when the Lord takes us into heaven. There is no limit to the amount of grace and beauty that a soul can attain before reaching its eternal destination.

As our catechism reminds us, Jesus commanded his disciples to prefer Him to everything and everyone, asking them to renounce all that they had. Jesus gave the example of the poor widow of Jerusalem who, despite her poverty, gave away all that she had to live on. In fact, detachment from riches is "obligatory" for entering Heaven; we are to avoid "adherence to riches which is contrary to the spirit of evangelical poverty (*LG* 42 § 3)," according to the catechism (*CCC*, 2544, 2545).

To highlight the fact that Jesus was not kidding about work He expected followers to do, early saints urged the faithful to get off their duffs.

St. Justin Martyr, slain for the faith in Rome around 165 A.D., warned that words were not enough:

> Let those who are not found living as He taught, be understood not to be Christians, even though they profess with the lips the teachings of Christ. For it is not those who make profession, but those who do the works, who will be saved.

St. Barnabas, ranked as an Apostle by Scripture although he wasn't one of the original Twelve, wrote, "The way of light, then, is as follows. If anyone desires to travel to the appointed place, he must be zealous in his works" (*Epistle of St. Barnabas,* c. 70-130 A.D.).

St. Clement of Rome taught that we must not be "lazy or slothful in any good work" and that "we are justified by our works, not by our words" (*First Epistle to the Corinthians,* c. 96 A.D.).

All Aboard the Soul Train

If we have any grace at all on our soul when we die, we will receive a ticket to Heaven. But some trains travel more slowly than others.

If we die with souls as holy as the ones of Mother Teresa or St. John Neumann, our souls may immediately find themselves in Heaven after death. Later, on the Last Day of earth, our body will rise to join us in its newly glorified state.

If we die less holy than certain saints, but still with grace, then our soul will need to be purged of its last traces of self-love before fully experiencing God in all His glory. This is painful, but we know we will be better off for it once we are in Heaven. Our glorified bodies will still meet us on the Last Day, and a great new world will be ours. The catechism states:

> The visible universe, then, is itself destined to be transformed, "so that the world itself, restored to its original state, facing no further obstacles, should be at the service of the just," sharing their glorification in the risen Jesus Christ.
>
> *"We know neither the moment of the consummation* of the earth and of man, nor the way in which the universe will be transformed. The form of this world, distorted by sin, is passing away, and we are taught that God is preparing a new

dwelling and a new earth in which righteousness dwells, in which happiness will fill and surpass all the desires of peace arising in the hearts of men (GS 39 § 1)."

— *CCC,* 1048

Some theologians believe that God will destroy the current universe and create a new Heaven. Others say God will completely remake the existing earth into a Heavenly one. Either way, we will have round-the-clock, one-on-one personal access to our God, who will live in us, giving us constant joy.

In Heaven, we will no longer be married to our spouse, but don't fret: we will know and love our spouses and other family members even more deeply once in Heaven, and we will be thrilled to see them there.

Our vision of God will not be limited to our physical eyes. God will live in us in an intense and all-consuming way.

Some theologians say God will actually be connected to our minds. That's because an infinite God could not be experienced in visual images, which are finite. The late Rev. William G. Most, in his book *Catholic Apologetics Today,* noted that Pope Benedict XII believed there would be no image at all between God and us, while St. Thomas Aquinas completed the thought, saying that God must directly link Himself to our intellect. That kind of vision, Most concludes, "is possible only for a creature that is part divine."[35]

Heaven: The Eternal Wedding Feast

The up-close experience of God in all His glory is known as the Beatific Vision. Our whole lives are leading up to this homecoming, which alone can provide true and everlasting happiness.

Our secondary source of happiness will be the company of family and friends, with whom we will be reunited (the ones that were not too naughty, of course!).

The little things will also be nice: no pain, no disease, no disabilities, no worries, no drudgery, no stress, no exhaustion, no aging . . .

In Heaven, we will not be confined by time or space. In fact, time is a dimension created only for those of us on earth. The Bible assures us that "with the Lord one day is as a thousand years, and a thousand years as one day" (2 Pet. 3:8). This may sound confusing, but less so when one considers that time travel is not only theoretically possible, but that we already can detect time slowing down or speeding up, each time we accelerate or decelerate. Of course, it's much easier to detect such time changes while traveling in a high-speed space shuttle than in a sluggish automobile.

In Heaven, will not have to wait in line at the airport to visit our cousins overseas. Rather, we will be able to communicate with others freely, without restraint. Envision sending 100 e-mails to 100 different people at once, in full hologram, but without having to type anything. Imagine being able to watch and absorb every cable television station simultaneously, including the foreign channels (but only the wholesome stuff, of course).

Everyone in Heaven will love us to no end. Right now, they may think we are a pain in the neck, but in Heaven, nobody will have a single complaint about us!

We will not doubt the sincerity of their love for us because the moral, spiritual state of all will be apparent to all, with the saints and martyrs having the highest degrees of glory shining through them, and with not one soul retaining the slightest selfish or jealous thought.

Meanwhile, our ability to process information will have exploded. On Judgment Day alone, we will have the ability to see every day of our own life and of the lives of others unfold before us.

In Heaven, questions we have long pondered will be answered.

In Heaven, we will not have to break our backs to put food on the table.

But there will be things to do, not one of which will be boring. If there is work to do in this dynamic new environment, it will be the kind that puts a smile on our faces. Nobody will be working for self-gain or selfish glory. In Heaven, we will be ultimately fulfilled and perfected, sharing our gifts in the way we were made to. We will know what we were designed for.

Ironically, the more we labor for God on earth, and the more we give up our own ambitions in order to focus on others, the more fulfilled we will feel in Heaven.

Different Rewards: All Good

For in Heaven, there are different rewards for different people. The Bible refers to different mansions in the Father's house.

St. Augustine and other Church Fathers said that the many mansions refer to different levels of reward in Heaven for different levels of merit accumulated by believers on earth. St. Augustine, in particular, said that although those with more merit will shine more brightly than those with less merit, all will shine nonetheless, and none will envy a brighter star.

In his masterpiece *Summa Theologica,* St. Thomas Aquinas agreed, saying that increased merit translates to increased happiness in Heaven.

> The more one will be united to God the happier will one be. Now the measure of charity is the measure of one's union with God. Therefore the diversity of beatitude will be according to the difference of charity.[36]

The Catechism of Trent puts it this way: "For in my Father's house, says our Lord, there are many mansions," in which shall be distributed rewards of greater and of less value according to each one's deserts.

In his second letter to the Corinthians, St. Paul also preached that our charity on earth has a direct correlation with our rewards in Heaven.

> ... he who sows sparingly will also reap sparingly, and he who sows bountifully will also reap bountifully.   — 2 COR. 9:6

St. Paul assures us that the glories to be revealed in Heaven will dwarf any amount of suffering one could endure on earth.

> ... and if children, then heirs, heirs of God and fellow heirs with Christ, provided we suffer with him in order that we may also be glorified with him. I consider that the sufferings of this present time are not worth comparing with the glory that is to be revealed to us.   — ROM. 8:18

The prizes of Heaven are ours so long as we avoid getting distracted by the prizes available on earth.

> ... But Jesus said to them again, "Children, how hard it is to enter the kingdom of God! It is easier for a camel to go

through the eye of a needle than for a rich man to enter the
kingdom of God."   — MK. 10:24-25

"Enter by the narrow gate; for the gate is wide and the way is
easy, that leads to destruction, and those who enter by it are
many. For the gate is narrow and the way is hard, that leads to
life, and those who find it are few."   — MT. 7:13-14

Finally, Jesus promised eternal life to those who eat His flesh and
drink His blood.

"Truly, truly, I say to you, unless you eat the flesh of the Son
of man and drink his blood, you have no life in you; he who
eats my flesh and drinks my blood has eternal life, and I will
raise him up at the last day."   — JN. 6:53-54

For the most part, details on our existence in Heaven will be a
surprise, but the Bible does make a few suggestions:

And we all, with unveiled face, beholding the glory of the
Lord, are being changed into his likeness from one degree of
glory to another; for this comes from the Lord who is the
Spirit.   — 2 COR. 3:18

Then the eyes of the blind shall be opened, and the ears of the
deaf unstopped; then shall the lame man leap like a hart, and
the tongue of the dumb sing for joy. For waters shall break
forth in the wilderness, and streams in the desert; the burning
sand shall become a pool, and the thirsty ground springs of
water; the haunt of jackals shall become a swamp, the grass
shall become reeds and rushes. And a highway shall be there,
and it shall be called the Holy Way; the unclean shall not pass
over it, and fools shall not err therein. No lion shall be there,
nor shall any ravenous beast come up on it; they shall not be
found there, but the redeemed shall walk there. And the ran-
somed of the LORD shall return, and come to Zion with
singing; everlasting joy shall be upon their heads; they shall
obtain joy and gladness, and sorrow and sighing shall flee
away.   — IS. 35:5-10

In Heaven, we will not even need the sun or electricity, because God will be the source of light.

> And night shall be no more; they need no light of lamp or sun, for the Lord God will be their light, and they shall reign for ever and ever. — REV. 22:3-5

Theologians generally describe four qualities that our glorified bodies will have in Heaven.

1. Impassibility: We will be immune to suffering, pain, sorrow, and death. We will be immortal.

2. Clarity, or splendor: The bodies of the elect will radiate like the sun. The Bible tells us Jesus' Body did this during the Transfiguration. While every saint shall shine, some shall shine with greater glory, depending on the merits of each. St. Paul described this phenomenon in the Bible:

> The brightness of the sun is one kind, the brightness of the moon another, and the brightness of the stars another. For star differs from star in brightness. So also is the resurrection of the dead. — 1 COR. 15:41-42

3. Agility: We will have the capacity to move at supernatural speeds wherever we please.

4. Subtlety: Material objects will not prevent us from passing. We will have the power to penetrate solid barriers.

It is ironic that the existence of such a strange world, one that lacks physical barriers to movement and communication, was taken for granted by theologians long before physicists came up with theories and proofs that we on earth had the potential to tap into such phenomena.

Today, we have proof that our universe is not limited to three dimensions; we know that we reside in a world where time and motion are intimately connected; a world in which speeding up causes time to slow down, a world where energy can be changed into matter, and matter into energy. One by one, barriers to communication have been stripped away with the advent of telephones, radio, television, the Internet, and electronic mail.

Although physical obstacles still prevent modern society from traveling in time, Albert Einstein's Theory of Relativity proved that time travel is theoretically possible. Recent developments in the mathematics of quantum mechanics, quantum tunneling, and String Theory make benefits such as time travel and quantum teleportation even greater likelihoods of the future.

But those in Heaven are already enjoying the perks of freedom of movement. And they don't have to go to the trouble of harnessing large reserves of energy from black holes in order to do so.

"Earning" Heaven

If you are a Catholic who has many friends from evangelical or nondenominational churches, then you've probably heard the phrase "earning salvation." If you asked your friends what in the world this means, they might have told you that it means "relying on one's own works for salvation." Catholics, of course, do not hold to this, but many non-Catholics are erroneously taught that we do.

Hopefully, you were able to spout out what you learned during your Catholic elementary school days: that salvation is by grace alone, and that grace, like faith, is a free gift from God. Only works rooted in the selfless love that springs from God's grace can accomplish God's work.

Using typical evangelical terminology, Catholics would say they cannot "earn their salvation," but they can "earn" their damnation (by rejecting the graces showered on them).

In other words, if we are going to Heaven, it is purely due to God: He gave us the graces we need, He gave us the work we should be doing, and He gave us the desire and strength to accomplish His work and avoid temptation. All we did was cooperate with His plan, and the cooperation itself was only made possible by God's grace.

But, if we wind up in Hell, it is our own fault. It has nothing to do with God.

The belief that people could be saved by their works apart from faith was an early heresy called Pelagianism, which, along with Semi-Pelagianism, was denounced by the Catholic Church from the start. The Church has continued to condemn these heresies. According to the Council of Trent in the mid-1500s:

> If any one saith, that man may be justified before God by his own works, whether done through the teaching of human nature, or that of the law, without the grace of God through Jesus Christ; let him be anathema.[37]

It seems to me that the difference between the Catholic and Protestant evangelical doctrines of justification is less about whether one can earn salvation (which is impossible) than whether one can lose saving grace after receiving it.

The Catholic Church has taught for 2,000 years that it is, indeed, possible for a human being to lose saving grace — and, therefore, lose justification — through mortal sin. That's because the Bible distinguishes between sins that are deadly and sins that are not.

> If any one sees his brother committing what is not a mortal sin, he will ask, and God will give him life for those whose sin is not mortal. There is sin which is mortal; I do not say that one is to pray for that. All wrongdoing is sin, but there is sin which is not mortal. — 1 Jn. 5:16-17

The idea that it is impossible to lose justifying grace — a tenet of many evangelical Protestant churches — wasn't part of any Christian belief system until sixteenth-century Protestant Reformers posed it. On the other hand, critics of the ancient Catholic teaching on justification argue that Catholics try to "pay" for grace with their works, instead of receiving grace freely.

So I will try to clarify the Catholic position on grace with the following analogy.

Picture two guys walking down the street. A funnel hovers over the heads of both. Grace in the form of vanilla pudding is being poured into both funnels. The pudding is falling onto the heads of both men.

Let's say the first guy lifts his arm and places his thumb under the opening of the funnel to stop the flow of pudding. This guy has taken action to stop the free flow of grace. He rejected the free gift of grace. He exercised his free will to choose damnation.

But let's say the second guy does nothing. The grace keeps falling on him. By doing absolutely nothing, he has received the free gift of

God's grace. Now, he can use this grace to do Christ's work just like Popeye the Sailor Man used spinach (also originating outside of himself) to accomplish things.

Catholics believe that our faith is a gift from God.

Catholics believe that our prayers and works stem from grace that comes from God.

Catholics believe that every drop of grace that falls on us, Jesus earned through His sufferings, death, and resurrection.

But we also believe that every sin we commit originates from ourselves, with no involvement from God. Salvation comes from God, but damnation comes from us.

Faith Alone?

As any good Catholic school child knows, faith is a free gift, and it is a prerequisite for Heaven. Our works are not even valuable if we don't have faith first. Only work done out of our love for God is worth anything to Him.

But can someone with "faith alone" get into Heaven? This is a trick question. It depends on the definition of faith, and on the Greek word from which "faith" was translated. There are several different Greek words for "faith," all with slightly different connotations.

The Bible, in fact, says that justification[38] is not by faith alone: "Justification is by works and not by faith alone" (Jas. 2:24). Therefore, if "faith" refers to "belief alone," then one cannot be saved in that manner, according to the Bible. Nowhere does the Bible say that justification is by faith "alone." When St. Paul preaches about faith, he is expressing something more than belief alone. His writings imply a faith that necessarily includes obedience and trust.

Martin Luther, the founder of "justification by faith alone" theology, was not aware of the full connotation of the "faith" discussed by St. Paul. According to the Rev. William G. Most, Luther did not adequately investigate the context or origin of the Greek words *pistis* or *pisteuein* before formulating his faulty doctrine of justification. If Luther had been aware that St. Paul's reference to "faith" would have to include obedience in order to be true to its Greek origin,[39] he never would have arrived at his well-thought-out — but defective — theology.

Furthermore, St. Paul repeatedly shows that faith and obedience are inseparable, with phrases such as the "obedience of faith" (Rom 1:5, 16:26). Most continues:

> Clearly, such a concept of faith as that given in the councils of Trent and Vatican is radically different from Luther's concept. So sadly, Luther's "discovery" is not really a discovery but a mistake, since he did not get the true Pauline meaning of faith in the words "salvation by faith."[40]

Unfortunately, Luther started out with a faulty "faith alone" formula, and then applied it to most other areas of teaching. He decided that man did not have the free will to cooperate with God's grace or with anything relevant to his salvation.

In his work *On the Bondage of the Will* (1525 A.D.), he wrote:

> ... with regard to God, and in all that bears on salvation or damnation, [man] has no free will but is a captive, prisoner and bondslave, either to the will of God, or to the will of Satan.

For Luther, salvation depended purely on whether or not a person was lucky enough to have received faith. Luther came up with a well-organized system of beliefs, but the assumptions on which they were based were influenced more by his passion and zeal than by the original and consistently held teachings of the Church.

Imagine walking into a classroom with one giant mathematical equation that takes up an entire blackboard. Albert Einstein is scribbling away furiously, and at last arrives at a solution. But then someone scurries in to inform Einstein that he's been using the wrong value of "x" from the start. Even the brilliant Einstein, when working with faulty input, would produce a faulty conclusion.

So it was with Luther, who, lamentably, approached all of Scripture with his erroneous understanding of St. Paul's words. The tragic divisions in Christianity that resulted have never been healed.

As historian Bard Thompson put it:

> The chief issue of the Protestant Reformation was never better expressed than by Charles V when he said of Luther, "It is preposterous that a single monk should be right in his opin-

ion and that the whole of Christianity should be in error a thousand years or more."[41]

How do Catholics view Christians in the Reformed traditions? Here is how Pope John Paul greeted 90,000 young people at the Mile High Stadium in Denver on August 12, 1993:

"Most of you are members of the Catholic Church, but others are from other Christian Churches and Communities, and I greet each one with sincere friendship. In spite of divisions among Christians, 'all those justified by faith through baptism are incorporated into Christ . . . brothers and sisters in the Lord.'"[42]

The Teaching of Jesus

One does not need to understand a complex theory of justification or sanctification to understand the type of life Jesus expects from those who desire Heaven. The words He left for us are simple.

. . . Then Jesus told his disciples, "If any man would come after me, let him deny himself and take up his cross and follow me. For whoever would save his life will lose it, and whoever loses his life for my sake will find it."   — MT. 16:24-25

But if any one has the world's goods and sees his brother in need, yet closes his heart against him, how does God's love abide in him? Little children, let us not love in word or speech but in deed and in truth.   — 1 JN. 3:17-18

"Greater love has no man than this, that a man lay down his life for his friends."   — JN. 15:13

"Every one to whom much is given, of him will much be required."   — LK. 12:48

"For if you forgive men their trespasses, your Heavenly Father also will forgive you."   — MT. 6:14

"Love your enemies and pray for those who persecute you."
— Mt. 5:44

"You shall love the Lord your God with all your heart. . . . You shall love your neighbor as yourself."   — Mt. 22:37-39

"Love your enemies, do good to those who hate you."
— Lk. 6:27

"Give to every one who begs from you; and of him who takes away your goods do not ask them again."   — Lk. 6:30

"Sell all that you have and distribute to the poor, and you will have treasure in Heaven; and come, follow me."
— Lk. 18:22

CHAPTER EIGHT

✝

Now I Get . . . Purgatory

Sister Lisa explained it this way to my first-grade class: people who had mortal sins on their souls, and weren't sorry for them, would go to Hell; people who were as holy as the saints would go directly to Heaven. The rest of us would spend time in Purgatory.

Sister briefly described Purgatory as a place of waiting that preceded Heaven. She was honest enough to let us know that most of the class would probably be detoured there.

Truthfully, I had no problem with Purgatory at that point. I erroneously envisioned it to be a nondescript sort of planet where people paced back and forth to kill time. I surmised it was not an appropriate locale for parties, pools, or piñatas, but at least there would be people to chat with. It seemed tolerable.

In the blink of an eye, Sister had skipped to other topics, and Purgatory would not resurface for the remainder of my religious education. I believe I completely forgot it existed.

Understandably, then, I gasped out loud when — in my late twenties — I encountered a book describing Purgatory as brutally painful. Many theologians evidently believed Purgatory involved fire, and lots of it. They also pondered that question often skipped over on those morning radio shows: would Purgatory involve a real, physical fire, or would it consist solely of our souls being made to perceive the tormenting sensation of burning fire, without a visible, tangible flame?

Yikes! All this time I had been wasting my "worry" energies on minor discomforts like tetanus shots or catching the flu, while all the time I might be facing years — perhaps dozens or hundreds of them — ahead, engulfed in the flames of unrelenting purgatorial fires.

I made sure to inform my mother of the news next time I saw her. She said she was surprised that I had never learned this common piece of information in school. Evidently, the truths of Purgatory are well known by her generation.

But when I mentioned it to a friend my age — a product of a Boston-area Catholic high school — the response was different. "I didn't know that," the Ivy League graduate responded. "Thank you for telling me before I commit my next sin!"

An unscientific poll conducted subsequently by a roving reporter demonstrated that more than 90 percent of Catholic Generation X-ers are in for a cruel surprise before reaching the pearly gates. If only they had picked up one of those best-selling paperbacks on the topic — *Purgatory Explained* by Father F.X. Schouppe, S.J., or *Charity for the Suffering Souls* by the Rev. John A. Nageleisen, for example — from one of the front display tables at Borders or Barnes & Noble. And, too bad the corner newsstand was fresh out of St. Catherine of Genoa's brief booklet, *Treatise on Purgatory,* when they went magazine hunting.

I do wish more of my teachers had thought to elaborate on Purgatory to my class. (I also hope that if I'm about to walk into a burning building someday, someone might give me a holler.)

Two Saints: Two Points of View

St. Catherine of Genoa (1447-1510) would have told me all about Purgatory if I had met her. God granted her not only a special glimpse into His view of her own soul, which led to her profound conversion, but also a glimpse into the experience of souls in Purgatory.

Unfortunately, the captivating observations of Purgatory in her Treatise would not make it onto the Internet for a good 500 years.

According to St. Catherine, the suffering souls in Purgatory are tormented more by their delayed union with God than by their intense physical pain. Yet their pain is coupled with an unimaginable joy that stems from their overflowing love of God. Like gold, each soul attains a more stunning level of purity as it is further melted and burned away, she observed. Souls that have not been purified to their fullest potential would not think of entering into the full presence of God. According to the Treatise:

. . . the soul in which there is even the least note of imperfec-
tion would rather cast itself into a thousand Hells than find
itself thus stained in the presence of the Divine Majesty.

— *Treatise on Purgatory*, viii

Once in Purgatory, a soul may do nothing to accumulate additional merits; those are only available on earth. Nor may a soul do
anything to lessen his or her divinely assigned penalty in Purgatory.
But they may receive assistance from the saints on earth, who can
offer prayers and alms for their benefit.

The souls in Purgatory have their sights fixed on God. They have
been rendered incapable of focusing on themselves even for a moment,
according to St. Catherine. Through God, they are more aware of
goings-on than we are. According to visionary St. Catherine:

[The souls in Purgatory] see all things, not in themselves, nor
by themselves, but as they are in God, on whom they are
more intent than on their own sufferings. . . . For the least
vision they have of God overbalances all woes and all joys that
can be conceived. Yet their joy in God does by no means abate
their pain. . . . This process of purification to which I see the
souls in Purgatory subjected, I feel within myself.

— *Treatise on Purgatory*, xvi, xvii

Another saint who received a vision of Purgatory was St.
Christina the Admirable (1150-1224) of Belgium:

The torments which they there endured and appeared to me
to be so excessive that it is impossible for me to give any idea
of their rigor. I saw among them many of my acquaintances,
and, deeply touched by their sad condition, I asked what place
it was, for I believed it to be Hell. My guide answered me that
it was Purgatory, where sinners were punished who before
death had repented of their faults, but who had not made worthy satisfaction to God.[43]

St. Christina saw these things after suffering a physical death at
the age of 32. She woke up from her obviously deceased state, and
rose out of her coffin for all to see. She reported that the Lord had

offered her the option of staying in Heaven, or postponing it in order to return to earth to suffer. The suffering would be used to deliver souls from Purgatory and to help save souls on earth from the path toward Hell. St. Christina warned the people of the town that she would be undergoing extraordinary penances for the rest of her life, which lasted 42 additional years.[44]

> Thenceforth Christina lived without house or fire; she threw herself into burning furnaces, where she survived the torment of flames. The Lord told her that she would endure great torments without dying from the effects — this would constitute a constant miracle. She prayed in winter in the frozen waters, and on and on. [St. Robert Cardinal Bellarmine] wrote that everyone could see Christina standing in the midst of the flames without being consumed, and covered with wounds, every trace of which disappeared a few moments afterwards.[45]

Painful But True

Despite the incredible drama that unfolds in Purgatory, this teaching — a corollary flowing logically from the doctrine of justification — has somehow escaped the radar of many modern-day Catholics, who naively anticipate smooth transitions into their eternal home. In the scheme of things, Purgatory is merely a wrinkle in the path to all eternity, a wrinkle that will fade away forever on the Last Day along with the earth as we know it, leaving behind only Heaven and Hell.

Nevertheless, anything involving pain lies close to my heart, and I would not wish any unsuspecting friends to pass without having heard about it.

The doctrine of soul purification between death and Heaven makes sense, because we know that no sinning occurs in Heaven. Yet, the elect on earth are still sinning as we sit here. Something needs to happen to us before we are ready to see God, for the Bible tells us that "nothing unclean shall enter" Heaven (Rev. 21:27).

The thick catechism devotes only a few paragraphs to our final purification.

All who die in God's grace and friendship, but still imperfectly purified, are indeed assured of their eternal salvation; but after death they undergo purification, so as to achieve the holiness necessary to enter the joy of Heaven.

— *CCC*, 1030

The Church gives the name Purgatory to this final purification of the elect, which is entirely different from the punishment of the damned. The Church formulated her doctrine of faith on Purgatory especially at the Councils of Florence and Trent. The tradition of the Church, by reference to certain texts of Scripture, speaks of a cleansing fire (cf. 1 Cor. 3:15; 1 Pet. 1:7):

As for certain lesser faults, we must believe that, before the Final Judgment, there is a purifying fire. He who is truth says that whoever utters blasphemy against the Holy Spirit will be pardoned neither in this age nor in the age to come. From this sentence we understand that certain offenses can be forgiven in this age, but certain others in the age to come (St. Gregory the Great, *Dial.* 4, 39: PL 77, 396; cf. Mt. 12:31).

— *CCC*, 1031

The teaching is also derived from the Scriptural account of Judas Maccabeus atoning for the dead to make reparation for their sins (2 Mac. 12:44-46), according to the catechism.

First and foremost, the Church recommends that we offer Eucharistic sacrifices to assist the dead. Almsgiving, indulgences, and works of penance are also suggested.

The Catholic Church has not defined whether or not Purgatory is in a physical location, or what lengths of time — if any — are associated with the cleansing of the soul. Neither has the Church said definitively whether Purgatory involves fire, although private revelations to saints have indicated the presence of fire. We won't know such things for sure until we die. What we do know is that Purgatory is a process. It is a process of purification whereby our souls are purged of any attachments we still have to earthly temptations as of our final day on earth. It is also a finishing-up of the punishment or penance we still owe for sins already forgiven.

As Christians know, Christ already suffered, died, and rose to pay the price for freeing us from the eternal damnation that would have awaited us. But after we receive the forgiveness merited for us by Christ, there is still work for us to do.

For example, a fellow who has been stealing money each week from the collection basket may suddenly be overcome with sorrow for his wrongdoing. He may confess his crime to the congregation and receive instant forgiveness. But he will still want to start contributing as much as he can to the basket, to help make up for the hurt he caused to the poor.

Our sins have caused temporal damages, so we must make temporal amends with the help of God's grace. When we have paid the last "penny" for the sins we committed, our purging will be complete, and we shall be clean enough to enter Heaven and see Christ face to face.

A "Purgatorial" cleansing of our souls can, in fact, begin on earth. Anyone who has endured a prolonged illness or trial that resulted in a stronger bond with God, and a shedding of sin to some degree, has already experienced purification, or purging, of the soul. Some have experienced this phenomenon multiple times in a life. Purgatory is just the final stage of the same process. Those who have further to go in their purification process at the moment of death can, and will, finish up between death and entrance into Heaven.

While we are all so wrapped up preparing for our retirement days, we should take a queue from a Christian man named Abercius, who, in 190 A.D., was wise enough to make provisions for his Purgatory days. He left this message on his gravestone, requesting prayers:

> The citizen of a prominent city, I erected this while I lived, that I might have a resting place for my body. Abercius is my name, a disciple of the chaste shepherd who feeds his sheep on the mountains and in the fields, who has great eyes surveying everywhere, who taught me the faithful writings of life. Standing by, I, Abercius, ordered this to be inscribed; truly I was in my seventy-second year. May everyone who is in accord with this and who understands it pray for Abercius.
>
> — Epitaph of Abercius (190 A.D.)

The Beginning of the End

Okay, let's take it from the beginning (of the end of life). We die. Upon dying, we immediately learn whether we will spend eternity in Heaven or Hell. If Johnny B. Bad dies one hour from now, and is not in a state of grace, then he will be directed to Hell in exactly one hour. There are no second chances for those who die apart from God's grace.

On the other hand, if Johnny B. Good dies in a state of grace, with no mortal sin on his soul, he will be relieved to hear the news that he will spend eternity in paradise with his beloved Savior. But if he is like most human traffic en route to Heaven, he will first be directed toward Purgatory to be cleansed.

The souls headed for Purgatory will feel profound sorrow, suddenly fully aware of the pain inflicted on Jesus by their own sins. They will sincerely desire to make reparation for the temporal damage caused by their sins. Some souls will be making more reparations than others.

Even some of the holiest saints were told by God that they still had a day or so owed in Purgatory. The Lord told St. Faustina she had the choice between spending one day in purgatory or spending a brief time on earth devoted to intense penance. We also have reports of life-long sinners who, having waited until a moment before death to repent, were assigned to suffer in Purgatory until the final day of earth.

God's plan did not call for any of us to suffer like this. But neither did His plan call for any of us to sin. It is not God's decision but our own that puts us in this predicament.

If God did not refine our souls to the purity of gold, and instead, admitted us as we are today, then Heaven would be flawed. The purging of our own souls is necessary not only for the peace and happiness of the other residents of Heaven, but to make us capable of seeing the holy, living God as He is.

The perfect Heaven that God has prepared for is a love feast so powerful that our hearts will be set on fire for all eternity.

Just because there is a Purgatory, though, doesn't mean everyone has to participate in it. In fact, Jesus prefers that we bypass it all together. He prefers that we be prepared to go straight to Heaven when we leave this earth. He calls us to be saints here on earth, and supplies us with everything we need to reject the last traces of self-love within ourselves.

Even one little sin undermines our relationship with God. Just one little sin causes reverberations throughout the world that we will not be fully aware of until Judgment Day.

One dot-sized sin might take seconds to commit, and another second for God to forgive. But the reparation or punishment involved may take years. For justice to be served, it seems reasonable that the pain of the punishment should outweigh the pleasure derived from the sin.

St. Augustine, the most revered of the Church Fathers, wrote:

> Man is forced to suffer even after his sins are forgiven, though it was sin that brought down on him this penalty. For the punishment outlasts the guilt, lest the guilt should be thought slight if with its forgiveness the punishment also came to an end.
> — Tract. cxxiv, *In Joann,* n. 5, in P.L., XXXV, 1972

The concept of the penalty outlasting the sin really isn't news to most of us; it was probably ingrained in us as kids. Knock down a crystal vase? Work all summer to pay for it. Betray a friend? Work for several years to gain back the trust. Rob a bank at gunpoint? Spend twenty years in the slammer. But let's say the bank robber drops dead his first day in prison. He dies before the reparation is made. That's where Purgatory comes in.

As unpleasant as Purgatory sounds, it is a wonderful alternative to that dreaded place of no return, where sin abides forever. It is only through Christ's suffering, dying, and rising for us that has made forgiveness available and opened the gates of Heaven after the fall of Man. It is only the merits and graces of Jesus Christ that give us the awesome power to undo the effects of our past sins and become more perfectly united to Him.

Like Purgatory, surgery hurts. But a doctor may order it anyway, for the sake of the patient's future health and happiness.

Unsurprisingly, some theologians compare the pain of Purgatory to a woman in labor. The woman endures intense pain, yet she rejoices in knowing what is to come. The same is true with the glowing bride who smiles as she walks up the aisle to marry her dream groom, oblivious to the fact that her heels are digging through the flesh of her feet.

A "Hellish" Experience

On earth, our days are a mixed bag: punishment and purification one day, but celebrations the next day. Purgatory, on the other hand, involves one solid streak of nothing but purging. Therefore, theologians believe it will be the most severe and most prolonged pain we will ever experience.

In fact, some Church Fathers theorized that the fires of Purgatory were the same as the fires of Hell, except that the purgatorial fires were temporary cleansing fires rather than the eternal punishment of Hell.

St. Thomas Aquinas, one of the greatest Catholic theologians of the last millennium, wrote an opinion that I hope and pray was a terrible mistake. In his masterpiece, *Summa Theologica,* St. Thomas proposed that the worst pains we feel on earth are not as painful as the least pains in Purgatory. According to this thirteenth-century saint, "It is the same fire that torments the reprobate in Hell, and the just in Purgatory. The least pain in Purgatory," he says, "surpasses the greatest suffering in this life. Nothing but the eternal duration makes the fire of Hell more terrible than that of Purgatory."

Summa Theologica also cites St. Augustine as promoting the idea that the fires of Hell and Purgatory are connected. St. Augustine wrote:

> Even as in the same fire gold glistens and straw smokes, so in the same fire the sinner burns and the elect is cleansed.
> — *Summa Theologica*, Supplement to the Third Part,
> Appendix 2 (Here, St. Thomas Aquinas quotes
> Gregory the Great, quoting St. Augustine.)

Faced with the unsettling truth about Purgatory, you may be wondering how to lessen the penalty accumulated thus far. Pray, fast, receive the sacraments frequently, and be kind and charitable to all, especially those least cherished by society. Offer up daily Mass not only for your own good, but for the souls already in Purgatory.

A brief prayer said this moment for a deceased loved one will be deeply appreciated by the individual, whose punishment will be lessened. In fact, any suffering that comes our way — a flu, a broken bone, or a bee sting — can be offered up to God as a sacrifice to benefit souls. In the Old Testament, atoning for the dead was called "a holy and pious thought":

He [Judas Maccabeus] also took up a collection, man by man, to the amount of two thousand drachmas of silver, and sent it to Jerusalem to provide for a sin offering. In doing this he acted very well and honorably, taking account of the resurrection. For if he were not expecting that those who had fallen would rise again, it would have been superfluous and foolish to pray for the dead. But if he was looking to the splendid reward that is laid up for those who fall asleep in godliness, it was a holy and pious thought. Therefore he made atonement for the dead, that they might be delivered from their sin.

— 2 MAC. 12:43-45

As Christians, we believe in the Communion of Saints. The members of the Body of Christ — in Heaven, on earth, and in Purgatory — form a spiritual communion. With Christ as our Head, we can help one another out.

"So we, though many, are one body in Christ, and individually members one of another," St Paul wrote to the Romans. (Rom. 12:5)

Our God is so fully of mercy that He has provided repentant sinners on earth various ways to reduce or even eliminate the justly deserved punishment in Purgatory that our sins have earned for us. Baptism, which can only occur once in a lifetime, is so powerful that is wipes our souls clean not only of all sin, but of all punishment accumulated during a lifetime up to that point. After Baptism, the Church grants partial indulgences — which can eliminate part of a person's future punishment in Purgatory — and plenary indulgences, which eliminate all of a person's Purgatorial punishment accumulated from Baptism up to that point.

Lists of available indulgences are available on the Internet. The many indulgences approved by the pope include meditating over the Stations of the Cross, reading Scripture, and adoring Jesus before the Blessed Sacrament. As a condition for receiving an indulgence, the person is often required to go to Confession, receive Communion, and to pray for the pope. For plenary indulgences, the person not only must be free from mortal sin, but also must be free of any attachment to venial sin.

Some indulgences can be gained for oneself; others may be done for a soul already in Purgatory.

In the meantime, is there any soul for whom we should not pray? It would be fruitless for a Christian to pray for a soul who is definitely in Hell, since there is no escape from that prison. It would also be useless to pray for someone we believe is in heaven. If the Church has canonized a person a saint, we can be sure the person is already in heaven. Although Mother Teresa and Pope John Paul II have not yet been canonized, most people I know believe they are in heaven. As long as someone is in heaven, whether it is a well-known saint or a pious great-grandmother, we may as well ask the person to pray for us. Prayers from those who behold the face of God are powerful.

...And It's Ancient News

Christians have been praying for the dead ever since the Apostles walked the earth.

Jews were hip to the practice even earlier.

Before Christ's time, Jews were teaching that we undergo a final purification between death and final glory. Today, devout Orthodox Jews who lose a loved one pray a prayer called the "the Mourner's Qaddish" for 11 months after a death, for the purpose of speeding up the purification process. Prayer is stopped before a full year passes in order to avoid implying that the person is guilty of an inordinate number of sins that need purging. However, St. Augustine was still asking for prayers for his saintly mother even 15 years after her death.

To my own friends, I say: when I die, please don't stop praying for me 11 months after my death. Furthermore, I do not wish to hear gooey, sappy stuff, such as "She's in a better place" or "She's at peace" while I'm undergoing a purging fire and am desperate for your prayers. Please make a note of this on your refrigerator!

While in Purgatory, I would hope for some extra prayers on special holidays.

> We offer sacrifices for the dead on their birthday anniversaries (the date of death — birth into eternal life).
> — Tertullian, *The Crown* 3:3 (211 A.D.)

The Writing on the Walls

Evidence that the earliest Christians prayed for the souls of the dead lies in inscriptions on underground tombs, or catacombs, that were determined by archeologists to date back to the first century. The inscriptions say things like "Peter and Paul, pray for Victor."

> In a word, so overwhelming is the witness of the early Christian monuments in favor of prayer for the dead that no historian any longer denies that the practice and the belief which the practice implies were universal in the primitive Church. There was no break of continuity in this respect between Judaism and Christianity.[46]

St. Augustine's mother, St. Monica, asked her son to remember her at the altar after she died. Augustine complied, and noted in his work *Confessions* that "the sacrifice of our redemption" was offered up for his mother. He said there was no doubt such sacrifices benefited the dead.

> ... But by the prayers of the Holy Church, and by the salvific sacrifice, and by the alms which are given for their spirits, there is no doubt that the dead are aided, that the Lord might deal more mercifully with them than their sins would deserve. For the whole Church observes this practice which was handed down by the Fathers.
>
> — St. Augustine of Hippo, *Sermons* (c. 411 A.D.)

In another work, St. Augustine said the "authority of the Catholic Church" was "clear" on this teaching (*The Care to be Had for the Dead* 1:3, 421 A.D.).

In 392 A.D., St. John Chrysostom argued that if Job's sons could be purified by their father's sacrifice, then the dead could be purified by our offerings (*Homilies on 1 Corinthians*, c. 392 A.D.).

Like the words "Trinity" and "Incarnation," the term "Purgatory" does not appear in the Bible. But have no fear, the doctrine was part of Christianity even before the Bible was put together. The second book of Maccabees calls it a "holy and pious thought" to pray for the dead who have not reached Heaven, so that they can be freed from their sin. In the New Testament, St. Paul discusses baptizing people for the dead (1 Cor. 15:29-30), and he prays for the soul of a man named Onesiphorus, who is dead (2 Tim. 1:16-18).

The Gospel of Matthew refers to a time beyond the earth where we can be cleansed of our sins. We know this refers to Purgatory, since reparation for sins is not possible in Hell —and is no longer needed in Heaven.

> "And whoever says a word against the Son of man will be forgiven; but whoever speaks against the Holy Spirit will not be forgiven, either in this age or in the age to come."
>
> — Mt. 12:32

Enduring the punishment for a sin previously forgiven is a common theme in the Bible. For example, the Lord forgives David for his sin, but David still must face a brutal penalty: the death of his first child (2 Sam. 12:13-14).

So, if a non-Catholic catches you atoning for sins and chides you with that pesky question — "Wasn't the cross of Jesus enough?" — just show your friend what the Bible says. And tell your friend that the cross was, indeed, enough to open the gates of Heaven. It was enough to make forgiveness available to the world. It was enough to deliver hope to a world of fallen people. But it was also enough to make God's own grace available to us: grace so powerful that our own prayers and sufferings become valuable for the atoning of sins already forgiven. Christ's awesome Sacrifice was enough to merit graces for the faithful that can be used for works to reverse the temporal damage caused by us. We call this penance.

Once your friend realizes that the ability to use Christ's graces to atone for our sins was God's plan, and a gift at that, your friend will jump for joy. (Good luck!)

While the holiest saints may receive their reward immediately upon death, most of us will first have to suffer loss before we are prepared to enter the Kingdom:

> . . . the fire will test what sort of work each one has done. If the work which any man has built on the foundation survives, he will receive a reward. If any man's work is burned up, he

will suffer loss, though he himself will be saved, but only as
through fire.   — 1 COR. 3:13-15

Since we cannot suffer any loss in Heaven, we know that this loss
occurs on the way to Heaven, during the purification process, which
perfects our souls.

> "You, therefore, must be perfect, as your Heavenly Father is
> perfect."   — MT. 5:48

It is only when our souls have been refined to the utmost purity
that they may bask in the presence of the Lord in all His glory. For,
the Bible instructs us to strive "for the holiness without which no one
will see the Lord" (Heb.12:14).

Once our earthly attachments and disorders have been burned
off of us, we will be ready to say those last few words of Pope John
Paul II as he lay on his deathbed: "Let me go to the house of the
Father."

The beloved Christian writer, C.S. Lewis, generously prayed for
the souls of his deceased friends so that they, too, could enter the
Father's house. In a letter, Lewis once mused:

> Our souls demand Purgatory, don't they? Would it not break
> the heart if God said to us, "It is true, my son, that your
> breath smells and your rags drip with mud and slime, but we
> are charitable here and no one will upbraid you with these
> things, nor draw away from you. Enter into the joy"? Should
> we not reply, "With submission, sir, and if there is no objec-
> tion, I'd rather be cleaned first." "It may hurt, you know" —
> "Even so, sir."[47]

✝

Now I Get . . . Judgment Day

My rudimentary impression of Judgment Day was that this was the day all of my acquaintances and myself would be judged worthy of heaven, and some other creepy folks would be sent along the other way. It sounded simple enough.

I sure wish my religion teachers had reviewed the itinerary. I probably would have done things a tad differently while growing up.

On Judgment Day, the entire world will have full and instant knowledge of everything I've done in my life. Every sin. Every deed, good or evil. Every word, nasty or kind. Every piece of gossip uttered behind someone's back. Every fib. You get the idea.

And not just the things that I've done. There will be a thorough public review of your entire life as well! The Gospel warns:

"I tell you, on the day of judgment men will render account for every careless word they utter; for by your words you will be justified, and by your words you will be condemned."
— Mt. 12:36-37

Yikes.

I had always imagined the event to be — well, largely, noneventful for those written in the Book of Life. I presumed it would be as stress-free as picking up a final grade for a pass-fail class, where you know you came in between A and D, and therefore passed.

Our final grades, in the form of Heaven or Hell, will be assigned to us on Judgment Day. But that will only make up part of the day's festivities.

Not only will we be subject to giving an account of all our past actions and our time spent idle, we will also learn the extent to which each of our actions caused hurt and damage — or goodness — in the world. We will be shown the fruits of our prayer, our fasting, our charity, and our love. The Bible says:

> Nothing is covered up that will not be revealed, or hidden that will not be known. Therefore whatever you have said in the dark shall be heard in the light, and what you have whispered in private rooms shall be proclaimed upon the housetops.
>
> — Lk. 12:2-3

According to St. Jerome, some sins will cause us mere embarrassment, while others will result in "agony for a long time." But both the venial and the mortal sins need to be accounted for (*Against Jovinian,* c. 393 A.D.).

The sheer mental capacity that humans will have on this day — enough to comprehend every moment of one's own life as well of billions of other people's lives — seems to shed some light on the type of enhanced perception and wisdom we will possess in Heaven.

In Heaven, the final spiritual condition of each and every person will be visible to all. We will plainly see who were the Mother Teresas while on earth, and who were the ones who just slipped in by the seat of their pants. The holiest saints, the ones who poured out the most love and who sacrificed themselves most for the least of Christ's brothers, will receive the greatest rewards.

According to the catechism:

> In the presence of Christ, who is Truth itself, the truth of each man's relationship with God will be laid bare (cf. Jn. 12:49). The Last Judgment will reveal even to its furthest consequences the good each person has done or failed to do during his earthly life.
>
> — *CCC,* 1039

For example, if you felt moved one day to offer the coat on your back and all the cash in your wallet to a homeless girl you encountered on the street, and that girl was so touched by the incident and so filled with Christ's love that she wound up becoming a nun, then you will enjoy that part of the movie.

On the other hand, if your past stint as a hit man caused impressionable children to develop ill-formed consciences leading to careers as serial murderers as adults, then you may want to hide behind your tall bag of popcorn during the show.

This movie is guaranteed to have a happy ending, for it will demonstrate how God's justice ultimately prevails.

Show Time!

When, you might ask, can we expect to see this Mother of all Reality Shows on the celestial silver screen?

This legendary biographical tale of the world, whose plot is updated daily, is slated for broadcast on the earth's Last Day. We will know that day is upon us when Jesus appears in the sky for His Second Coming. The scene will bear resemblance to His Ascension into Heaven less than 2,000 years ago.

The cast of characters will include everyone from Adam and Eve to Ludwig von Beethoven, and from Princess Diana, kings, and queens to the natives of the most obscure Amazonian tribes. The stars will include a long parade of Apostles, popes, and saints (known and unknown). Even the folks with names in the end credits, whether representatives of evil or virtue, will play pivotal speaking roles. The theme will be the triumph of God's love, peace, and communion over sin and strife. The plot will involve the rescue of humanity by a divine Savior whose heart is aflame with love. The love affair will culminate in the eternal wedding feast of the Church and Christ, the bridegroom. Things will once again be restored to the way they were before the Sin of Adam.

Referring to the revelations to be made on this Day, the catechism states:

> We shall know the ultimate meaning of the whole work of creation and of the entire economy of salvation and understand the marvelous ways by which his Providence led everything towards its final end. The Last Judgment will reveal that God's justice triumphs over all the injustices committed by his creatures and that God's love is stronger than death (cf. Song 8:6).
> — *CCC,* 1040

Some Words From the Judge

But there is more to this Day. Besides the colorful multi-media presentation, there may be some remarks. Advance copies of the transcript have been made available for perusal in the Bible. The message is to be delivered by the Son of Man, Jesus Christ, after He comes in glory with all His angels and sits on His glorious throne. To those who helped out the hungry, sick, and poor, He will say, "Come, ye blessed." To those who "forgot" to heed his commands, He will say, "Depart from me."

According to the Gospel of Matthew, after separating the sheep from the goats, Christ the King will say to those on His right:

> "Come, O blessed of my Father, inherit the kingdom prepared for you from the foundation of the world; for I was hungry and you gave me food, I was thirsty and you gave me drink, I was a stranger and you welcomed me, I was naked and you clothed me, I was sick and you visited me, I was in prison and you came to me."   — Mt. 25: 34-36

But Jesus will say to those on His left:

> "Depart from me, you cursed, into the eternal fire prepared for the devil and his angels; for I was hungry and you gave me no food, I was thirsty and you gave me no drink, I was a stranger and you did not welcome me, naked and you did not clothe me, sick and in prison and you did not visit me." Then they also will answer, "Lord, when did we see thee hungry or thirsty or a stranger or naked or sick or in prison, and did not minister to thee?" Then he will answer them, "Truly, I say to you, as you did it not to one of the least of these, you did it not to me."   — Mt. 25:41-46

As for the text of Christ's speech as laid out in the Bible, many theologians believe the message will not be spoken, but rather will be imparted to us in a more supernatural way. According to the Catholic Encyclopedia, it is likely that "Divine illumination" will instantly allow each person to comprehend the moral states of all souls.

Theologians believe the great Judgment will take place on earth, which will subsequently undergo a mighty fire that will completely transform the planet as we know it. By the end of the Day, all of God's children will be in Paradise. Those who finished life unrepentant will be locked in the dungeons of Hell forever, never again to wreak havoc on the elect. One thing is for sure: the Judge will be fair, balanced, and infallible.

There is no telling when this Day will come, so we must pray and stay on guard. It will appear like lightning for all to see.

> For as the lightning comes from the east and shines as far as the west, so will be the coming of the Son of man.
>
> — MT. 24:27

Scripture tells us the Second Coming will come like a thief in the night. I suppose some will be rollerblading along Boat House Row on the Schuylkill River in Philadelphia, others will be hiking up the Inca Trail to Machu Picchu, Peru, and still others will be checking their e-mail, or chatting outside the basilica after daily Mass. A blink of an eye later, Jesus will have come again, and the end of the world will be at hand.

> Then two men will be in the field; one is taken and one is left. Two women will be grinding at the mill; one is taken and one is left. Watch therefore, for you do not know on what day your Lord is coming. But know this, that if the householder had known in what part of the night the thief was coming, he would have watched and would not have let his house be broken into. Therefore you also must be ready; for the Son of man is coming at an hour you do not expect.   — MT. 24:40-44

The state of our souls at that moment will be preserved for all eternity more pristinely than the crystallized meteorites that fell to our planet a billion years ago. Just as we are still unable to change our high school yearbook photo decades later, neither shall we be able to change the final condition of our soul.

In Heaven, souls will sparkle with varying degrees of beauty and brilliance. The greatest glory will shine through the souls who most detached themselves from earthly riches and goals. Jesus said:

Do not lay up for yourselves treasures on earth, where moth and rust consume and where thieves break in and steal, but lay up for yourselves treasures in Heaven, where neither moth nor rust consumes and where thieves do not break in and steal.

— MT. 6:19-20

Despite the inability of experts to intelligently predict the timing of the Last Day, there are some Coming Attractions we can be on the lookout for. Scripture teaches us that certain events will occur before Judgment Day.

Those signs will include:

- A Great Apostasy, whereby many nations around the earth will abandon the Christian faith (2 Thess. 2:3).
- The reign of the Antichrist, a sinful man who will oppose Christ and the Church, exalt himself to god status, and lure many of the faithful to follow him (2 Thess. 2:3-12).
- A conversion of the Jews to Christianity, possibly spurred on by the return of Elijah to earth.

  ... and thus all Israel will be saved, as it is written: The deliverer will come out of Zion, he will turn away godlessness from Jacob; and this is my covenant with them when I take away their sins (Rom. 11:26).

- A host of calamities, such as wars, famines, pestilences, and earthquakes.

But not even the saints in heaven are privy to the date when God will be closing things down on earth. The day when Christ returns in glory shall remain the world's best-kept secret.

For the world will come to an end by no created cause, even as it derived its existence immediately from God. Wherefore the knowledge of the end of the world is fittingly reserved to God.

— St. Thomas Aquinas, *Summa Theologica*,
Supplement to the Third Part,
Question 88, Article 3

On the big Day, Christ will judge both the living and the dead, the just and the unjust. We know the court proceedings will, in some way, involve the Twelve Apostles, sitting on "twelve thrones, judging the twelve tribes of Israel" (Mt. 19:28).

Interestingly enough, those who are still alive and milling around on earth the day of the Second Coming will be brought up into the sky to meet the Lord in the air. Unlike us, they won't have to die, nor will they have to have their souls separated from their bodies first (in that way, they will be like Elijah and Enoch). Some call this meeting in the sky "the Rapture."[48]

> . . . the dead in Christ will rise first; then we who are alive, who are left, shall be caught up together with them in the clouds to meet the Lord in the air.　　— 1 Thess. 4:16-17

The rest of us, the already-dead folks, will finally have our souls reunited with our bodies, which will rise up from our graves. We will then keep our physical bodies forever, whether we are in Heaven or Hell.

> And every one who has left houses or brothers or sisters or father or mother or children or lands, for my name's sake, will receive a hundredfold, and inherit eternal life. But many that are first will be last, and the last first.　　— Mt. 19:29-30

Besides the General Judgment on the Last Day, which involves the whole world, each one of us also has a private judgment at the moment of our death. This is when we learn our eternal destination.

Okay, let's recap some of the more subtle points of the chapter. If any of you — and this is important — if any of my friends among those reading this feels the least fleeting temptation to mock, chuckle, or chortle at my expense in the near future . . . well, then, I will definitely be hearing all about that on the Last Day. A word to the wise may spare you all some embarrassment.

For we must all appear before the judgment seat of Christ, so that each one may receive good or evil, according to what he has done in the body . . .   — 2 Cor. 5:10

[God] . . . will render to every man according to his works: to those who by patience in well-doing seek for glory and honor and immortality, he will give eternal life; but for those who are factious and do not obey the truth, but obey wickedness, there will be wrath and fury. There will be tribulation and distress for every human being who does evil, the Jew first and also the Greek, but glory and honor and peace for every one who does good, the Jew first and also the Greek. For God shows no partiality.
— Rom. 2:6-11

. . . all were judged by what they had done.
— Rev. 20:13

For thou dost requite a man according to his work.
— Ps. 62:12-13

"For the Son of man is to come with his angels in the glory of his Father, and then he will repay every man for what he has done."   — Mt. 16:27

[God] judges each one impartially according to his deeds.
— 1 Pet. 1:17

Does not he who keeps watch over your soul know it, and will he not requite man according to his work?
— Prov. 24:12

For God is not so unjust as to overlook your work and the love which you showed for his sake in serving the saints.
— Heb. 6:10

Their end will correspond to their deeds.

— 2 COR. 11:15

Whatever your task, work heartily, as serving the Lord and not men, knowing that from the Lord you will receive the inheritance as your reward.   — GAL. 6:9

. . . knowing that you will receive from the Lord the due payment of the inheritance; be slaves of the Lord Christ. For the wrongdoer will receive recompense for the wrong he committed, and there is no partiality.

— COL. 3:24-25

CHAPTER TEN

†

No Getting Out . . . of Hell

Clever enough excuses can get us out of a parking ticket, jury duty, or jail. But not even the most creative among us has a remote chance of escaping the eternal prison known as Hell.

That's because the choices we make against God have permanent consequences. Sin makes our souls incompatible with eternal union with our holy God. That union is the purpose of our lives, and the only thing that can make us truly fulfilled.

In the original scheme of things, not one human being was supposed to go to Hell. The Bible says God "desires all men to be saved" (1 Tim. 2:4). And no believer will ever go to Hell without first using his or her free will to commit serious sin and refusing to repent. The catechism explains:

> Mortal sin is a radical possibility of human freedom, as is love itself. It results in the loss of charity and the privation of sanctifying grace, that is, of the state of grace. If it is not redeemed by repentance and God's forgiveness, it causes exclusion from Christ's kingdom and the eternal death of Hell, for our freedom has the power to make choices for ever, with no turning back.
> — *CCC,* 1861

If sociologists could conduct a survey of the poor men and women residing in Hell, I would venture to guess that most of the residents had convinced themselves either that Hell did not exist or at least that they were not deplorable enough to merit it. Still there would be a remaining five percent who realized their sins were hell-worthy, but planned on repenting at the last minute (but just didn't see death coming).

Polled as to the top reasons for wishing to escape, survey participants would surely cite physical agony, emotional torture, personal
humiliation, darkness, and unquenchable fires as reasons for wanting out.

Referring to Hell, the Bible uses images such as a "lake of fire that
burns with sulfur" (Rev. 19:20), "unquenchable fire" (Mt. 3:12),
everlasting burnings (Is. 33:14), a lake of fire and sulfur (Rev. 20:10),
and a "land of gloom and chaos, where light is as darkness" (Job
10:22). The bodies in Hell will be "an abhorrence to all flesh" (Is.
66:24).

But the number one reason given for dissatisfaction would prove
to be the torment of separation from God.

The Church teaches us that the worst pain experienced in Hell
is the pain of loss — the pain of eternal separation from our loving
God, "in whom alone man can possess the life and happiness for
which he was created and for which he longs" (CCC, 1035).

Souls entering Hell are immediately haunted by the realization
that they will be forever deprived of our loving God. These damned
individuals instantly realize they have forfeited an amazing relationship with an awe-inspiring God, and as a result, will never love again;
for love will never again be possible. They suffer profound loss.

Meanwhile, these souls also become aware of the elect going on
to eternal glory.

As if that were not distressing enough, the lack of love will be
accompanied by unrelenting pain. Could Hell involve poor souls
drowning in a river of flowing lava, at a temperature rivaling the sun's,
with no option of dying or even going unconscious for a moment?
All we know for sure is that Hell is a permanent and "eternal fire" (Mt
25:41).

Whether our souls travel to Heaven or Hell, they are incapable
of dying.

Fortunately, God is pulling for us, ready to shower His mercy on
anyone who repents of past sins. The Bible tells us God does not wish
"that any should perish, but that all should reach repentance" (2 Pet.
3:9).

It goes without saying that God would not want any of his children to go to Hell, any more than loving parents would want to kick

a child out of the house for drug use that endangers younger siblings. But justice demands that the non-repentant souls be locked out of God's household. Only those who freely choose to love God can be with Him.

On the Last Day, the souls in Hell will be permanently reunited with their old physical bodies to experience Hell forever. Believe it or not, a few theologians have even theorized that Hell is located in the core of the earth. If I had heard this, I never would have tried to dig a hole in the sand to China from the Jersey Shore when I was little!

The concept of Hell being inside the earth seems to have stemmed from Scripture. In one instance, Moses announced that God would punish some Old Testament characters in a very particular way for being schismatic: if the men in question, Dathan and Abiram, died an ordinary death, then it was not the Lord who had sent Moses. But if the ground opened up and swallowed them alive into the netherworld, Moses declared, then it would be known that the men had defied the Lord. The Bible continues:

> And as he finished speaking all these words, the ground under them split asunder; and the earth opened its mouth and swallowed them up, with their households and all the men that belonged to Korah and all their goods. So they and all that belonged to them went down alive into Sheol; and the earth closed over them, and they perished from the midst of the assembly. — NUM. 16:31-33

So far, the Church has not formally defined the location of Hell. She is much more concerned with leading sinners outs of Hell's path.

Wherever Hell is, we know it is a short trip away. Faster than a scramjet-powered hypersonic flight, the ride there will get the damned soul to its destination an instant after death. The person's body will follow, but not until the Last Day of earth. Unlike the glorified and beautiful bodies that will join the souls in Heaven, the bodies descending into Hell will be hideous and deformed.

Thus is the fate of those who die while loving themselves more than others. The Bible makes it clear that refusing to care for those who suffer the most, including the poor, hungry, homeless, sick, and imprisoned, will earn someone Hell (Mt. 25:31-46).

We know from the Bible that it is possible many people are already there.

> Enter by the narrow gate; for the gate is wide and the way is easy, that leads to destruction, and those who enter by it are many. For the gate is narrow and the way is hard, that leads to life, and those who find it are few.   — Mt. 7:13-14

Although the Church has officially declared certain people to be in heaven (the saints), the Church has never officially proclaimed any specific person to be in Hell. Many believe the Apostle Judas Iscariot, who betrayed Jesus for 30 pieces of silver only to hang himself afterwards, resides in Hell, but we just cannot say for sure.

Many who strive for Heaven will get distracted by earthly rewards and pleasures. According to Jesus, many "will attempt to enter but will not be strong enough" (Lk. 13:23).

From the earliest centuries, the Catholic Church has taught that Hell is for those who die while still refusing to repent of their mortal sins. How many mortal sins does it take to get to Hell? Just one. In a sermon in 395 A.D., St. Augustine warned:

> But do not commit those sins on account of which you would have to be separated from the Body of Christ, perish the thought!
> — St. Augustine, *Sermon to the Catechumens on the Creed* 7:15 (395 A.D.)

Choosing to not go to Mass on Sunday, without a serious reason, is one way to break off a relationship with God. Another way to be "separated from the Body of Christ" and reserve a place down under, according to the Bible, is adultery:

> But I say to you that every one who looks at a woman lustfully has already committed adultery with her in his heart. If your right eye causes you to sin, pluck it out and throw it away; it is better that you lose one of your members than that your whole body be thrown into Hell.   — Mt. 5:28-29

Sister Josefa Menendez (1890-1923), a Spanish nun to whom the Lord granted multiple visions of Hell, recorded in her notes that the majority of people she saw in Hell seemed to be there for sins of impurity, stealing, or unjust trading. During one of her visits to hell, Josefa saw priests and nuns who had broken their vows of chastity or poverty and died without repenting. In obedience to the Lord's commands, Josefa wrote down her observations, which are now compiled in the book *The Way of Divine Love.*

Hell will be so intolerable that people there will beg to die, but death will not be an option, according to the Book of Revelation (Rev. 9:16). It would be better for them to have never been born (Mt. 26:24).

The Bible even mentions the kinds of things people in Hell utter once they find themselves there.

> So it was we who strayed from the way of truth, and the light of righteousness did not shine on us, and the sun did not rise upon us. We took our fill of the paths of lawlessness and destruction, and we journeyed through trackless deserts, but the way of the Lord we have not known. What has our arrogance profited us? And what good has our boasted wealth brought us? All those things have vanished like a shadow, and like a rumor that passes by. — WIS. 5:6-9

Some people just refuse to believe that sin leads to Hell. Others will not believe high blood pressure and cholesterol can cause a heart attack. But, if all contributing factors are present, the heart attack and the Hell will arrive nonetheless. None can say he hasn't been warned.

Those who have already devoured the Bible and catechism for teachings on Hell, and who are hungry for more insight into the torment involved, can try the 23-page booklet *What Will Hell Be Like?*

This booklet contains the writings of the great eighteenth-century Church missionary, St. Alphonsus Liguori. St. Alphonsus, a fan of St. Thomas Aquinas, makes the following hypotheses:

- The damned in Hell desire others to be damned with them;
- The damned retain memory of their sins on earth, and are tormented by them;

- The damned who sin in greater number and measure suffer more than those with fewer sins;
- The damned are mocked by the demons in Hell.

Also consider the 488-page *The Dogma of Hell* by Father F.X. Schouppe, S.J. It includes handy tips for the whole family, such as "How to avoid Hell."

But let us not jest. Hell is a painful reality already being endured by many. The prayers and Masses we offer up today for the salvation of sinners can change the fate of people all around us.

In 1917, the Virgin Mary granted a vision of Hell to some children in Portugal, precisely so they would know how crucial it was to pray and make little sacrifices for the conversion of sinners. If you happen to have Salvador Dali's painting *Vision of Hell* hanging over your fireplace, then you might be interested to know the Fátima children's visions[49] inspired that painting.

During her apparitions, Mary told the children many souls would go to Hell because they had nobody to pray or make sacrifices for them. As you may recall, it was these same children for whom Mary performed the Miracle of the Sun, during which more than 80,000 people in Portugal saw the sun dance around the sky, plunge, and rise. (The miracle is discussed in Chapter 14.)

One of the children was Lucia, who died in 2005 after a long life of prayer. The following is a transcript of Sister Lucia's description of Hell as she saw it.

She opened Her hands once more, as She had done the two previous months. The rays [of light] appeared to penetrate the earth, and we saw, as it were, a vast sea of fire. Plunged in this fire, we saw the demons and the souls [of the damned]. The latter were like transparent burning embers, all blackened or burnished bronze, having human forms.

They were floating about in that conflagration, now raised into the air by the flames which issued from within themselves, together with great clouds of smoke. Now they fell back on every side like sparks in huge fires, without weight or equilibrium, amid shrieks and groans of pain and despair, which horrified us and made us tremble with fright (it must have been this sight which caused me to cry out, as people say they heard me).

The demons were distinguished [from the souls of the damned] by their terrifying and repellent likeness to frightful and unknown animals, black and transparent like burning coals. That vision only lasted for a moment, thanks to our good Heavenly Mother, Who at the first apparition had promised to take us to Heaven. Without that, I think that we would have died of terror and fear.

CHAPTER ELEVEN

†

Got Morals?

We certainly don't want to wind up in Hell. But do we have to do everything the Church says?

Well, let's see. You have a moral dilemma. You cannot decide whether a certain action you are contemplating can be justifiable. You sit up all night, thinking about it, praying about it, reflecting on the potential downsides as well as the intrinsic merits of the action at hand. Admittedly, the action has traditionally been considered sinful, and clearly, it has a bad rap. But the more you think about the action — polygamy, let's say — the more you are able to envision a very many good things coming out of it, at least in this particular case.

By morning — or perhaps after some long, contemplative hikes up the mountain —you conclude that, in your specific case, the action in mind would be okay, after all.

The problem here is that truth is not subjective.

The method for determining truth as described above sounds impracticable, if not ridiculous. Yet, I've had acquaintances of diverse creeds who have professed taking the precise route described above to reach a moral conclusion.

In the end, in every case, the person concluded that the action under consideration would be quite acceptable, to the great delight of the person. In a mammoth coincidence, the decision to take up the action was exactly the more convenient and more desirable path for that person to take, especially in light of new circumstances and opportunities that had surfaced. Despite the fact that some of these deeds had been proclaimed wrong throughout all of Christian-Judaic history, and despite the fact that the person previously had opposed the action, the person had now succeeded in altering his or her perception of the deed.

The human mind is exceptionally adroit at the game of rationalization, as I know from my own skill in the sport. But the Catholic Church stands firm, divinely proclaiming the unchanging moral truths of Jesus Christ. It is the Catholic Church, and not each individual sinner, who possesses, in the words of St. Augustine, "the crown of teaching authority" (*The Advantage of Believing* 35, 392 A.D.).

If the Church has already resolved the moral dilemma we face, we will not do any better on our own.

Chances are, the first hunch we have about a sin is the correct one. Chances are, the first hunch will also be the one to lead us down the more difficult road.

God has written natural law on our hearts, but our minds get clouded by sin. Each time we submit to sin, we lose grace. By losing grace, we not only lose strength and power to avoid other sins, we also lose our ability to recognize sin.

So, because of our fallible nature, we have the duty to form our conscience by turning to the Church Jesus founded. In the business of morality, our Church is utterly incapable of pronouncing error. How do we know this?

From the beginning, our Church was promised the truth by Jesus Himself. As recorded in the Bible, Jesus said His Church would be guided by the Holy Spirit into "all truth" (Jn.16:13). The Bible also assures us that the Church is "the pillar and bulwark of truth" (1 Tim. 3:15).

Our God was wise enough to establish a Church that would not only last until Christ's Second Coming, but one that would accurately preserve His teachings. To believe the Church supplies us with false teaching, therefore, is to doubt Christ's own promise.

Can we suppose for one moment that Jesus would have left us helpless, with nothing but our own feeble and flawed minds to discern which actions would lead us to Hell? Would He have left us with no way to distinguish harmless deeds from toxic deeds that would contribute to the Lord's Cross? And with no way to ascertain whether a doctrine we think Scripture is communicating to us is actually a doctrine of the devil?

There is no doubt the Holy Spirit helps all of us bring Scripture into our hearts. However, we cannot fool ourselves into thinking that, as individuals, we are capable of infallibly extrapolating all the intricacies of moral theology found in the Bible. Promises along that line are granted to the Catholic Church alone.

If we really want to know how Christ wants us to behave, we listen to the Church. We pray for God's help to obey. If the Church tells us to stay away from things like witchcraft, astrology, palm reading, tarot card readings, and horoscopes — and if the Church says these endeavors are not from above, and possibly are of the underworld — then we probably don't need them.

Anyone's conscience might figure out that physical assault, suicide, and even the sullying of a person's reputation, are wrong, perhaps even falling under the Church's classification of the sin of murder, albeit in different degrees. But what about things like purchasing a poison for an elderly uncle who wants to end his life, or cloning a human being to then destroy the new life for the sake of manufacturing organs?

Must each individual Christian spend years reading and re-reading the Bible to determine the ethics of such things for oneself? Is each of us obliged to examine generations of philosophical and theological thought to arrive at an informed decision on the proper classification of each possible sin, only to realize that the next person's assessment may diverge from our own?

In more cases than we realize, the Church has already done the work for us. The Holy Spirit has spoken. The Church declares both human cloning and poisoning to be wrong. Like a mother who teaches her child not to run into the street, our Church, which is our guardian of truth, has been put here by God to keep up safe.

The Facts of Life

In its continual affirmation of life, the Church cautions us not to remove the feeding tube of a mentally handicapped person who is not otherwise dying. We are taught that a human being, of any level of intelligence or mobility, is made in the image of God and possesses a soul destined for God. Therefore, whether the person is sleeping, unconscious, disabled, or just an infant, a human being cannot ever be compared to a vegetable, a mineral, or an animal, Pope John Paul II instructed us. Only children of God have spiritual life.

Even if artificial means are required, providing food and water "always represents a natural means of conserving life, not a medical act," Pope John Paul II told doctors and ethicists at a conference in Rome on March 20, 2004. The late pope called the administering of food and water "obligatory" and said that, since no one knows when a person might come out of a vegetative state, even after more than a year has passed, one cannot ethically justify "interruption of minimal care for the patient, including food and water."[50]

The very notion of depriving a mentally handicapped person of a simple feeding tube on the grounds that she is disabled sets a dangerous precedent for society. Not surprisingly, every major advocacy group for people with disabilities in the United States publicly opposed the deprivation of food and water in the Terri Schiavo case.[51]

What disabilities might be targeted next as potential rationales for deeming a person's life not worth continuing? Do we want to live in a world where it is illegal to starve an animal, but legal to starve a former love interest?

Perhaps Michael Schiavo thought he was being a good husband by fighting for the cessation of water and food into Terri's body. Maybe he even thought he was being a good "husband" while he was "going on with life" and bedding another woman, even as Terri lay helpless in the hospital. But in the end, it doesn't much matter what he thought. Our Church teaches us that he was *wrong;* we are obliged to feed the hungry and meet the basic needs of healthy, albeit disabled, human beings.

Of course, change the scenario and you also change the moral parameters. If a person was dying from a degenerative disease, and food would just prolong the person's pain, then perhaps such a drastic action could be legitimately considered. If the lungs or heart of a sickly person required permanent intervention of advanced machinery, the removal of that machinery could be legitimately considered. If a person with cancer felt a prescribed treatment would be too painful and unbearable to endure for the possible benefit involved, the person could legitimately refuse the treatment.

But food and water are basic needs a civilized society must provide to those unable to feed themselves. That is what our popes have taught us.

A Supreme Court judge in Queens agreed when he ruled in April of 2005 that a feeding tube was basic care and could not be considered medicine. As a result of Judge Martin Ritholz's ruling in the *Borenstein v. Simonson* case, an 86-year-old Orthodox Jewish woman, Lee Kahan, was not subjected to starvation.

In a seventeen-page document, the judge not only discussed New York state law, but also mentioned the view of Orthodox Jewish law, since the woman's devout religious beliefs came up during the trial. He wrote:

> Judaism views nutrition and hydration by feeding tubes or intravenous lines not as medical treatment but as supportive care, no different from washing, turning, or grooming a dying patient.

Fighting for justice for the smallest and weakest among us has always been a priority for Christians. Over the centuries, our ancestors rejoiced when equal rights were granted to various groups of people through amendments to the U.S. Constitution.

The Thirteenth Amendment gave people the right not to be held as slaves; the Fifteenth and Nineteenth Amendments extended the right to vote to blacks and women. Still, there is no amendment in sight recognizing the inalienable rights of a human being in the womb to not be killed, whether by poison, stab wound, or smothering. The meekest and most powerless human beings among us still have no protection against discrimination based on gender, health, or size. In China, in particular, notorious population control laws have led to horrific persecutions of the female sex, persecutions resulting in gender imbalances that threaten the family and economy there.

In America, those wishing to abort sometimes claim the generous motive of not wanting to bring an unwanted child into the world. The first problem with this is that a unique human being *has already been* brought into the world; the second is that the child is not unwanted, as evidenced by notoriously long adoption waiting lists filled with names of loving couples. Of course, the life of the pregnant mother is to be equally valued and respected. Young mothers who carry their children until birth and adoption carry a significant burden and must be offered assistance and compassion.

Our Church is not unreasonable. Consider the case of a mother, three months pregnant and diagnosed with a type of cancer that will kill her within weeks if she doesn't take chemotherapy. Her doctor warns her the treatment will be lethal to the fetus in her womb. Can the mother take the medicine? Sure. In fact, the Church says she can, and should, take it.

The Church explains that taking medicine is an intrinsically good, life-saving action; this contrasts sharply with the evil action of murdering a baby with a doctor's knife. The baby's resulting death from the chemotherapy is an unintended, bad side effect of the otherwise life-giving medicine.

Across the board, the Church teaches that intrinsically good actions are acceptable, even in cases with unintended bad side-effect results, provided there is balance. On the other hand, an evil action can never be tolerated, even if it produces laudable results. The unjust condemnation of an innocent person cannot be permissible, even if it would save a nation (CCC, 1753).

Therefore, the woman who says she will become a prostitute for a week to raise money for displaced hurricane victims commits a grave wrong. The executive who siphons a million dollars out of her company's coffers, for the purpose of distributing it to the impoverished Zulu people, is wrong.

The Church has always rejected the views of Renaissance philosopher Nicolo Machiavelli, who declared, "The ends justifies the means."

That is why the Church rejects in vitro fertilization. Even though the end result or goal — procreation — is laudable, the action taken to achieve it violates God's designs for creating new life. Whenever procreation is removed from the conjugal union of the spouses, God's plans get trampled upon. God's designs are further thwarted in cases where embryos that have been implanted are removed and destroyed. Because of the high failure rate of IV fertilization, some doctors implant extra embryos in the woman. Then, if "too many" of them survive, some are removed.

Another scenario falling into the Machiavellian category would be medical research that relies on violations of the sanctity of human life. Because the Church holds that destroying a human embryo unjustly ends a human life, the Church condemns stem-cell research that requires the destruction of human embryos. On the other hand, the Church encourages and funds research on adult stem cells and stem cells from umbilical cords. A simple rule of thumb is: Never do evil to accomplish good. It follows that investors should do research before purchasing a stock to ensure they do not unwittingly support biotechnology firms that profit from sacrificed human life. Overall, the Church is one of the world's largest healthcare providers, especially to the poor, and is a frontrunner in the care and treatment of AIDS patients around the globe.

Striking a Balance

In predicaments where a good action leads to a negative side effect, the Church offers its blessing if — and only if — there is balance: the good desired must equal or outweigh the damage done, and all steps are taken to prevent or minimize the bad consequence. Therefore, a mother could not in good conscience take a medicine for her own non-fatal condition that would lead to the baby's death. Nor could she take a cough medicine that would permanently blind or cripple the baby.

The lives of both human beings are equally sacred.

Sometimes, a person is faced with the choice of two unavoidable evils. According to the Church, we are obliged to choose the lesser of the evils. The pilot who, at the last second, must choose between crashing into a home or a school must choose the home.[52]

Just when modern society catches us by surprise with a seemingly new scenario, we realize there is nothing new since the start of the human race. From the earliest times, our ancestors have experienced the same struggles and the same threats to human justice and virtue. They have generated the same arguments and rationales for justifying their actions.

The reasons people offer today for wanting to extinguish a life within them are no different from the reasons they had in ancient cultures. Starting in fourth-century B.C., physicians would solemnly recite the Hippocratic oath, promising to do no harm. Named after the ancient Greek physician and philosopher Hippocrates (although more likely formulated by Pythagoras), the oath long included a pledge against two specific harms:

> I will not give poison to anyone though asked to do so, nor will I advise such a plan; and similarly, I will not give a woman a pessary to cause abortion. But I will keep pure and holy both my life and my art.

It wasn't until the middle of the twentieth century that some medical colleges began deleting the part about euthanasia and abortion.

Societies change; sins don't.

There are no new sins under the sun, only new tools for committing them.

The Church has always known the woman and the man were created to complement each other in a way that reflected God's own inner unity. The design has not changed since Adam and Eve. According to the Bible:

> So God created man in his own image, in the image of God he created him; male and female he created them. And God blessed them, and God said to them, "Be fruitful and multiply, and fill the earth and subdue it."   — GEN. 1:27-28

As perfect gifts to one another, the man and woman become co-workers with God himself in the awesome creation of human life. As the catechism tells us, God's creation has never been compatible with fornication, masturbation, sodomy, or adultery.

Contrary to a popular view, the invention of the birth control pill in the 1960s did not introduce an entirely new ethical conundrum. Ancient Egyptian writings reveal various options for contraception dating back to more than a millennium before Christ's time. Onan, who lived approximately 1,500 years before Christ, was struck dead for spilling semen on the ground, according to the Old Testament (Gen 38:6-10). The sin of Onanism, or withdrawal, as well as other contraceptive devices and potions, are mentioned in a variety of ancient writings.[53]

From the beginnings of Christianity, the Church cautioned its flock against defiling the marital act, which, by definition, must be open to procreation. As long as a man's seed is expelled, it must land in the birth canal of the wife.

In 195 A.D., Clement of Alexandria wrote:

> Because of its divine institution for the propagation of man, the seed is not to be vainly ejaculated, nor is it to be damaged, nor is it to be wasted.
> — *The Instructor of Children,* 2:10:91:2

Somewhat later in 255 A.D., Hippolytus of Rome also wrote:

> On account of their prominent ancestry and great property, the so-called faithful (certain Christian women who had affairs with male servants) want no children from slaves or lowborn commoners, [so] they use drugs of sterility or bind themselves tightly in order to expel a fetus which has already been engendered.
> — *Refutation of All Heresies,* 9:12

In the late fourth and early fifth centuries, St. Augustine repeatedly condemned marital acts that blocked procreation, saying that they turned spouses into adulterers.

Even Protestant Reformers condemned contraception. Martin Luther called it "more atrocious than incest and adultery" while John Calvin labeled it "monstrous."

And none other than Sigmund Freud described as "perverse" any sexual activity that aimed to shed its reproductive aspect, isolating pleasure as the sole goal.[54] According to author Christopher West:

> Wise men and women throughout history (not only Catholics) have recognized that respect for the procreative function of sexual union is the linchpin of all sexual morality. Even Sigmund Freud recognized this. He wrote that 'abandonment of the reproductive function' is the common feature of all perversions. We actually describe a sexual activity as perverse if it has given up the aim of reproduction and pursues the attainment of pleasure as an aim independent of it.
> — *Introductory Lectures in Psychoanalysis*

All of Christianity condemned contraception even until the 1930s, when the Anglican Church started allowing it for special cases. One by one, each Protestant denomination lifted the ban, but the Catholic Church is prevented by the Heavens from opposing natural law. It will never give the green light for the defiling of the sanctity of marriage or of the design of the female and male as ordained by God. Fortunately, God's love and forgiveness is forever available to those who return to his laws.

Many of even the most sincere Catholics lack an awareness of the history of the Church's moral codes. Through no fault of their own, many are not even aware that the Church has teachings on certain topics, much less what the reasons are for those teachings. One read-through of the *Catechism of the Catholic Church* can clear up a world of questions for the curious. The book — with about ten million copies sold — is replete with footnotes so that readers know where to go for background information. Here is a quiz to get you started.

Sin or Not?

Cloning an animal? No problem.

Cloning a human? Big problem.

Pornography, the selling of slaves, the worshipping of golden calves? Sin City.

Gambling? It's okay in moderation, but check the catechism for the required conditions.

Alcohol? Also okay in moderation, but sins include drunkenness and being a stumbling block to someone trying to fight an addiction.

Uttering obscenities? The Bible speaks out against them. "But now put them all away: anger, wrath, malice, slander, and foul talk from your mouth" (Col. 3:8).

Gluttony? It's one of the "Seven Capital Sins," which include pride, avarice, envy, wrath, lust, and sloth. The virtues paired up with these sins are: moderation, humility, generosity, charity, meekness, chastity, and zeal.

Autopsies? Perfectly acceptable for scientific or police investigations.

Cremation? The church earnestly encourages burial of the whole body, but permits cremation if the remains are buried respectfully in an urn, rather than sprinkled over a river. By keeping the remains in one place, Christians testify to their belief that bodies will be raised whole on the Last Day.

Cocaine? Using it is sinful. Our bodies are temples of the Holy Spirit and we have no right to assault or abuse them.

Taking the name of the Lord in vain? Thou shalt not do this, according to the Second Commandment.

Reincarnation? Heresy. God created each person to have one soul that corresponds to one specific body. The two will be separated at death, but reunited on the Last Day for all of eternity.

Ouija boards, séances, necromancy, nihilism, Marxism, post-Enlightenment rationalism? Rejected!

Evolution? Fine. Catholics are welcomed to believe or not to believe that human beings physically evolved from another form of life. However, we may not say that there was an evolution of the soul. God directly infused a newly created soul into the first human being, as He continues to do for each new human life that He creates.

"Big Bang" Theory? We are permitted to believe or not to believe that the creation of the universe was prompted by a chain reaction in which one super dense little blob of matter and energy exploded into a whole universe 10 to 20 billion years ago. If we choose to believe this, however, we must also acknowledge that the first speck of matter (a speck that, incidentally, weighed as much as the whole universe) was created by God out of nothing, and that the entire process was designed and guided by God, rather than by coincidence. In fact, many cosmologists are in awe of the universal order that governs our universe, and the way in which each element has come together in a precise way so as to allow for the existence of human life on earth.

The Bible says that God created the world in six days, but it also says that with the Lord, one day is like a thousand years, and vice versa. I, personally, believe that God did billions of years' worth of work in six 24-hour "earth" days, and left it here to appear in its billion-years form for humans, from their limited human perspective, to analyze and unravel.

Not believing in the miracles of the saints? Not a sin. Catholics are not required to believe in specific miracles attributed to the intercession of a saint, nor are we obliged to believe messages stemming from private revelation (as opposed to the public revelation that was deposited when Jesus and the Apostles walked the earth). Of course, we must believe in the miracles of Jesus, especially His resurrection and ascension, and others as recorded in the Bible.

Web surfing for hours at the office? This would be stealing, unless you made up the time later (after careful tracking of the minutes) and your employer was open to the idea.

Cow tipping? Don't be mean! Although there are no encyclicals devoted to the mischievous sport of cow tipping, the Church teaches that Christians owe kindness to animals, and should not desire that any suffer needlessly. Therefore, the frustration and pain suffered by a fallen cow would make this activity wrong. On the other hand, if a cow were about to trample a child, and toppling the cow was the only way to save the child, then the action would be admissible, and even required.

We are also permitted to use animals for food, clothing, labor, and medical research, but we should take steps to keep suffering at a minimum. "God entrusted animals to the stewardship of those whom he created in his own image (cf. Gen. 2:19-20; 9:1-4)," according to the catechism (*CCC*, 2417).

Jumping into a shark-filled aquarium? Sinful, if your intention is to be eaten, but heroic, if your intention is to save a child who fell in.

Not attending Mass on Sunday? Serious sin. The Mass is the heart of Christian life and worship. On the other hand, if we are on the way to Mass and pass an injured person lying on the ground, then it would be a sin to attend Mass and ignore the helpless person. Outward, visible, public, and regular worship has been part of Christianity since the time of the Apostles. In the New Testament, the letter to the Hebrews reminds the faithful about "not neglecting to meet together" (Heb 10:25). As for the rest of the day, the catechism teaches that the focus should be relaxation of mind and body, prayer, and the cultivation of our familial, cultural, social, and religious lives. On the other hand, the Church cautions us to be mindful of Christians who are unable to rest from work on Sundays due to poverty and misery (*CCC*, 2186).

Claiming you are younger or older to obtain a discount at the amusement park? The sin of stealing.

Refusing to tithe? Not sinful. Mosaic Law is no longer in effect, having been replaced by the New Covenant. Christians are encouraged to give as much as they can to their church and other religious charities, whether it be less than a tenth of their salary or much more. Tithing continues to serve as a useful guideline for Christians.

Buying stock in a corporation that grossly violates pollution laws, pushes cigarettes on children, conducts forced sterilization of women in Third World countries, and has a subsidiary in the pornography industry? A shameful, shameful sin.

Buying and selling of slaves? Mortal sin.

Buying and selling of relics? Mortal sin, in some cases. The Church prohibits the sale of first-class relics (bones or body part of a saint) and second-class relics (clothing worn by a saint), but not third-class relics (cloth touched to a saint's clothing). Vendors may charge for the reliquary or container that houses a relic. In the same way, vendors may not sell the Holy Word of God, but they may sell the paper and binding on which it is printed. Relics have always been part of Christianity. In the early Church, the relics of St. Peter, the other apostles, and their successors were vehicles for many of God's healings. In about 150 A.D., the Christians of Smyrna referred to the bones of their deceased bishop, Polycarp, as "more valuable than precious stones." In 2004, the relics of St. Augustine made a special tour in Italy in commemoration of the 1,650th anniversary of the birth of the great philosopher and theologian. Recently, a few unprincipled entrepreneurs have been caught trying to sell first-class relics on eBay. Shame on them!

Today, a parish in Pittsburgh is said to have the largest collection of authentic relics of saints outside the Vatican. In fact, St. Anthony Chapel, located in the Troy Hill section of the western Pennsylvania city, houses relics from the majority of the saints in the history of Christianity — including St. Mary Magdalene, St. John the Baptist, and St. Anthony — as well as splinters from the Cross of Jesus.

Telling friends whom you voted for in the election of pope? A sin worthy of excommunication, as every cardinal knows.

Doing too many good works? Opposite of sinful. In fact, the more devoted to good works a person in a state of grace is, the more he or she will accelerate the coming of God's Kingdom. As we will see in the next chapter, God uses every good work in some way. St. Paul said we should abound in good works, and assured Christians that their efforts would not be in vain (1 Cor. 15:58).

Informing somebody about the faults and failings of another? This is a sin, according to the catechism (cf. Sir. 21:28) (*CCC,* 2477). An exception exists when there is an urgent need to notify a certain party of the wrongdoing. For example, if Robby has never entered a house without leaving with a pocketful of jewelry, and Robby plans to attend your brother's housewarming celebration, notifying your brother might qualify.

Receiving Communion at a Protestant church? Not permitted. Plus, it can be seen as impolite.

Receiving Communion at an Orthodox church? Permitted only if no Catholic Church is available to you. Besides having our seven sacraments, Orthodox churches have a valid Mass by virtue of their valid apostolic succession of priests. So, it is truly Jesus you are receiving.

Possessing a statue? Encouraged. Keeping statues and paintings of Christ, saints, or angels nearby helps call to mind God's glory and can help increase our devotion. Just imagine how strange it would be if we had never seen a picture of Jesus! Muslims oppose artistic representations of the human form, which they equate with idolatry. The first Christian art came in the form of painted Biblical scenes in first-century catacombs. The idea that it is wrong to use images in Christian devotion is a heresy known as Iconoclasm, which was condemned by the Second Council of Nicea in 787 A.D. In the Old Testament, God ordered the making of statues, including two gold cherubim with wings (See Ex. 25:28-30).

Opponents of the use of religious images generally cite Ex. 20:4-5 as their base for objection, but the intention of these verses is to guard against the making of images to be worshipped. Catholics don't worship objects, of course, nor would we ever accuse somebody of idolatry who displayed a Christmas manger on their mantle or who watched images of Biblical figures in movies such as *Moses* or *The Passion of the Christ.* The Early Church did not believe that Scripture opposed the use of religious images in art.

In vitro **fertilization?** Not permitted. However, many technologies and treatments for fertility are compatible with God's designs, and are thus sanctioned by the Church. The basic rule of thumb is that the primary cause of human reproduction must be conjugal union. Science can assist the marital act but cannot replace it. Therefore, hormonal injections (if used safely) or surgeries to repair tubal blockages would be permissible. On the other hand, creating human embryos in lab dishes is condemned. For more information, visit www.popepaulvi.com or write to the Pope Paul VI Institute in Omaha, Nebraska.

Sterilization, condoms, spermicide, the pill, the birth control patch, and other contraceptives? Not permissible. The marital act must always be open to the possibility of life. Although the couple may abstain from the act, the couple may not the defile the act itself by deliberately blocking its inherent life-giving aspect. Even in the Old Testament, we see a condemnation of the common method of the times for making one sterile: "No one whose testicles have been crushed or whose penis has been cut off may be admitted into the community of the LORD" (Deut. 23:1).

Natural family planning? Childbirths may be spaced naturally through the monitoring of the women's fertile period each month. The latest monitoring methods are far superior to the "rhythm" method of the old days. For information, do an Internet search of terms such as "Natural Family Planning," "Billings Ovulations Method," "Creighton Method," or "Sympto-Thermal method." Women also have the option of monitoring their fertility using ovulation detection devices sold at most drug stores.

Studies have shown NFP is 98 to 99 percent effective when the couple has been trained by a certified instructor, and NFP couples' divorce rates are a mere fraction of those who contracept.

Legitimate reasons for delaying the next childbirth might include serious emotional issues, a financial situation where a couple could honestly not afford to feed another baby, or a wife awaiting surgery. Non-legitimate reasons would include a desire to travel the world before settling down, or a yearning to appear slim at cocktail parties. God said, "Be fruitful and multiply" (Gen. 1:28).

Separation? Can be permitted for serious reasons.

Remarriage? A Christian marriage is a permanent spiritual bond that can end only with the death of one spouse. Remarriage would be considered adultery, unless the man and woman are living as brother and sister. Jesus said, "Whoever divorces his wife and marries another, commits adultery against her; and if she divorces her husband and marries another, she commits adultery" (Mk. 10:11-12).On the other hand, if a person's first marriage was annulled, then the person is free to marry. Annulments are only to be granted where a true marriage never took place. In other words, the conditions necessary for a Christian marriage did not exist when the couple took their wedding vows. Grounds for annulment are spelled out in the Church's canon law and can be discussed with a priest. A few of the many scenarios might include a spouse who had planned to cheat from the start; a spouse with a severe mental illness that rendered the person incapable of fulfilling his or her marriage obligation; or a couple who had set out to permanently block all chances of conceiving, despite having the ability to have children. Nothing that occurs after a marriage can nullify a true marriage, if one took place.

Donating your liposuctioned fat for stem cell research? A thoughtful gesture! The Church encourages scientific research on stem cells, whether they come from adult human tissue, umbilical cords, placentas, amniotic fluid, bone marrow, adult cadavers, or fat derived from liposuction. The only thing opposed by the Church would be research on stem cells from human embryos that were purposely killed or destroyed by another human (since these little guys have not given their consent). Advocates for using these embryos sometimes argue that not all cell types or tissues can be manufactured from adult stem cells. This does not make the destruction of human embryos any less immoral. Not to mention, in talks around the country, priest-neuroscientist Fr. Tadeusz Pacholczyk has noted that not a single person has yet been cured by research on embryonic stem cells, while thousands have been cured by the more promising adult-type and umbilical-cord stem cells. Fr. Pacholczyk, education director for the National Catholic Bioethics Center, did his doctoral work in neuroscience at Yale and his postdoctoral work at Harvard. (A final note: we certainly do not recommend liposuction unless your doctor has ordered it!)

Research on aborted embryos? Unethical, if human (as mentioned above). Ethical if animal. In the words of Archbishop Renato Martino, "The principle that human beings (embryos) should not be used as an object or 'sacrificed' is always valid, even when others might benefit from that practice."[55]

Fr. Pacholczyk has said that as "a former embryo" himself, he is grateful he was "never offered up on the altar of science" to be used for embryonic stem cell extraction. Fr. Pacholczyk testified, "We can never allow for the sanctioned creation of a subclass of human beings, made up of those still in their embryonic or fetal stages, who can be freely exploited and discriminated against by those fortunate enough to have already passed beyond those early stages."[56]

Destroying a human embryo that was going to be discarded anyway — for the sake of research? Immoral. In Fr. Pacholczyk's published list of ten stem-cell research myths, the priest responds to such faulty reasoning:

> The moral analysis of what we may permissibly do with an embryo doesn't depend on its otherwise "going to waste," nor on the incidental fact that those embryos are 'trapped' in liquid nitrogen. If we think about a schoolhouse in which there is a group of children who are trapped through no fault of their own, that would not make it okay to send in a remote control robotic device which would harvest organs from those children and cause their demise.

Although we must not destroy human life for research, the Church has not voiced an objection to research on cells from life that has died naturally. If a woman has had a miscarriage, cells may be obtained from the embryo or fetus. These cells — known as "embryonic germ cells" — may be five to nine weeks old and therefore older than the five-day embryos that researchers generally uses for extracting stem cells. But Fr. Pacholczyk told me that "embryonic germ cells" derived from fetal cadavers behave similarly to ones derived from five-day-old embryos.

Waging war? After all peaceful policies and diplomacy have been exhausted, war can be permitted to protect against an existing aggressor inflicting great damage, provided the war will not cause more damage than the enemy aggressor would. But read up on the four strict conditions of Just War Theory, as developed by St. Augustine and St. Thomas Aquinas.

Manipulating the DNA of a human fetus? Pope John Paul II said this could be acceptable for the correction of serious hereditary illnesses, but not for making designer babies.

Premarital sex? Everyone knows this one is wrong, but few are aware that the spread of sexually transmitted diseases among young people has reached epidemic proportions. A recent report estimated that by age 25, one of every two sexually active youths in America will have an STD.[57] In the United States, there are 65 million people currently living with an incurable STD, according to the Centers for Disease Control and Prevention. One of the commonly transmitted STDs today is the Human Papillomavirus, which is the major cause of cervical cancer. The effectiveness of condoms in preventing HPV has shown to be poor, according to the CDC.

Just being a good person? Being a good person is imperative, but as saints throughout history will tell you, even they could not have accomplished what they did without frequent reception of the sacraments plus long hours in prayer, for it is mainly through the sacraments that Christ makes people into what He wants them to be. Through the sacraments, He pours His life-giving grace onto us in a direct way. Acting upon us, this grace helps us form our conscience, avoid temptation, increase our love for God and others, and shape us into something worthy of eternal union with Christ, which is the hope of every Christian.

Racism? This is not only evil; it is a ridiculous stance. Each of the six billion people on this planet has a common ancestor, and therefore is a genetic relative of every other person on this planet. Scientists have confirmed that all living human beings are biological descendants of a woman who has been dubbed the "Mitochondrial Eve." We have all inherited a piece of mitochondrial DNA from this woman, who is believed to have lived in eastern Africa between 100,000 and 200,000 years ago. Whether or not this woman was the first person on earth — the Biblical Eve — remains a mystery, but it seems that we are all descended from Adam and Eve. Their first sin caused each of us to inherit a wounded human nature.

St. Paul wrote: "Therefore as sin came into the world through one man and death through sin, and so death spread to all men because all men sinned" (Rom. 5:12).

Those interested in reading about mitochondrial DNA and our ancestral heritage can consult the research of Rebecca Cann, Mark Stoneking, and the late Allan Wilson.

Those interested in participating in a major study to trace the migratory patterns of early human beings as they left Africa can go to www.nationalgeographic.com to purchase a DNA kit for $99.95 with instructions on sending in a swab of saliva for analysis. Participants will be provided information such as what percentage of their DNA from the maternal line and the paternal line is from each of four population groups: Indo-European, sub-Saharan, East Asian, and native American.

Marrying a Neanderthal? If Neanderthals were still alive, we would be able to marry them if and only if they were determined to be creatures with rational souls and with an anatomy that would allow the males and females of the two groups to become one flesh. They would have to be true human beings, and thus, children of God. The Neanderthals, a hominid species or subspecies believed to have disappeared from the planet at least 28,000 years ago, settled in Europe long before the appearance of the first modern humans, but co-existed with us modern *Homo Sapiens* for a time. Scientists discovered the first Neanderthal fossil in 1856 in Düsseldorf, Germany, but we still do not know if these large-brained, muscle-bound characters were capable of making tools more complex than an ax or spear, or to what degree these bipedal hunters could contribute to creative, philosophical, literary, or scientific thought. One thing is for sure; they left us no page-turning *Oedipus Rex,* no architecturally masterful Taj Mahal, and no mysteriously fascinating Mona Lisa.

What about marriage to an alien, you ask? If aliens from other planets existed, they, too, would be eligible for betrothal if they met the aforementioned conditions. But we would want to baptize and evangelize them before planning the ceremony.

Permitting a married man to be a priest? In certain parts of the world, a married man can become a Catholic priest, though not a bishop. While the majority of the Catholic Church (i.e., those whose

Mass adheres to the Roman Rite) has a mandatory vow of celibacy for priests, a few of the Eastern-rite communities of the Catholic Church allow married men to enter the priesthood.

Eastern-rite churches, which are more common in Eastern Europe and the Middle East than in the Americas, are in union with the pope but maintain different liturgical rites and ancient languages during the Mass. They include the Byzantine, Coptic, Syrian, Armenian, Chaldean, Maronite, and Syro-Malabar rites.

Even in the majority Roman Rite, exceptions to the rule have been made to allow some married ministers who converted to the Catholic faith from other Christian denominations to be accepted into the priesthood. But each of these men had to promise he would not remarry if his wife were to die. Similarly, newly ordained Eastern-rite priests must pledge not to remarry, should they be widowed, or to not take a wife if they are entering the priesthood while still single.

Celibacy rules for priests are a Christian discipline and tradition, rather than dogma or doctrine. Therefore, the Church has the authority to change them or make exceptions to the rules to best serve the flock. On the other hand, the rule that only men are eligible for priesthood is part of Church dogma, which can never change.

The theory that allowing priests to marry would have stemmed the priest scandal is a tad illogical. In fact, the guilty priests were generally not ones who would have wanted to marry otherwise.[58]

My personal view is that the ones who are willing to make the greatest sacrifices to enter the priesthood — the ones who would otherwise most likely be married — are the ones most likely to exhibit the holiness of life so sorely needed in our churches, and the ones likely to bring the most people to Jesus. We need priests whose love for and faith in Christ are so overwhelming that they do not hesitate to hand themselves over fully to Him. We need priests who understand and exemplify the unique and sacred role of priests as representatives and imitators of Christ.

There are also practical reasons for celibacy in the priesthood. St. Paul, who opted for the celibacy of Christ, noted that a celibate clergy member would be able to dedicate himself fully to his flock, not having to divide his time between Church and family. After all, a devoted married priest with a wife and ten children might crowd up the rectory! Add to that a scenario with a severely disabled child, a child with a drug addiction, and few flu-stricken toddlers, and St. Paul's advice seems all the wiser.

St. Jerome, the famed Doctor of Biblical Science who, like St. Augustine, pledged celibacy, wrote in the late fourth century that both marriage and virginity were gifts from God, but he compared virginity to gold, saying it was the more precious gift, while comparing wedlock to silver.

Despite my own preference for celibate priests, there are plenty of holy married priests who have served as blessings to diocese around the world.

As of 2003, the Church counted a total of 405,450 priests worldwide, according to the 2005 edition of *Annuario Pontificio,* the official Vatican Yearbook. According to Church statistics, the total number of priests in the world has increased over the past decade, while the number of priests in the United States has decreased.

Saying the Bible has mistakes? Don't even try. The Bible is the Word of God. God speaks without error or contradiction in the 27 books of the New Testament and the 46 books of the Old Testament. Once I thought I found a mistake, but, alas, I was wrong. Ecclesiastes 1:5 seemed to be implying the earth was the center of the universe: "The sun rises and the sun goes down, and hastens to the place where it rises." But then I recalled my cousin Kate telling me she slept under the boardwalk to catch the sun "rising" over the ocean. She, too, was using the language of appearance as we all do to communicate real events. In fact, it would have been quite bizarre if she had waxed scientifically: "I slept under the boardwalk until the longitudinal line at which I was positioned had approached the point at which the sun became visible."

Likewise, writers of the Bible sometimes use the language of appearance and other literary styles to convey truths, but they never lie or err. The Book of Revelation, which is the last book of the New Testament, is famous for its use of symbolism and imagery. A lamb, a dragon, a lampstand, seven heads of the Beast, seven trumpets, and seven bowls of God's wrath are among the symbols employed to provide information about God's warnings to sinners, God's plans for end times, and the ultimate triumph of goodness over evil.

Sometimes, Jesus used parables in his preaching to convey moral truths; it does not require a particularly sharp eye to recognize some of these instances. Meanwhile, Matthew, Mark, Luke, and John set out to provide accurate and literal eyewitness accounts of what Jesus preached and did. The reports of St. Peter walking on water, Lazarus being raised from the dead, and Jesus healing the deaf, blind, and sick are presented as plain, matter-of-fact testimony. The Church teaches that the literal sense of the words of Scripture (the intent of the sacred author) is the first principle of Biblical interpretation. The spiritual (including allegorical, moral, or anagogical) is then built on the literal sense. St. Thomas Aquinas agreed, writing, "All other senses of Sacred Scripture are based on the literal."

Understanding what the sacred author has set out to communicate is key to interpreting Scripture. The task demands familiarity with the linguistic trends of the author's day for writing, conversing, and narrating. Try parachuting into a tribal community deep in a Brazilian rain forest, and making a speech filled with sarcasm, irony, parodies, and American idioms. The natives will not properly understand your message, and they may just filet you for dinner.

Apparent contradictions in the Bible stem from misunderstandings on the part of the reader. Obstacles to comprehension include lack of familiarity with the original language in which the Scripture was written and with the culture and personal background of the author. Those who seek to excel in the proper interpretation of Scripture should enroll in courses in hermeneutics and exegesis, and should study Hebrew, Aramaic, Greek, and Semitic languages.

No time for all that? Well, we still need to read the Bible. The Church "forcefully and specifically exhorts" us to do so, reminding us of St. Jerome's admonition: "Ignorance of the Scriptures is ignorance of Christ"(DV 25; cf. Phil. 3:8 and St. Jerome, *Commentariorium in Isaiam libri xviii prol.*: PL 24, 17b) (*CCC,* 133).

Being an astronomer and a priest at the same time? A serendipitous combination! Scientist-priests are a time-honored tradition in the Catholic Church. Today, we've got Fr. George Coyne, an astronomer who is director of the Vatican Observatory, Fr. Cyril Opeil, a physicist recently stationed at Los Alamos National Laboratory, Fr. Kevin Fitzgerald, a top researcher in molecular genetics who is based at Georgetown University, and countless others. Religious brothers, or friars, and religious sisters, or nuns, have also contributed their talents to the cause of science.

The Vatican curator of meteorites is currently Brother Guy Consolmagno, a Jesuit Brother who has a Ph.D. from the Massachusetts Institute of Technology. Brother Guy spends part of the year in Italy, analyzing and overseeing the Church's extensive collection of meteorites, which are currently housed in the papal summer palace outside Rome. He also spends plenty of time in Arizona, where Jesuit astronomers built the world-renowned Vatican Advanced Technology Telescope on Mount Graham, about an hour's drive northeast of Tucson. (Religious brothers, like nuns, generally take vows of chastity, poverty, and obedience, but do not receive priestly powers to perform sacraments.)

The brother — a science fiction fan honored when an asteroid was named after him — often expresses his delight that 35 moon craters were named after Jesuit priests and brothers. Like many religious scientists, Brother Guy has said his discoveries about the universe have increased his love for God by increasing his understanding the personality of our Creator. Astronomers, physicists, and chemists are particularly touched by Bible verses such as Wis. 11:20, which teaches that God "arranged all things by measure and number and weight."

Unsurprisingly, the Catholic Church has a longstanding tradition of placing telescopes on top of basilicas and other churches.

"Cathedrals in Bologna, Florence, Paris, and Rome were designed in the seventeenth and eighteenth centuries to function as world-class solar observatories. Nowhere in the world were there more precise instruments for the study of the sun," writes Thomas E. Woods, in *How the Catholic Church Built Western Civilization.*[59]

In his book, Woods mentions characters of the Church such as Fr. Roger Boscovich, sometimes credited as the father of modern atomic theory; Fr. Giambattista Riccioli, an astronomer and geographer who helped map the moon; Fr. Athanasius Kircher, often called the last Renaissance man thanks to his groundbreaking work in such a vast array of fields (geology, math, biology, astronomy, botany, electromagnetism, and Egyptian hieroglyphics, to name a few); St. Albert the Great, one of the world's renowned natural scientists of his time; Fr. James B. Macelwane, who wrote the first seismology textbook in the United States; Fr. Christopher Clavius, whose impeccable astronomical calculations helped give us the Gregorian calendar that replaced the mathematically flawed Julian calendar; Roger Bacon, the Franciscan friar and mathematician who advanced the study of optics and refraction of light, and who was theorizing about the potential for cars, submarines, and airplanes even back in the Middle Ages; and the early Catholic founders of modern economics, who were forerunners of Adam Smith and other later pioneers in the field.

As noted in Woods' book, the Jesuits (a religious order of priests and friars) alone contributed to the development of tools ranging from pendulum clocks to reflecting telescopes, and to advances in the understanding of everything from circulation of the blood to the nature of light waves.

The Catholic Church, which invented the university system itself,[60] has been an indomitable force in the advancement of almost every scientific field; in light of that, it's almost amusing that those who wish to bash the Church by painting it as anti-science, almost without fail, latch on to the case of astronomer Galileo (an admittedly embarrassing incident for the Church). However, embarrassing as this incident is, those who cite it as "proof" inevitably botch the facts.

First, Galileo (1564-1642 A.D.) was not the first to scientist to stumble across the reality of heliocentrism (meaning that the earth orbits around the sun, and not vice versa). Polish astronomer Nicolaus Copernicus (1473-1543 A.D.), a devout Catholic — who, it is believed, entered the priesthood later in life — had already proposed the theory in his work *De Revolutionibus Orbium Coelestium* (On the Revolutions of the Celestial Bodies). This work, dedicated to Pope Paul III, was welcomed by Churchmen — although, admittedly, it would have received a greater welcome had Church leaders not felt pressured amidst the cry of Luther, and other Protestant Reformers, that heliocentrism was "unbiblical."

Furthermore, plenty of ancient scientists had previously uncovered clues pointing to a sun-centered universe. Aristarchus of Samos, for one, had published a treatise more than 200 years before Christ, hypothesizing that the stars and sun were fixed, and not the planets.

As for Galileo, the Church allowed his proposal to be held as a theory or hypothesis, but said greater proof would be necessary before Galileo would be permitted to proclaim it as truth. To that point, Galileo had not had any luck providing evidence of a stellar parallax (a change in angular position of nearer stars against the background of more distant stars), the lack of which was considered the strongest argument used by opponents of heliocentrism.

Galileo initially agreed to regard his work as a theory, but eventually broke his promise and started declaring his work as truth. It was his defiance that spelled trouble; he was subjected to accusations of suspected heresy, an inquisition, and punishment for this disobedience.

Heliocentrism, of course, turned out to be correct, although some of Galileo's arguments turned out to be wrong. For example, he made the mistake of using the tides of the oceans (a result of the moon's gravitational pull) to explain the earth's rotation on its axis. What you won't hear from Church critics who comfort themselves by aligning themselves with Galileo is that Galileo himself remained Catholic after the incident, was sent a blessing by Pope Urban VIII while he was dying, and was buried on consecrated grounds at a Catholic church in Florence.[61]

The Galileo case does remind us not to regard the Bible as a science textbook, but as a guide for salvation. It is also demonstrates the prudence and patience of a Church not willing to jump headfirst into a compelling view before receiving and scrutinizing all the evidence.

The Rev. Stanley L. Jaki, a historian of science and honorary academician of the Pontifical Academy of Science, has suggested that the Church's adherence throughout the centuries to a rational and omnipotent God who ordered Creation was what allowed the Church to make grand strides in science where everyone else failed. Lacking the depth, vigor, and philosophy required for self-sustaining scientific progress, Jaki says, the cultures of the Hindus, Chinese, Mayans, Incas, ancient Greeks, and Egyptians all suffered a "stillbirth" in the sciences, having been doomed to cycles of discovery and destruction. (Jaki, a prolific author now in his 80s, has given lectures at Princeton, Yale, Harvard, and Oxford.)

Anthony Rizzi, director of the Institute for Advanced Physics in Baton Rouge, adds:

Modern science was not born in China, or in undiscovered North or South America, or anywhere else but Catholic Europe. Does the beautiful flower of modern science bloom in the area of the garden that is poisoned? To the contrary, it does so in the fertile part.[62]

Rizzi, who gained worldwide attention in 1997 when he solved an 80-year-old dilemma of physicists — the definition of angular momentum — will tell you that science came from "the heart of the Church."

Being too open-minded? One can never be too open-minded, unless a matter has already been firmly established as truth. For example, it has been established that humans need oxygen, the sun produces energy through nuclear fusion, and the earth has a magnetic field. So, it would be foolish to insist on "open-mindedness" regarding such scientific facts. Over the centuries, theological truths have also been settled for those who believe in Christ's promise of divine guidance to His Church into "all the truth."

As Catholics, we understand that practices, canon law, the pope's personal opinions, and even the prevailing view on non-doctrinal matters can change from time to time. But we have a promise from above that our official dogma — core teachings on faith and morals — is the settled and revealed truth of the Holy Spirit.

Truths in this world which are not open to debate by historic Christians would include the Incarnation, the Resurrection, the Trinity, the contents of our Bible, the Real Presence in the Eucharist, the unbreakable bond of a Christian marriage, the necessity of penance for sin, God's design for a male priesthood, and so on.

These doctrines and others are the official faith of the Church that Jesus promised to be with always. If the Holy Spirit's guidance were not promised to our Church, then we might be facing a lifelong fate of questioning and rehashing of even the most basic doctrines of Christianity. Fortunately, our doctrines have come down to us through the safe and secure lines of succession that stretch from the Apostles to our bishops and pope. We need not wonder if the Church was built on partial truth when Christ promised it "all" truth.

Not even the pope can discard Church truth. As Pope Benedict XVI pointed out at an Ascension Sunday vigil Mass in 2005, the pope "must not proclaim his own ideas, but constantly bind himself and the Church in obedience to God's Word in the face of all attempts to adapt that Word or to water it down, and in the face of all forms of opportunism."

Just as astronomers are able to see our galaxy and others more clearly with time, our Church sees phenomena related to our salvation more clearly. But everything was there from the start.

Consider the doctrine of the Trinity. The Father, the Son, and the Holy Spirit have always existed, but it was during a span of centuries that our Church comprehended this sacred mystery more deeply, and officially defined it. God would not expect individual believers in this millennium to wake up each morning only to tackle such an issue from scratch again and again, much less to reach a conclusion by the end of their lifetime. Nor would God expect us to awaken each morning to the task of developing the entire range of Christian doctrines as if we were still in the first century.

Fortunately, we need not sit down to dinner each night — with an open mind, of course — to sort through piles of early Church writings with the goal of discerning which writings should really have been put in the Bible.

The Church has spoken on these matters. Those who trust in Christ's promises to His Church are obliged to listen. (Mt. 16:18, Lk. 10:16, Mt. 18:17)

Our Church, like a wise grandparent, understands things more fully as it ages. But the Church has an advantage over the human mind; it neither withers nor expires within the span of a century or less. Author G.K. Chesterton once mused that the Church represents "completed human nature."[63] It's been getting wiser for 2,000 years. It has retained its knowledge, discarding none.

If this Church has proclaimed since its inception that certain premarital or marital behaviors are wrong, would it be reasonable for a Christian at any point in history to reply, "Sorry, I've thought about these behaviors and they seem beneficial and edifying to me"?

I can just picture Adam in the sunny Garden of Eden, moments before the apple-eating incident that spawned death and suffering for all of humankind, sitting there feeling proud of his own independent rationalizations that freed his conscience to try a new pleasure. Perhaps he said to himself, "By exercising my intelligence and free will, I have concluded that in such a bountiful land teeming with glorious fruit trees, the consumption of one piddly apple could not hurt anyone."

Perhaps he also rationalized to himself: "The apple would be pleasurable. Pleasure is natural. God created me with a desire for pleasure and apple."

Ironically, by exercising his freedom and choice to disobey, Adam lost all the freedoms and choices that were originally granted to man. Ironically, the pleasure from an apple is temporary, whereas the types of pleasures God has prepared for us in heaven are eternal.

As Archbishop J. Michael Miller once explained, "Freedom only makes sense when it is tied to the truth, what is objectively hard-wired into human experience and into the world." The archbishop, who is secretary of the Vatican's Congregation for Catholic Education, made the comments to the *Vermont Catholic Tribune* in Burlington, Vermont, in May of 2005. Freedom that is not based on truth, he said, is nothing more than power or license.

God programmed the world with His own truth, which we may or may not understand at the moment. For example, the fact that Earth is the third planet from the sun may be taught to us or shown to us by external sources (a teacher, a telescope, a satellite photo). But without such external aids, reaching such a conclusion would be impossible using only our internal mental skills and logic.

Still, the science pupil would hardly question the fact or reply, "Sorry, I cannot accept the logic of what you are saying. It seems more rational that earth would be the first planet or farthest planet from the sun."

Similarly, the first Christians would not have dared to reply to the Apostles, "You have told us about Baptism, but as rational beings, we cannot accept the logic of water being able washing away our sins." Nor would any early Christian martyr have told an Apostle, "You have reported seeing Christ rise up into the air and into heaven. But, logically, He could hardly do this without wings."

Logic cannot explain why humans were programmed to feel romantic attraction, why humans were programmed to grow to five or six feet instead of fifteen, or why the ocean covers more of the earth's surface than land.

In this world, some things have already been set. God has set them.

Once we ascertain what exactly has been set, we move forward. We do not subtract; rather, we delve deeper. Knowledge becomes a base for catapulting us ahead into further discoveries in this world.

People like Albert Einstein, Isaac Newton, or Benjamin Franklin relied on their own past discoveries, and discoveries by scientists who went before them, to further the progress of humankind. Neither scientists nor the Church create the laws governing the universe; rather, they identify and study the ones devised by a Creator.

Despite the fact that God's designs for human beings and their eternal life were established long before we arrived here, and despite the fact that these designs have been ascertained rationally and consistently by a Church that does not cave to human opinion, opponents of a given Catholic doctrine will cry, "My open-mindedness shall lead me to a better conclusion."

For them, truth is not a fixed state, but rather a creative exercise that is severely limited by the person's isolated experiences.

All too often, the battle cry claiming that the Church wants us to "suspend reason" comes straight from the very souls who have not bothered to delve into any of the reasons offered for a doctrine, much less the historical background involved. In their worlds, we would wind up back at square one on each issue at every juncture for the rest of our lives, while grooming our descendants for the same fate. No truth would ever be reached. No truth would ever be accumulated.

In the words of the late author G.K. Chesterton, "The Catholic Church is the only thing which saves a man from the degrading slavery of being a child of his age."[64]

The possibility of a mistake — an inevitable consequence of personal determination of morality and a wildly open mind — may or may not lead to years of unwitting violations of God's laws accompanied by nails added to Christ's cross. But the open-minded soul is hardly concerned; for how can one be blamed when one was innocently ignorant with no clear means of affirming truth?

To those attempting life's voyage outside the Catholic Church, St. Francis de Sales warned: "Sailing thus then without needle, compass or rudder on the ocean of human opinions, you can expect nothing but a miserable shipwreck."[65]

Chesterton, a convert to Catholicism who debated atheists such as dramatist George Bernard Shaw, eventually concluded that the Church offered a more rational system of philosophy than the volumes of atheist writings he had devoured. He wrote:

> To become a Catholic is not to leave off thinking, but to learn how to think. . . . The Catholic convert has for the first time a starting-point for straight and strenuous thinking.[66]

Like many converts to the Church, Chesterton initially attempted to disprove the Catholic faith. He later declared:

> The moment men cease to pull against it they feel a tug towards it. The moment they cease to shout it down they begin to listen to it with pleasure. The moment they try to be fair to it they begin to be fond of it.[67]

CHAPTER TWELVE

☩

Now I Get . . . Penance

God's rules are not made to be broken. But once we have broken them, Lent is the perfect time to repair the damage.

When I was in third grade, on the Mondays leading up to Easter, each of us would randomly choose a card from the pile of index cards Sister Carol had prepared for us. Each contained a special Lenten assignment suitable for eight-year-olds.

Two of the Lenten lottery cards are still vivid in my mind. "Give up lunch dessert" was the one I dreaded pulling out. Instead, I deviously hoped for the one that said, "Help Mom wash the dishes." Of course, I knew full well that my mother strictly prohibited me from going near her dishes or dishwasher at that age. In other words, I would be off the hook for the coming week.

The shameful attitude displayed by this pitiful third-grader is the opposite of the Christian one. If we love Jesus, we should want to do penance and make significant sacrifices. We should be prepared to pull out the real whopper cards in life: "Give up your house," "Give up your friends," or "Give up your life." We should want to make amends for our many sins that have added to Christ's agony on the Cross. We should jump at the chance to comfort the crucified Christ by taking on some of the suffering of His Body. That's what St. Francis of Assisi, St. Padre Pio, and most of the saints did. Walking with Jesus in His suffering is precisely the response of a converted heart that grieves for past sins and the agony Jesus took on because of them.

The Apostle St. Peter, who died a martyr, wrote that we should patiently endure suffering "because Christ also suffered for you, leaving you an example, that you should follow in his steps" (1 Pet. 2:21).

As for the dessert that awaited me in my lunch box each day? It wasn't that I was unwilling to give up those tasty vanilla sandwich cookies; I just didn't see the point. I failed to perceive the connection between my suffering from cookie "starvation" and others benefiting from my sacrifice.

Giving blood. Donating to charity. Running errands for an elderly person. These were actions that directly corresponded with relieving another's plight.

But fasting for the sake of fasting? Penance for the sake of self-sacrifice? Self-denial — purposely squashing one's own fun? Why do any of that?

Because these were all things Jesus did, and there was a reason for them. He fasted in the desert. He lived in abject poverty. He endured emotional and physical torture. He allowed his flesh to be torn apart. He made the ultimate Sacrifice; He gave up His body. Not one ounce of His suffering was endured in vain. Rather, every ounce of His suffering benefited humankind.

I was watching the coverage of World Youth Day 2005 in Cologne, Germany, on television. A young sister, dressed in the garb of a Poor Clare, told the host of the Eternal World Television News that she wanted her whole life to be a sacrifice.

If we have been baptized into His Body, then God makes whatever sacrifice we offer up, whether small or large, valuable. Once we are living and motivated by supernatural grace, our prayer, fasting, almsgiving, or other penance can help undo some of the damage we, or others, have done to the whole Body.

Our sufferings, when united to His Cross, increase our friendship with Jesus. As intricate parts of the mystical Body of Christ, we have become co-workers with Christ, who divinely converts our efforts into valuable work for His saving plan. There is no limit to the work that can be done by the Communion of Saints.

In fact, the degree to which you and I unite our selves to the Cross determines the number of hearts converted and souls saved. It determines the degree to which love, peace, and joy will fill the earth. It influences the length of time our loved ones will have to suffer in Purgatory. It determines the condition of our own soul and our future happiness with God.

When done in the spirit of love and charity, nothing is wasted. Just as donations for the victims of the South Asian tsunami that touched down December 26, 2004, were carried across the ocean from caring Americans to battered countries, the prayers and penance that we offered up for the victims were also carried over to recipients by God in the form of blessings.

Amidst all the generosity and helping hands from around the world, a scene of bronzed European tourists relaxing on their beach towels on the sands popped up on our TV screens. What were they doing vacationing on the Thai island of Phuket just six days after the tsunami tragedy struck the region? The world was quick to declare them guilty. In reality, these tourists deserved no more blame than any of us at home who happened to be lounging in front of our TV sets making judgments. Why were we relaxing as if no homeless and dying people were suffering in our own cities? When God looks down and sees some of His children hurting, He expects the others to pitch in, no matter where they are. Sometimes we don't see them out our own windows and we forget to look a little harder.

As long as there are people who are hurting in this world — whether it is the five million orphans in Ethiopia, the tens of thousands of villagers slaughtered in Sudan's Darfur region, the street kids of Mongolia who live in steamy sewers, the young *basureros* of the Philippines who forage for food at garbage dumps, or the victims of wars, famine, and AIDS all over — the rest of us are called to contribute in some way.

To what extent should we give of ourselves? Mother Teresa said we must "give until it hurts." She said that as long as there is something left in us that we are not willing to give, we still have sin in us. She viewed the opportunity to share Christ's Passion as the greatest gift we could have.

The truth is: love hurts.

Little did I know as I crafted Valentine cards for my little classmates each February from white doilies, red lollipops, and colorful paper hearts, that the three men named "St. Valentine" who were associated with the romantic holiday were all martyrs for the faith. Little did I know as my mother tied a green ribbon in my hair, and attached a green shamrock pin to my school uniform, that St. Patrick deliberately slept on a hard rock, wore a rough hair shirt, and spent 40 days of fasting, prayer, and penance atop a mountain, enduring cold winds and rains for the love of God and the Irish people.

St. John the Baptist? Beheaded.

St. Rose of Lima? This Peruvian saint and virgin wore a metal-spiked crown, covered by roses, and slept on a bed of broken glass, thorns, and other sharp objects.

St. Bernadette Soubirous? This suffering saint to whom Mary appeared offered up her painful illnesses to God, saying: "The more I am crucified, the more I rejoice."

St. John Vianney? It is said that the amount of sleep and food he permitted himself could not have sustained a human being.

St. Francis of Assisi and St. Padre Pio? They endured the agony of the wounds of Christ in the form of the stigmata.

St. Jerome? To tame his flesh, he would fast weeks at a time.

St. Rita of Cascia? After praying to join Jesus in his suffering, she was hit in the forehead with a thorn that seemed to have come from an image of Christ's crown of thorns. Her forehead bled for her last fifteen years of life; the wound is still visible on her body at her shrine in Italy.

According to St. John of the Cross, a monk and philosopher of the sixteenth century, the soul cannot enter into, or attain, the hidden treasures of God "unless it first crosses into and enters the thicket of suffering, enduring interior and exterior labors . . . "

So where is the good news in all this suffering? Starting the moment we enter Heaven, we will forever be immune from pain. The hidden, supernatural riches of God, only available after dying to oneself, will be ours forever.

Just as the sufferings of a dedicated triathlon competitor may culminate in the glory of an Olympic gold, the sufferings of a Christian have an end point, and will culminate in eternal glory.

The sufferings that we patiently offer up to God will blossom into eternal goodness and blessings so breathtaking that they are beyond the scope of our earthly senses.

St. Paul, who was stoned, flogged, and beaten for the sake of the Gospel, had his sights set on these promised rewards.

> For this slight momentary affliction is preparing for us an
> eternal weight of glory beyond all comparison, because we
> look not to the things that are seen but to the things that are
> unseen; for the things that are seen are transient, but the things
> that are unseen are eternal.   — 2 COR. 4:17-18

In the beginning, of course, love wasn't supposed to hurt. God created Adam and Eve in an original holiness, purity, and justice meant for all of us, and placed them in a paradise untouched by problems, pain, or death. But they disobeyed, thereby wounding human nature for all future generations. That's why sin and suffering will forever be bound up together as long as we are on earth. But neither one will follow us into the Heaven that Jesus has won for us.

In Heaven, we will see the fruits of all our works that were performed in Christ. Done in the Lord, "your labor is not in vain" (1 Cor. 15:58), according to St. Paul. In his letter to the Romans, the same Apostle wrote that God will repay everyone "according to his works" (Rom. 2:5-8). He says much the same the Corinthians — each person who appears before the judgment seat of Christ will receive "good or evil, according to what he has done in the body" (2 Cor. 5:10).

Recognizing the power and value of his sufferings, St. Paul rejoiced in them: "Now I rejoice in my sufferings for your sake, and in my flesh I complete what is lacking in Christ's afflictions for the sake of his body, that is, the church" (Col. 1:24).

If members of the Church were not supernaturally bound together in the Body of Christ, then penance would be for the birds. If our souls did not keep on living after our earthly departure, then prayer and penance would be more suited for the insane.

We were created not for this world but, rather, a supernatural one. The souls that cling to Jesus the most by embracing the countercultural Way of the Cross while on earth will be the souls that enjoy the most intense joy and most intense bond with Jesus in heaven.

Blessed Mother Teresa told her order of nuns at the Missionaries of Charity that those who helped the poor at no cost to themselves were not sharing in the supernatural work of Christ; their efforts would be useful, but nothing more than social work. To redeem us, the Albanian-born nun explained, Jesus had to become one with us, sharing our life, loneliness, agony, and death. As Christians, then, we are to treat the poor as Jesus treated us — which means we must become one with them.

Once God's grace enters our soul, we become part of the mystical Body of Christ. As active parts of Christ's Body, we become co-workers (1 Cor. 3:9) with Christ. We are called to share in Christ's sufferings, which are temporary, but also to share in the blessings of Heaven, which are eternal.

The Bible says that as "joint heirs with Christ," we may be glorified with Him. But the condition attached to the promise of inheritance is that we suffer with Him. St. Paul wrote:

> ... and if children, then heirs, heirs of God and fellow heirs with Christ, provided we suffer with him in order that we may also be glorified with him. I consider that the sufferings of this present time are not worth comparing with the glory that is to be revealed to us. — ROM. 8:17-18

How can we fit sacrifices into our busy days? Besides keeping a vigilant eye on the needs of the sick, the elderly, and those hurting in any way, we can do simple things like giving up the radio in the car, skipping our favorite television show, reading Scripture on the train, or fasting on bread and water for a day or an afternoon. The more that people unite themselves to His Cross, the more souls will be brought over to the grace Christ won for us.

St. Bernadette had the right attitude. As she lay on her deathbed and the pangs of pain got unbearably sharp, she pulled the crucifix close to her and cried, "All this is good for Heaven!"

The most powerful Sacrifice of all is the Mass, which many devout Christians all over the globe attend seven days a week. At the Mass, we witness, and unite ourselves to, the actual Sacrifice made by Jesus two millennia ago. The Sacrifice on Calvary, which becomes present to us when the priest holds up the gifts of bread and wine, is the only perfect Sacrifice that can be offered up to God.

With Christ, we become one victim for the reparation of sin through Eucharistic participation, according to Dom Hubert van Zeller, a Benedictine monk and writer who died in 1984.[68]

Even if we are only able to attend Mass weekly, we still must take up a cross daily. Jesus said:

"If any man would come after me, let him deny himself and take up his cross daily and follow me." — Lk. 9:23

Rest assured that no matter how inconvenient or painful our sacrifices seem, the rewards to come will be inversely and exponentially proportional to the sufferings.

St. Augustine and his mother, St. Monica, were once blessed with a momentary vision of some of the gifts awaiting God's family up above. After the experience, they lost any appetite for things of this world and were filled only with an unquenchable longing for Heaven.

By the end of her life on earth, St. Monica had already seen some of the fruits harvested from her years of continual fasting and prayer. Her unceasing petition to God had been that her pagan son, Augustine, would become a Catholic and would have salvation. God rewarded her with much more. St. Augustine became a Catholic priest, bishop, and Doctor of the Church!

St. Augustine embraced the Cross to the point of making a permanent commitment to celibacy, poverty, and obedience.

Jim Caviezel, the Catholic actor who played Jesus in Mel Gibson's *The Passion of the Christ,* got a tiny taste of the Cross during the filming of the 2004 blockbuster movie in Italy. Caviezel endured hypothermia and sleep deprivation, was struck by lightning, and underwent an accidental lashing from a real whip. During the crucifixion scene, strong winds pulled his shoulder out of joint while he was up on the cross. Caviezel offered up these sacrifices, as well as fasting, prayer, and daily Mass, for the sake of a performance pleasing to God.

The end result was a piece of cinematography that caused some 13 million adults to change aspects of their religious behavior after viewing the movie.[69] Criminals around the globe were moved to turn themselves in for crimes they had gotten away with. The repentant souls included a burglar in Arizona; a neo-Nazi bomber in Oslo, Norway; and a 21-year-old Texas man who had killed his pregnant girlfriend and initially passed it off as a suicide.

Theatergoers were touched to have witnessed what Jesus endured for us. Understandably, others bypassed the movie for its violent content. But to those individuals, I'd say, "Oh, come on. Just offer it up!"

After all, the violence on the screen will not compare to what Christ actually endured, nor will it compare to the eternal agony from which Christ saved us. But it will serve to remind us of Christ's boundless love for us. Perhaps, it will also motivate us to better follow the Bible's mandate to pitch in with our own corporeal sacrifices and disciplines. In a letter to the Corinthians, the great Apostle St. Paul wrote:

> I pommel my body and subdue it, lest after preaching to others I myself should be disqualified.   — 1 COR. 9:27

Penances keep our souls strong, giving us some resistance to the temptations of mortal sin. Even St. Paul, who seemed to possess an unassailable faith, vigorously disciplined his body in order to avoid the risk of disqualification from his Heavenly reward.

The Church emphasizes that a true conversion of heart must precede and accompany our acts of penance in order for our sufferings to be valuable. One cannot wake up one morning and announce, "Today I shall abstain from meat to make up for the bank robbery I shall commit tomorrow," or "It is true I work as a hit man by day, but I devote my evenings to the delivering of meals to shut-ins." The penances of these individuals are not worth the price of a dirty rag.

A true conversion requires sorrow for all past sins and a sincere intention to do all in one's power to avoid sin in the future. Our actions must be motivated by grace rather than by rewards or praise by people. In fact, the Bible encourages us to do our penances in secret, and to help people who cannot possibly repay us. In the end, it's all between us and God, and God alone can satisfy.

Considering that our curtain call on this planet could come the next time we walk out the door or put down this book, the time for conversion is now. As I look through my old freshman directory from college, I recall the faces of numerous classmates who are no longer with us. Upon waking up on their last mornings here, they could scarcely have imagined they would be meeting their Maker that day. Not the one who got on his bicycle. Not the one who boarded a Pan Am plane from London to New York. Not the one who reported to work at the World Trade Center. Not the one who had a heart attack in his twenties. And certainly not the one who was on his honeymoon, enjoying a hike through the Himalayas in Nepal, when he was robbed and killed by natives.

Compared to the magnitude of all eternity, our life expectancy on this planet is minuscule, and our hourglass is running out of sand. St. Paul viewed our time here as a life-long race with a prize at the end. Our opportunity to offer up sacrifices — for the sake of our own souls and for the good of all — comes with a deadline, which is the moment our heart stops.

In early 2005, I was present for a homily at St. Colman Church in Ardmore, Pa., a homily meant to prepare us for the penitential season of Lent. Father Tadeusz Pacholczyk spoke about denying and renouncing ourselves to allow God to enter our lives more powerfully. He offered a striking metaphor that was difficult to forget.

On a train ride in Italy, the priest told us he struck up a conversation with a student of art and sculpture in Florence. The student mentioned seeing a museum collection of partially finished statues of Michelangelo and said by examining the pieces, he could envision the final form that Michelangelo had in mind for each marble chunk. The priest continued:

> Sometimes Michelangelo had to decide on the placement of an arm or leg on a statue in such a manner as to avoid a knot in the marble which he could then chisel out. Michelangelo had the gift of being able to peer into a crude block of marble and discern the inner design, the inner figure waiting to be released, even if the marble was less than perfect. Each of us is like a particular piece of marble in the hands of God, being chiseled and shaped to become something beautiful. He shapes us continually throughout our lives, through the experiences, sufferings and joys that come our way. We are different from a block of marble, though, because we have to cooperate with the hand of the craftsman who chisels us.

We may not know what God is doing, but we have to trust that He has a masterpiece in mind. We have to let God have dominion over our lives, Father told us, and to chisel away all that is not Christ-like, so that the "real inner beauty that is buried" can surface.

That is where penance comes in.

The *Catechism of the Catholic Church* offers a few penance options (*CCC*, 1434-1436) that open us up to God's work: fasting, prayer, and almsgiving; efforts and gestures aimed at reconciliation with others; concern for the salvation of one's neighbor; the intercession of the saints; the practice of charity, concern for the poor; the exercise and defense of justice; admission of faults to one's brethren; revision of life and examination of conscience; and endurance of persecution for the sake of righteousness. According to the Bible, the practice of charity "covers a multitude of sins" (1 Pet. 4:8, Jas. 5:20).

Those willing to give up dessert are on the right track, but Jesus longs for friends who are willing to give up their house, their pals, or their lives at the drop of a hat.

As it turned out, I learned many devout Catholics were fasting on bread and water on Wednesdays and Fridays. Hundreds of thousands had made lifelong vows of poverty, chastity, and obedience, all for Jesus. Millions of Christians have gone, and continue to go, to bloody deaths for the Faith.

Here, I had been groaning about giving up a few cookies.

CHAPTER THIRTEEN

✝

Now I Get . . . the Saints

Speaking of hard penances, my elementary school teachers had plenty of them in the form of homework for our mothers. In third grade, one class project concocted by hard-working Sister Carol required students to come to school dressed as our patron saint for a day. Mine was St. Clare of Assisi from medieval Italy. After paging through a pile of books, my mother was lucky enough to spot the saint's picture so that she could promptly get busy at the sewing machine with all the brown fabric she had to go buy.

I turned out to be a perfect replica, visually. The simple brown robe reached right to my ankles and the veil fit decorously on my head. I wrapped the St. Clare cord around my waist. But I wasn't willing to cut off my long hair, or to arrive barefoot, as this holy nun was known to do.

My mother took a look at me and blurted out, "Well this is wonderful! This can double as your Halloween costume!"

After I let out a horrified whimper (I was not going to be running around our neighborhood trick-or-treating in such garb), my mother admitted she was just kidding. She would make another costume.

I mention this experience only because it is one of the few memories that I have of learning about the lives of saints in school.

If I had known how powerful saints' prayers were, I would have put them to work! One of their primary tasks in Heaven is to pray for us. And, evidently, the holier a person is, the more Christ lives and works through the person.

"The prayer of a righteous man has great power in its effects," according to the Letter of James in the New Testament (Jas. 5:16). So powerful, in fact, were the prayers of the great prophet Elijah that it did not rain for three and a half years (Jas. 5:17).

God sometimes uses even relics of the saints as instruments of miracles.

Elijah's successor, Elisha, was so holy that after he died, contact with his bones brought a dead man to life (2 Kings 13:20-21). In the New Testament, cures were also worked by St. Peter's shadow (Acts 5:15-20) and St. Paul's face cloths (Acts 19:11-12).

Even the relics of Santa Claus have been reported to heal people! Well, at least the relics of St. Nicholas, around whom the legend of Santa Claus arose. St. Nicholas, Bishop of Myra, Lycia (modern-day Turkey), died in either 345 A.D. or 352 A.D. His relics are currently preserved in Bari, Italy, and are said to produce an oily substance, known as Manna di San Nicola, with a medicinal affect.

Yes, the saints are more alive in Heaven than we are on earth.

Having given us the saints as family members, God would be insulted if we ignored those spiritual brothers and sisters. Since the saints in Heaven see Christ face to face, they are made knowledgeable of our requests through our mediator, Christ. In Heaven, all see and hear more clearly. Communication is not a problem in the afterlife.

Christians have sought the intercession of saints and angels in Heaven since earliest times. In a first-century book called *The Shepherd,* a work so respected by the early Christians that it was read at church, the author Hermas referred to intercessions being obtained by an angel.

> ... having been strengthened by the holy angel [you saw], and having obtained from him such intercession, and not being slothful, why do not you ask of the Lord understanding, and receive it from him?
>
> — *The Shepherd* 3:5:4 (80 A.D.)

St. Clement of Alexandria adds: "... though he pray alone, he has the choir of the saints standing with him [in prayer]" (Miscellanies 7:12 [208 A.D.]).

In the Book of Revelation, angels in Heaven offer our prayers up to God in "gold bowls filled with incense, which are the prayers of the holy ones" (Rev 5:8).

Although some Christians stopped praying to saints after the sixteenth-century Reformation, most Christians continue to pray for the intercession of saints even today.

Some protesters of the intercession of the saints will argue that it is wrong to honor a human being. They need only look at the fourth commandment, which says we must honor our parents, who are human. It's a requirement! Some critics will even try to say that Catholics "worship" saints, but, as every Catholic school child knows, only God can be worshipped.

Find me a Catholic who pays no attention to Mary or the saints; chances are that this person also lacks a strong relationship with Jesus.

Alternatively, find me a Catholic who loved Jesus so much that he or she took up religious life in a Third World country, committing to life-long vows of celibacy, poverty, and obedience, and I will bet my money this person's relationship with the Communion of Saints is also beautiful.

Even saints need saints. Mother Teresa looked to St. Thérèse of Lisieux, who, in turn, derived strength from the life of St. Teresa of Ávila. St. Frances Xavier Cabrini, the missionary nun known as Mother Cabrini who founded schools, hospitals, and orphanages in America, chose St. Francis de Sales and St. Francis Xavier as her patron saints. If Christians of this magnitude needed help from the saints in Heaven, then how much more do we need them?

Besides showing us the tricks of the trade for cultivating a close relationship with God, the saints in Heaven can help us by interceding before Christ's throne with our petitions. St. Monica would pray fervently at the shrines of the saints for the conversion of her sinful son, Augustine, who later became a great saint and Church Doctor.

As we pray the Apostles' Creed, we profess to believe in the Communion of Saints. This means that all of God's children, whether on earth or in Heaven, are connected through God. We cannot be separated from them since we are all part of the One Body, with Christ as head.

Thanks to this cohesive bond, one part of the body can compensate for damage done by another part of the body. It operates the same way as a literal physical body: if your left foot is broken, your right does extra work to compensate. If one of us is suffering, another of God's children can pray for us whether from earth or from Heaven.

If world leaders can gain wisdom and inspiration by studying the strategies and legacies of leaders before them, then Christians have everything to gain by examining the lives of the holiest saints, for saints are precisely what we are called to become.

One . . . Two . . . Three Steps to the Saints

With so many saints who have shone with God's love over the centuries, it would be impossible to mention each one. Therefore, I am forced to draw up a method to narrow down the list. In the tradition of the trivia game "Six Degrees of Kevin Bacon," I have determined to include only saints that I could get to from myself in three connections or less.

As fans of the Kevin Bacon game (inspired by the film *Six Degrees of Separation*) know, players normally attempt to connect movie actors to actor/singer Kevin Bacon in as few steps as possible.

So, just for fun, here are my "connections" to some saints, as well as some miraculous happenings associated with them.

ST. JUAN DIEGO (1474-1548)

I chose this poor peasant because I once stood on the grounds where the Mother of God and Queen of Heaven appeared to him — three miles northeast of what is now downtown Mexico City — in December, 1531. Mary appeared to the devout Juan Diego, sending him to the bishop several times with a request to build a church to glorify Her Son on the grounds on which she stood. When the bishop asked for a sign to verify the request, Mary supplied Juan Diego with a resplendent array of flowers during a season conducive only to weeds and cacti.

Back at the bishop's palace, when the flowers fell out of Juan Diego's *tilma,* or cloak, all knelt down upon the sight of a brilliant life-sized figure of the Virgin Mary glowing on the cloth. Today, more than 475 years later, the fabric shows no sign of fraying or fading. The image retains its color and luminosity, despite the fact that the *tilma* was woven with Mexican ayate fibers, which rot after 20 years.

The Findings of NASA Scientists and Other Experts

The image's divine origins were evident to all who saw or examined the *tilma* from the beginning. Even in the eighteenth century, scientists found that it was impossible to paint a similar image onto a tilma made of identical fibers. But it wasn't until the twentieth century that more advanced techniques were used to study the *tilma*.

After taking 40 infrared photographs of the image, NASA scientists Philip Callahan and Jody B. Smith concluded that the image had not been coated with preservatives. No trace of paint could be found. No stroke of a paintbrush was detectable. The technique for transferring an image onto the *tilma* was not recognizable or repeatable, and the scientists concluded it could not be verified as human work.

Richard Kuhn, who won the Nobel Prize for chemistry in 1938, found that the image contained no natural, animal, or mineral colorings. Synthetic colorings did not even exist in the sixteenth century.

But my favorite discovery comes from Dr. Jose Aste-Tonsmann, an engineer from the Mexican Center of Guadalupan Studies. In 1979, he magnified the corneas of the Virgin Mary's eyes 2,500 times. He discovered the outlines of various human figures reflected in the eyes! The use of satellite digital imaging techniques resulted in the identification of a bearded white man who resembles a portrait of Bishop Zumárraga, as well as an Indian with a beard and mustache, unfolding his cloak before the bishop. There is also a younger man thought to be interpreter Juan González; a dark-skinned woman, and a man with Spanish features.

In other words, if Mary was present in the room during the unveiling of the cloak, this is the scene that would have been reflected in her eyes! The same people reflected in the right eye are also present in the left eye, but in different proportions; in fact, in the same proportions that would have been expected based on different angles of vision from each eye. Ophthalmologists who have examined the images say Mary's eyes appear to be strangely "alive." They have also stated that the visual distortion of the images precisely corresponds to the curvature of the cornea.

But, back to the story of Juan Diego. Originally named Cuauhtlatoatzin, this widowed Indian man was baptized in Mexico just a year after the first dozen Franciscan priests arrived in the country. His new Christian name was Juan Diego. A few years earlier, in 1521, the Aztec capital in Mexico had fallen to Hernan Cortez, leader of the Spanish conquistadors.

In 1531, ten years after the conquest of Mexico City, at a time peace was flourishing, the devout Juan Diego would walk 14 miles barefoot to Mass. One morning, Mary called him from a hill called Tepeyac. The beautiful woman shone like the sun, and the rock on which she stood seemed to be sending out beams of light.

The once scrubby plants seemed transformed into emeralds and gold. Mary expressed her desire for a temple to be built in the place she appeared. In this church, she would exalt her Son. The Indian peasant visited Bishop Juan de Zumarraga, who had only arrived in the New World a few years earlier. The bishop was unconvinced of Juan Diego's story.

Mary again appeared to Juan Diego, who, in turn, begged the beautiful maiden to choose someone more respected and esteemed than he to transmit her message. Mary assured him he was the chosen messenger. This time, after questioning Juan Diego thoroughly, the bishop believed that it was Mary that the Indian had seen, but said he would need a sign in order to proceed. Mary appeared to Juan Diego for the third time, telling him to return the next day to receive a sign to bring to the bishop.

The following day, instead of going straight to the hill to meet Mary, Juan Diego attended to his gravely ill uncle, who begged Juan Diego to fetch a priest immediately to hear his Confession before he died. On the way to Tlatilolco, Juan Diego reached the foot of the hill where Mary had appeared, and decided to take the roundabout path so that Mary wouldn't see him until after he had fulfilled his uncle's request. But Mary came to meet him, and assured Juan Diego that the uncle would be healed.

At that same moment, Mary appeared to the uncle and cured him. The *tilma* with Mary's image was later brought to the uncle, who confirmed that it was the same woman in his room. Back at the hill, Mary had Juan Diego climb to the peak to cut flowers. The frost of December usually allowed only for weeds and cactuses, but Juan Diego encountered an opulent bed of vibrantly colored flowers of many types. He thought he might be in paradise. He cut them and placed them in the fold of his *tilma*, or cloak.

Mary said not to show anyone the flowers until he was in the presence of the bishop. Juan Diego set out to the bishop's palace. Upon his arrival, some servants tried to grab the flowers, but each time they tried, the flowers no longer seemed real, but rather as if they were painted or sewn onto the *tilma*. The servants told the bishop what they had seen, and the bishop believed.

When Juan Diego unfolded his *tilma* before the bishop to release the flowers, an image of the Virgin Mary in full size appeared on the cloak. The bishop and other witnesses in the room fell to their knees. The bishop shed tears and asked for Mary's forgiveness for not fulfilling her wish previously. Juan Diego showed them the site where the church was desired. Then he returned with a group of people to his uncle, who testified that he had been cured by Mary. Juan Diego's uncle said that Mary had told him to see the bishop, and to testify to what he had seen. The image would be called the "Perfect Virgin, Holy Mary of Guadalupe," Mary had told the cured man.

As a result of the miracle, millions of indigenous people in Mexico were converted to Christianity from their polytheistic Aztec religion. Mary was declared patroness of Mexico, patroness of Latin America, and patroness of all the Americas from North to South. Juan Diego was canonized a saint by Pope John Paul II in 2002.

The *tilma* has survived heat, humidity, storms, smoke, soot, and contact with skin and lips. When nitric acid accidentally spilled on it, the acid transformed to a water drop and dried. In 1921, a bomb placed next to the *tilma* by an anti-religious group heavily damaged the marble altar, smashed stained-glass windows, and twisted a cast-iron cross out of shape, but the *tilma* was left untouched. It is on display today at the Basilica of Guadalupe outside Mexico City. A tiny piece of the *tilma* is preserved as a relic in the Our Lady of the Angels Cathedral in Los Angeles.

Much of the above account can be found in a translation of the *Nican Mopohua,* which was written within 20 years of Mary's appearance to Juan Diego.

TWO STEPS TO ST. PADRE PIO (1887-1968)

To complete the link from this author to the great St. Padre Pio of Pietrelcina, I simply need Salvatore Petroccia, the father of one of my dearest friends from high school. At a recent Padre Pio festival in Vineland, N.J, Mr. Petroccia smiled and reminded me that he had once received Communion from Padre Pio in Italy. He had seen the dark gloves Padre Pio wore on his hands to camouflage and absorb the blood from his stigmata wounds. He had participated in his Mass. Mr. Petroccia, who was seventeen or eighteen at the time, had come from his hometown of Reino on a bus of villagers who believed. Word had spread that Padre Pio was blessed by God.

Mr. Petroccia was just one of the hundreds of thousands that would travel from all over Italy and beyond to hear this Italian friar say Mass. It is astonishing how many participants in his Mass came away with the same impression: they were overwhelmed with a feeling that they had truly participated in the Passion of Christ, having stood in the very presence of God.

Padre Pio was probably even more known for hearing Confessions, having heard about two million in his lifetime. People would wait all day in long lines for their turn to confess to the bearded Capuchin monk, who frequently, already knew their sins, the status of their souls, and much more. If one "forgot" to mention a sin, he wasn't too shy to remind the person of the specific sin withheld, even the most secret ones. He was even known to shoo away unrepentant souls arriving at his church.

Padre Pio is also credited with the gift of bilocation, appearing in two places at once, as confirmed by a long list of reputable witnesses, including cardinals. He bilocated to cure people, to save lives from danger, and to offer spiritual support to those in need. While still at home in his monastery in San Giovanni, he visited the Vatican, hospital rooms, and even other continents.

For 50 long years, Padre Pio bore the stigmata, willingly sharing in the intense suffering of Christ in order that more souls could be saved. The stigmata were imprinted on him by an Exalted Being, which Padre Pio identified as Christ.

Padre Pio is said to be one of only two saints that bore all five of the main wounds of Christ: the wounds from the nails through the feet and the hands, as well as the lance through the side. Padre Pio's deep wounds bled constantly, regardless of whether he applied ointment or wore cloth mittens to hide the large amounts of blood.

He lost a cup of blood per day just from the gash in his side. The blood had a sweet and fragrant odor, which was especially strong when God's graces were being bestowed through him. Characteristic of true stigmata, the wounds never festered, got infected, or showed any signs of healing, as normal wounds would. The wounds on the tops of his hands and feet lined up with the wounds on the bottoms. Doctors examined Padre Pio endlessly, unable to find a medical explanation.

The deep wounds miraculously disappeared without a trace at the end of his ministry, leaving no scars on his corpse.

According to St. Pio, "The life of a Christian is nothing but a perpetual struggle against self; there is no flowering of the soul to the beauty of its perfection except at the price of pain."

Among the countless healings that God performed through Padre Pio, one often mentioned is the recovery of Dr. Wanda Poltawska, a friend of Pope John Paul II, who was diagnosed with a cancerous throat tumor, but had been informed there was a five percent chance that the tumor could be benign. When she was being prepared for surgery, the doctors surprised her with some news. She could go home. There was no tumor at all now. At first, Poltawska tried to convince herself that she had been misdiagnosed or had fallen into the "five percent" category.

She did not know until later that Archbishop Karol Wojtyla, the future pope, had written two letters to Padre Pio: the first requesting her cure, and second thanking the monk. Even after learning about the letters, she had trouble accepting the supernatural nature of her healing. Poltawska, who hadn't previously had any knowledge of Padre Pio, began hearing about the holy man and his many interventions. In 1967, she decided to join the crowds who arrived for his Mass in San Giovanni Rotondo.

After Mass, the monk was walking along when he picked her out, came over, patted her on the head, and said, "Now, are you OK?" That's when she believed. Years later, she learned that upon receiving the pope's request for her cure, Padre Pio replied, "I cannot say no to this request." This she learned from the man who delivered the future pope's letter to Padre Pio.

Like many participants in the Mass of Padre Pio, Poltawska has said she was made utterly aware that that the Passion of Christ on Calvary was truly present at the Mass. Padre Pio was in visible agony as he offered up the Holy Sacrifice, trembling, sweating, and bleeding from his five wounds, which he tried to keep hidden. When the pain was so intense that he could not turn the pages of his Mass book, Padre Pio was assisted by angels, according to the monk, who was known to communicate with angels as naturally as with people.

The agony he experienced at the altar was not separate from the agony of the cross. It was the same cross that he was united to. It was the same cross that St. Paul was united to. There are reports of Padre Pio's face being transfigured after the consecration.

Entire books have been written about healings worked through Padre Pio, but I will just mention a few more.

Her grandmother took a little blind girl with no pupils, Gemma DiGiorgi, to Padre Pio in the 1940s. Padre Pio requested that she receive her first Confession and first Communion from him. Then he touched her eyes and she was able to see, despite the fact that she still did not have pupils.

A construction worker named Giovanni Savino was injured so severely in a dynamite accident in 1949 that his right eye was annihilated, leaving his eye socket empty. The left eye and the rest of his face were severely damaged. As the man lay on his hospital bed, he felt a slap on the right side of his face and smelled the legendary aroma of Padre Pio. When the doctors arrived, his face was completely healed, and an eye had materialized in the empty socket.

Perhaps the most famous miracle associated with Padre Pio, however, was an occurrence in the sky in the vicinity of San Giovanni Rotondo during World War II. American bomber planes arrived to drop bombs on a target in Southern Italy. But one or more pilots encountered a giant monk in the sky who prevented them from following through. Padre Pio had previously promised God's protection of San Giovanni Rotondo.

After being told that the monk he saw was probably a saint named Padre Pio, the general went into San Giovanni full of curiosity. When he saw a group of monks outside the friary, he immediately picked out Padre Pio as the one that matched the monk in the sky. Padre Pio came over to him and said, "Are you the one who wanted to kill all of us?" According to accounts, the general knelt before the monk; afterward, the general also became a Catholic.

St. Padre Pio's canonization miracle — a miracle which, by Church regulation, must be officially approved after an exhaustive investigation — was the cure of seven-year-old Matteo Pio Colella in 2000, in a hospital founded by Padre Pio in his hometown of San Giovanni Rotondo. The boy was suffering from meningitis, and nine of his organs were gradually failing. After being told by doctors there was no hope for him, the boy's mother and some friars began praying to Padre Pio. While praying at the saint's tomb with closed eyes, the mother had a promising vision. She described it in writing: "With closed eyes, in black and white, [I saw] a Friar with a beard who advanced resolutely to a bed and picked up with both hands the small rigid body of a child and put him on his feet." The boy made a surprising recovery. When he awoke from his coma, the boy said that he had seen an elderly man with a white beard and long brown robe. The man said to him, "Don't worry. You will soon be cured." Doctors determined the recovery to be inexplicable from a medical standpoint.

ONE STEP TO ST. JOHN NEUMANN (1811-1869)

It is one short step from this author to the diminutive St. John Neumann, the fourth bishop of Philadelphia. I saw him myself. Well, at least I saw his body, which is on display behind glass at St. Peter the Apostle Church at Fifth and Girard in Philadelphia.

Known for his holiness of life, spiritual writings, and devotion to the needy, St. John Neumann is credited for laying the groundwork for the diocesan Catholic school system in the United States. He was canonized a saint in 1977, on a day I remember well. The canonization meant that both my parish church, and my school at the time, had to change names, with the word "Blessed" being replaced by "Saint."

Born in Bohemia (now the Czech Republic), St. John Neumann arrived in America in his mid-twenties. He desperately wanted to become a priest at a time marked by a glut of priests in Europe. So, he bade farewell to his family and friends and left for America, eager to use his foreign language skills to minister to the many immigrant groups here. He joined a group of priests called the Redemptorists, who were known for ministering to the weak and abandoned. The immigrant priest continued to hone his language skills, taking Confessions in at least six languages: English, Spanish, French, Italian, Dutch, and later, Irish Gaelic.

In western New York, the young priest helped build churches and schools for German and Irish immigrant children. He also served in Pittsburgh and Baltimore before being ordained bishop of Philadelphia, which was the country's largest diocese at the time. His territory extended from Pennsylvania into parts of New Jersey, Maryland and Delaware. He worked tirelessly, founding sorely needed Catholic schools and churches. While bishop, he also instituted Forty Hours of Devotion to the Eucharist.

The list of miracles that Christians attribute to this saint is lengthy. But the healings that the Church has actually gone to the trouble of scientifically verifying are those of Eva Benassi of Italy in 1923 (acute peritonitis), six-year-old Michael Flanigan (bone and blood cancer) in 1963, and Villanova, Pa.-resident J. Kent Lenahan, whose skull was crushed in a car accident in 1949.

St. John Neumann, who stood a bit over five feet tall, collapsed and died while crossing the street at Vine and Thirteenth Streets shortly before his 49th birthday.

I should mention that St. John Neumann is not to be confused with the great Catholic writer, John Henry Newman (1801-1890), the famous Anglican priest and scholar whose conversion to Catholicism was quite an event in nineteenth-century England. The conversion followed the writer's exhaustive study of Church and doctrinal history.

By the end of his research, Newman said he could no longer justify the Anglican Church's separation from Rome, nor could he reconcile his church with the "one, holy, Catholic and apostolic Church" of the creeds. After tracing the development of doctrines back from his time to the first century, he concluded that only the Catholic Church could claim legitimate development of doctrine. He became a Catholic priest, and later a Catholic cardinal. One of his most famous works was his book-length *Essay on the Development of Christian Doctrine,* first published in 1845.

It was John Henry Newman, the writer from England, and not the Philadelphia saint, for whom the Newman Centers at universities around the world were named. The Newman Centers, the first of which was established at the University of Pennsylvania in 1893, are collegiate organizations that assist the spiritual, academic, and social lives of Catholic students.

TWO STEPS TO BL. TERESA (1910-1997)

I wish I had met this little Albanian nun, who worked tirelessly to comfort the sickest and poorest of India. Rather, in order to connect the dots from this author to Mother Teresa, I must take a path through her friend, Pope John Paul II, whom I was lucky enough to see at the age of ten. Seated atop a parade vehicle, the pope rode right down City Avenue —the street that divides Philadelphia and its western suburbs — about eight minutes from my home. The pope even waved to my mother, my brother, and me — at least we think he did.

Mother Teresa is yet to be canonized a saint, but I feel she is bound to get this honor soon, thanks to her widespread reputation for living a virtuous life. Born Agnes Gonxha Bojaxhiu, the nun chose her new name for St. Thérèse of Lisieux.

Starting when she received Jesus for the first time in Holy Communion, Mother Teresa was overcome by a profound love for souls. At the age of eighteen, she left home to join an Irish order called the Sisters of Loretto. After a few months in Ireland, she arrived in Calcutta in January 1929, taught at St. Mary's School for girls, took her final vows in 1937, and declared herself the "spouse of Jesus" for "all eternity." In 1944, she became the school's principal.

But Jesus wanted more from her. Jesus told her that her vocation was "to love and suffer and save souls."

From September 1946 to October 1947, Mother Teresa had visions of Jesus and conversations with Him. Jesus begged her to start the "Missionaries of Charity," which he mentioned by name. He told her that He wanted Indian nuns, who "would be my fire of love amongst the poor, sick, the dying, and the little children." Jesus furthertold the nun she would suffer greatly, but to remember that even if she felt rejected by the whole world, this mattered not, because she was His own, and He was hers.

Jesus wanted her to dress as an Indian, simple and poor, wearing a sari. He said He wanted to see nuns clothed with the poverty, obedience, and charity of His own cross. The nuns He desired would "be so very united to me as to radiate My love on souls."

Jesus also told her how much it hurt Him when the souls of little children fell into sin; He longed for their pure love. He told the Mother Teresa to carry Jesus into the lives of the people of India, to offer more sacrifices, to smile more, and to pray more fervently. He requested that she "Come be my light. I cannot go alone," and told her that as the "Spouse of the Crucified Jesus," she would suffer great torments, but to trust Him blindly.

After Jesus had imparted His mission to her, He would never come to her in this way again for the rest of her life.

Mother Teresa started each day by receiving Holy Communion and, through her devotion to the Blessed Sacrament, saw Jesus in everyone that she served. She and the other nuns of the Missionaries of Charity would gather up the dying and the sick from the streets of the slums, to bring them to shelter and shower them with food, medical attention, and love. The organization grew to 450 centers around the world, with thousands of missionary workers. The nun helped launch the first Home for the Dying in Calcutta and some of the first AIDS hospices. Homes for abused women, abandoned children, drug addicts, prostitutes, and poor children also sprang up. Mother Teresa would remain in Calcutta until she died in 1997, at the age of 87.

When the nun won the Nobel Peace Prize in 1979, she insisted on foregoing the traditional banquet so that the $6,000 slated for the ceremony could be redirected to Calcutta's poor. She praised the charity of a starving Indian family who shared the little food they were given with their neighbors, and of an Indian woman who tore her coat in half to share it with someone in need. Mother Teresa reminded people that on the Last Day, only our efforts to feed the hungry and give drink to the thirsty would matter — not success nor material possessions. Work done without the motivation of love will have been done in vain, she said.

Mother Teresa said that any mother considering an abortion should give the child to her, and she would find a married couple who would love the child. As a result, her headquarters in Calcutta was able to give 3,000 children to adoptive families. To her, the right of an unborn child to live was a basic human right, not dependent on the pleasures of the parent or government.

On trips to the United States, the nun was often struck by the spiritual poverty of souls, something that she said was harder to overcome than material poverty. She spoke out against the legalization of abortion in the United States, claiming it had directly increased violence, damaged families, and "deformed a great nation."

Over the years, the nun suffered profoundly, just as Jesus had warned. Writings uncovered after her death showed she was haunted throughout her life with dark feelings of separation from and abandonment by God, the same type of feelings Jesus had while up on the cross.

Today, the message printed on Mother Teresa's so-called "business card" is familiar to many: "The fruit of silence is prayer, the fruit of prayer is faith, the fruit of faith is love, the fruit of love is service, the fruit of service is peace."

Mother Teresa was beatified in 2002, after her first miracle was confirmed. Another approved miracle — many more have been reported — would clear the way for sainthood.

Mother Teresa's approved miracle involved the overnight disappearance of a giant abdominal tumor from Monica Besra, a poor Hindu woman who was in the care of a hospice run by nuns of the Missionaries of Charity. On September 5, 1998 (the one-year anniversary of Mother Teresa's death), the nuns invited Besra to pray with them, letting her know it was a special day.

When Besra, who was 30 at the time, came in for prayers, she immediately saw a picture of Mother Teresa with rays of light beaming out from her eyes. Besra told the Associated Press that she began shaking, her heart went into a rapid beat, and she became scared and did not know what was happening to her. Later that day, the nuns placed a Mother Teresa medallion over the lump on Besra's stomach. The woman woke up at 1 a.m. to find that the tumor, which some said had made her look seven months pregnant, had vanished. She said she felt much lighter. "I was so excited, I woke up the woman in the bed next to me, Simira, and told her, 'Look, it's gone!'" Besra said in an interview.

Since the time of the healing — which was confirmed by the Church to be authentic after an exhaustive investigation — Besra and her whole family have converted to the Catholic faith.

TWELVE MINUTES TO ST. KATHARINE DREXEL
(1858-1955)

St. Katharine Drexel was born and raised in Philadelphia. Her favorite uncle lived on an estate just twelve minutes from my own home. The property is now the site of Archbishop Prendergast High School, a rival of my old high school, and the alma mater of my mother and all my aunts. Katharine's uncle, Anthony Drexel, founded the institute that became Drexel University, my husband's alma mater.

The wealthy heiress known as "Kate" grew up to become a nun, embrace a life of poverty, and, most notably, take on pioneering missionary work with blacks and Native Americans at a time these groups suffered great injustices in this country.

Katharine's father, Francis Drexel, and his brother, Anthony, made their millions after launching a successful banking house that eventually became part of the now-defunct Wall Street firm of Drexel, Burnham, Lambert, Inc. But riches never got in the way of the Drexels' passing on their strong faith and habit of philanthropy to the rest of the family.

Katharine's mother, Hannah, died soon after giving birth to the future saint, who was then sent to live with her Uncle Anthony and his wife until their grieving father could take her and her sister back. The two girls acquired a stepmother, Emma (Bouvier) Drexel. Emma was a faith-filled woman who welcomed the poor into the house three times a week, handing out money for rent, food, clothes, and whatever else was needed, from the Drexel residence on Walnut Street.

After Emma was diagnosed with cancer, Katharine, who was in her twenties, nursed her stepmother for three years until she died in 1883. Two years later, Katharine's father, Francis, died unexpectedly, causing the future saint additional grief and physical ailments. The three daughters began using their inheritance payments, about $1,000 per day, to launch charitable institutions. Katharine took an interest in helping Native Americans, whose plight she had witnessed on a family trip

In 1887, Katharine — who had been contemplating the religious life — and her two sisters succeeded in getting an appointment with Pope Leo XIII in Rome. When Katharine suggested to the pope that Indian missionaries were needed in the United States, the Holy Father replied, "Why not be a missionary yourself, my child?"

Katharine was visibly shaken by the suggestion, as she had planned a more uneventful life as a contemplative nun. But she took the advice to heart, ultimately founding the Sisters of the Blessed Sacrament. The women used the strength they derived from Jesus in the Eucharist to reach out to Native Americans and blacks, fight racism and injustice, and found and staff about 60 schools and missions in states such as New Mexico, Tennessee, Louisiana, Virginia, Ohio, New York, Illinois, and Pennsylvania.

The nuns are credited with establishing Xavier University, the first and only black Catholic college in America. By the time Mother Katharine died at the age of 96, she had pumped about $20 million of her inheritance into schools, churches, and centers.

Meanwhile, she committed herself to personal poverty. She would use pencils until they practically disappeared. She would use the insides of envelopes for writing notes. She would make use of discarded leftovers, and would generally refuse condiments at mealtime.

Pope John Paul II canonized Katharine Drexel in 2000, after the Church approved her two required miracles. One was the cure of little Amy Wall of Bucks County, Pennsylvania, in 1994. The girl, who was two at the time, was born with nerve deafness in both ears. After the family and community prayed for Katharine Drexel's intercession for four months, Amy's hearing was instantly restored in both ears.

Amy's preschool teacher told her mother that the girl she had come to pick up was a different girl than the one she had dropped off earlier. A thorough battery of tests, which had previously showed that Amy could barely detect shouting, now demonstrated perfect hearing. Dozens of physicians, including ear, nose & throat specialists, and 600 pages of documentation, confirmed that no medical explanation was possible. Not surprisingly, Amy's father, who had considered himself a nondenominational Protestant, converted to Catholicism after the miracle.

Other Connections . . . Other Saints

STS. FRANCIS (c. 1181-1226)
AND CLARE (1194-1253) OF ASSISI

Everybody loves Francis. Born in the Umbria region of Italy, this great thirteenth-century saint rejected the wealth and pleasures of his youth and married himself to the poverty of Jesus. Known for his profound compassion for the poor and lepers, as well as for animals, birds, and fish, St. Francis strived to stay clear of material goods and the little comforts of life. His fashion attire ranged from tattered cloaks to rough, itchy tunics. He was known to walk barefoot over rocks, mountains, and through snow, begging alms and joyously singing the praises of God.

As the founder of the order of Franciscans, he told incoming friars to give away all their belongings to the poor and follow him. The group eventually established a friary in small huts, a base from which to wander the country, preach the good news, and invite the poor in for a bite to eat.

In 1210, Francis and a group of fellow friars walked to Rome seeking approval for the group's simple Rule of Life from Pope Innocent III. The pope approved it, but only after having a dream in which he saw Francis holding up the Lateran Basilica, which was a symbol of the universal church. Years earlier, while praying before a crucifix, Francis had heard a voice, clearly saying, "Francis, rebuild my Church." The voice seemed to be coming right out of the cross.

Like all great Catholic saints, St. Francis had a great reverence for the Eucharist, the Sacrifice of the Mass, and the Mother of God, to whom he recited his own special salutation daily. He had the utmost esteem for the office of priest, because of the priest's role in making manifest the mysteries of the Holy Body and Blood of Christ. He took it upon himself to make sure that even the poorest churches had beautiful chalices worthy of holding the Blood of Christ, and that even the poorest priests had fine vestments worthy of celebrating Christ's Holy Mass.

As the first in a long line of saints to bear the painful stigmata, St. Francis was granted his wish to intimately share in Christ's pains. The wounds on his hands, feet and side were imprinted on his body by a fiery, supernatural being that came down on him on Mount Alverna after an explosion in the sky. St. Francis had been praying fervently to Jesus, begging Him to feel His sufferings.

Unlike Padre Pio's ever-bleeding wounds, the marks on St. Francis took the form of protruding flesh on both sides of his hands and feet in the shape of nails: the formations of four nail heads were matched with four long, pointy nail formations on the opposite sides of the feet and hands. One can still read a first-hand account of the whole event, which was recorded by Brother Leo, one of the three friars that accompanied the saint up the mountain in 1224.

Inspired by St. Francis' preaching, an eighteen-year-old noblewoman named Clare approached the saint about her desire to emulate Francis' strict Gospel-based way of life. An order of nuns called the Poor Clares was born. St. Clare lived in a poor house, fasted most days, never ate meat, and wore an uncomfortable hair tunic. She and her fellow nuns renounced all property.

She once mused, "They say that we are too poor, but can a heart which possesses the infinite God be truly called poor?"

Today, the world is blessed with 20,000 Poor Clares and more than a million Franciscans, including members of friar, priest, and secular orders. I, personally, have St. Clare to thank for my name!

ST. PATRICK, THE PATRON SAINT OF IRELAND
(387- 493 A.D.)

Saint Patrick, who converted pagan Ireland to the Catholic faith in the fifth century, earned his place in this chapter because, well, without him, I would not exist. That is to say, if my mother's pagan Irish ancestors had not become Catholic, then my mother never would have met my Italian father at a Catholic church dance, and I would be but a figment of your imagination.

Born in Scotland into a Latin-speaking Roman family of high ranking, St. Patrick admits that as youths, he and his friends ignored the laws of God and the teachings of priests. Kidnapped by pirates at the age of sixteen, St. Patrick would spend the next six years as a slave in Ireland. The experience jump-started his faith and prepared him for his future mission.

St. Patrick's time as a slave in Ireland — marked by constant prayer to God — ended when he escaped from his brutal master at the command of an angel, and journeyed 200 miles before reaching the coast and setting sail to Britain. He studied at a monastery, was ordained a priest, and, while working on papal missions, had visions of children who cried to him, "O holy youth, come back to Erin."

With the blessing and sendoff of Pope St. Celestine I in Rome, who commissioned the saint to gather the Irish race into the one fold of Christ, St. Patrick returned to Ireland. There, he would succeed in converting a nation to Christianity in just three decades.

Despite constant plots against him by the country's Celtic Druids, St. Patrick accomplished his mission in remarkably peaceful fashion. He became Ireland's second bishop and established schools, churches, and monasteries everywhere.

He worked wondrous miracles — or, that is to say, God worked wondrous miracles through him. The saint ordained many priests, accepted the vows of nuns, and consecrated hundreds of new bishops in Ireland. He brought back valuable relics from Rome. He met with Pope Leo the Great, who gave the saint his stamp of approval for the faith of Ireland. He prayed constantly. And he did penance like there was no tomorrow.

Besides his regular habit of sleeping on rocks and donning rough hair shirts, he spent forty days at the top of a mountain praying, fasting, and suffering in the unbearable cold, rain, and wind, all to obtain blessings for his people.

It was all worthwhile. St. Patrick received word from an angel that his penances had reaped many rewards: many suffering souls would be freed from Purgatory, the Antichrist would never penetrate Ireland, and, on the Last Day, St. Patrick would be judge of the Irish race.

St. Patrick's life was plagued with real attacks from demons, but was blessed with real visits from angels. He is the known as the Apostle of Ireland.

ST. CATHERINE OF SIENA (1347-1380)

One sunny morning, at the nunnery, I climbed up onto a table and stood up to see what I could see out the window. The panoramic view of Siena, Italy, was breathtaking. Music was streaming in, possibly from a church, and I bobbed my head to the beat. I felt on top of the world. That is, until it registered in my head that an angry nun was peering at me and yelling things in Italian at me from her own window in the next building. I promptly jumped off the table and hid under it, leaving my three traveling companions, Terri, Deb, and Susan, to fend for themselves.

Mea culpa! That was not the first impression that I would have wanted to make with the nuns of the same order of St. Catherine of Siena. The holy house where the saint grew up was right next to our nun-managed hotel, the Alma Domus, where carpet-less rooms with dishrags for towels reminded visitors of the austere lifestyle chosen by St. Catherine.

In her thirty-three years of life, St. Catherine read hearts, guided popes, served the poor, and saw visions of Christ, the Apostles — even people's guardian angels.

Most importantly, she proved that by dying to oneself while on earth, one could move mountains for the Church and for the life of souls. Privately, Catherine endured great penances and sufferings. Publicly, she radiated joy and love as she served the destitute, the imprisoned, and those dying from the plague and other hideous diseases.

Wisdom emanated from her as she settled conflicts between Church leaders and the republics of Italy, advised popes, settled political disputes, and fought for Church unity and peace. In 1377, she convinced Pope Gregory XI to return the Holy See to its rightful place in Rome from the pope's exile in Avignon, France.

Catherine's love affair with Christ started during her childhood. At the age of seven, she made a secret vow of virginity to God. At sixteen, she entered the Dominican order in the laywoman category, continuing to live at her father's house. Later, the Lord, in the company of Mary and the saints, appeared to her and adorned her with a gold wedding ring that featured a diamond surrounded by other jewels. But only Catherine could see it.

Catherine's early penances included scourging herself, sleeping on a board, cutting off her beautiful hair, wearing hair shirts, and severely limiting her sleep and food intake. Five years before her death, she received all five wounds of Christ when the stigmata descended on her from a crucifix still preserved in her old house. Thanks to Catherine's prayer, the stigmata were invisible to others during her life. But, upon her death, the wounds became clearly visible, producing testimony for all to see.

Miracles, visions, periods of ecstasy, conversations with Christ, and levitating in the air during prayer, all marked Catherine's holy life. Her first vision came when she was just six years old. While walking home with her brother, she saw a clear scene in the sky of Jesus, clothed like a pope, seated in glory with Apostles St. Peter, St. Paul, and St. John the Evangelist. At the age of twenty-three, she had visions of Heaven, Hell, and Purgatory. When she begged God to bring her dead mother, Lapa, back to life, God granted her wish.

Catherine, whose famous literary works include *Dialogue with Divine Providence* and *Letters,* is one of the first two female saints to be declared a Doctor of the Church. The other is St. Teresa of Ávila.

How Do Saints Do It?

And, so, we have seen what can happen if one dares to take the Gospel literally and strive to emulate the lifestyle of Jesus to the letter: the person just might end up a saint. The person just might risk helping the Lord guide thousands or millions of souls to salvation. Fueled by God's overflowing grace, the person might become so productive that orphanages, hospitals, churches, and missions spring up everywhere they turn. The person might live happily ever after in paradise, with the glorified Christ, in an indescribable world too beautiful for human minds to even imagine.

The biographies of the saints come not only with harrowing, life-altering stories of courage and humility, but also with the rich helpings of histories and culture from the countless countries and time periods from which the saints hail.

There were the martyrs, ranging from St. Joan of Arc to St. Maximilian Kolbe. There were saints who were both mothers and widows, such as St. Elizabeth Ann Seton and St. Bridget of Sweden. There were Catholic Reformation saints, such as St. Ignatius of Loyola, St. Francis de Sales, and St. Thomas More. There were Church Fathers, with names such as St. Augustine, St. Thomas Aquinas, and St. Anthony of Padua.

Despite the incredible diversity of their lives, the saints drew their nourishment from the same saint-making food. Each loved the Mass and received Holy Communion daily or as often as possible. Each led a life of simplicity marked by prayer, penance, and self-denial. Many, if not most, made lifelong vows of poverty, chastity, and obedience. Each took up a cross of suffering. Each shone with Christ's love, especially when it came to the poorest, sickest, and loneliest. The saints had a common friend and Savior, whose presence they knew well.

With Christ's grace, the saints were able to advance through all the easy and moderately difficult commands of Jesus, and leap right to the hardest ones:

"If any man would come after me, let him deny himself and take up his cross and follow me" (Mt. 16:24 and Mk. 8:34).

"One thing you still lack. Sell all that you have and distribute to the poor, and you will have treasure in Heaven; and come, follow me" (Lk.18:22).

The saints have proven to us that it is within the reach of human beings to be able to bow down to seemingly impossible instructions of Jesus. But human beings, left to themselves, are capable of nothing. Only by allowing the Word of God and the Flesh of God to enter us, do we allow God to supernaturally change us and prepare us for perfect union with Him.

Martyrs and Other Christian Witnesses

Amid all the clutter in our lives, thank heavens there are, even today, authentic Christian witnesses around us who remind us that our purpose here is serving God and others, and who remind us that this life is not the one to put stock in. They remind us that none of our days should be regarded as business as usual.

In China alone, many Catholic bishops have been kidnapped, killed, or imprisoned, but they continue to put Jesus first. In many parts of China, citizens must still choose between risking their lives at the illegal underground Catholic Church, or attending the false state-run Catholic churches, which are controlled by the communist government's Catholic Patriotic Association. Millions choose to risk their lives.

Christians in countries such as North Korea, Vietnam, Sudan, and Pakistan also risk severe oppression and violence for practicing their faith.

According to the *World Christian Encyclopedia,* more Christians were martyred in the last century than in all the other centuries put together. Specifically, 45 million of the 70 million Christian martyrs were killed in the twentieth century.[70]

In certain countries, the faithful walk miles to church in the sweltering heat every day; here in America, a dead car battery provides the perfect excuse not to worship half a mile down the road.

One bed and breakfast owner at the Jersey Shore told me that nobody in his new town ever bothered to greet or welcome his family after church, so he took his family to a church of a different creed around the corner. There, official church greeters immediately approached him and his wife, introduced them to other families, and promptly signed up the children for summer programs.

In certain countries, believers risk bombings and prison time each time they show up for Mass — yet here in America, we often don't even think to reach out to a newcomer at Mass. The tiny opportunities we pass up each day could be accomplishing valuable work for God and the whole world. Those four extra people offering up the Holy Sacrifice of the Mass in New Jersey could be helping to convert hearts and ease the sufferings of the persecuted around the globe.

While millions of us can hardly bear to give up a pastry after lunch, martyrs set their sights on the next world. Most of us set our sights on this one. We wake up each morning and start doing a million things that have nothing to do with the next life, which is the only life we were designed for. Imagine a person spending ten years studying nothing but oil painting in the years prior to entering medical school. That would be insane. We all must be insane.

In the aftermath of the World Trade Center attacks, TV reporters interviewed random people on the street. A few young adults mused that the tragedy had showed them the importance of "living it up" in the present. After all, one never knows when it will end, they reasoned. These responses would have been appropriate if nothing awaited us after this life. These responses would have been reasonable if Jesus had not told us to pick up our cross.

Much different answers would have come from Mother Teresa or the Apostle St. Paul. Or from St. Anna Wang, the fourteen-year-old girl who chose decapitation before denying her faith. Anna and other Christians were captured on July 21, 1900, by Boxer bandits in China during the Boxer Rebellion. Held prisoners in one room, the group was told that those who denounced their faith would be freed.

Anna and nine others did no such thing. They remained in captivity. Even after a bandit had cut off a piece of her flesh, and then her arm, Anna refused to deny her Catholic faith. Before her beheading, she was heard uttering, "The door to Heaven is open to all" and whispering the name of Jesus three times.

Another Chinese teenager who was martyred that same month was eighteen-year-old Chi Zhuzi. His right arm had just been cut off, and he was about to be flayed alive, yet he cried out, "Every piece of my flesh, every drop of my blood will repeat to you that I am Christian."

They understood well that the next life is the goal and the prize. The rest of us understand well what time our favorite TV show starts, and whether we need to replenish the ice cream in our freezers. We understand that we should be doing things differently, but we put it off. We are supposed to take up a cross daily, but we allow distractions to fill our lives.

As long as we are still exiled on this planet, we are supposed to be fighting members of the Church Militant. Those in Heaven make up the Church Triumphant. Those in Purgatory make up the Church Suffering. But we are the Church Militant, responsible for engaging in daily warfare, both physically and spiritually, against sin, temptation, and the devil. Our weapons are love, prayer, charity, fasting, and the sacraments, and our battles are daily.

Every now and again, someone in our midst reminds us of our purpose here. Every once in awhile, a dose of counterculture pierces us with Gospel truth. When a couple I met at a Bible study got married, they did not aim for the comfortable house on the Main Line. Instead, they moved into an old convent to help run a home for single pregnant mothers with no place to live.

A trip to Nicaragua in 2002 changed the life of a recent graduate of Villanova University. Instead of searching for a high-paying job after his 2004 graduation, as he had planned, the young man would devote the foreseeable future to spearheading the installation of purified water systems in fifty poor communities in Waslala. He could not ignore the poverty of this large Nicaraguan town, where many families continue to live in dirt-floor shacks without electricity, telephones, plumbing, or sanitation.

In my own college alumni bulletin, I saw that a former classmate was giving up her lucrative job at a Boston consulting firm to work at a Guatemalan orphanage that had caught her eye and heart during a trip to Central America.

A friend who had studied agricultural sciences at Pennsylvania State University moved to Bolivia in the 1990s and stayed a decade to teach advanced potato-growing methods in poor rural areas. A New England friend, Ali, took a three-year hiatus from her higher-paying job to manage an adult literacy program outside Boston.

A married couple I know was told by multiple doctors to abort their baby, whose internal organs were growing outside of the abdomen. Instead, the couple relied on the prayers of hundreds — friends, relatives, and their church community. The baby's organs began correcting themselves in the womb. Just after birth, a quick operation finished the job. Baby Zac turned out just as normal, just as cute, and just as loved as any other baby.

An old friend named Andrea also comes to mind. I haven't seen her in years, but I will never forget her inability to allow even one evangelization opportunity to pass her by. In her single days, she would sit at the bar and chat with guys who would flirt with her. They would want to know if she had a boyfriend. "Well, sort of," she would tease them. Eventually, she would reveal that she had a boyfriend in the Holy Spirit. This would lead to full-blown discussions about Christianity.

People like her remind us that none of our days should be regarded as business as usual. Full union with Christ will be anything but ordinary. Many who have gone before us are already basking in His glorious presence. That is what we need to set our sights on.

CHAPTER FOURTEEN

✝

Now I Get . . . Mary

Of all the saints in Heaven, only one was so blessed as to carry in her womb the Savior of the World. The Blessed Mother knew what she was talking about when she said in the first century, ". . . all generations shall call me blessed" (Lk.1:48).

Her image has been sculpted in marble by Michelangelo and painted in oil by Leonardo da Vinci. Mary's shrines at Fátima and Lourdes have been visited by millions of Catholic pilgrims. The crutches and wheelchairs of thousands of cured people hang at those sites.

The Coronation of the Virgin as queen of Heaven is depicted even on the door of the burial chamber of Protestant Reformer Martin Luther.[71]

The world knows that Mary brought her Son into the world, but seldom does it occur to some that she also helped bring her Son into the New World.

With the firm conviction that God wanted to guide him across the Atlantic Ocean to bring the good news of Jesus to a new land, the devout Catholic explorer Christopher Columbus, set out from Spain on August 2, 1492 with three ships, the *Niña*, the *Pinta,* and the *Santa Maria.*

For such a dangerous mission, Columbus had sought extra protection for his crew; he had named his flagship after the Blessed Mother, who has since been declared patroness of the Americas.[72]

During the ten-week voyage, Admiral Columbus committed himself to daily prayers and purity of language. He led his sailors in hymns honoring the Queen of Heaven. He made a decision that if land wasn't sighted by October 12, a Spanish feast day honoring

Mary[73], he would turn back to Europe. The ships reached land on precisely Mary's day.

After naming the first island San Salvador, or Holy Savior, Columbus named the second island Santa Maria — "Holy Mary" or "Saint Mary" in Spanish.

Throughout history, there have been Queen Mothers of England, of France, of Italy, of Denmark, and of African nations. Mothers of reigning kings have magnanimously served their countries and cared for their subjects throughout history.

But only the mother of the eternal King will reign as the eternal Queen Mother of Heaven. In the Heavenly family that God has prepared for us, Mary will forever be our mother and our queen.

As a queen mother is known to do, the Virgin Mary attached herself to a cause or two. The Virgin serves the Lord in her role as a promoter of peace, guiding her children to engage in penance and constant prayer for the conversions of hearts.

In this chapter, we will run some of the less understood Marian doctrines, such as the Assumption, the Immaculate Conception, the queen mother role, and Mary's place as the New Eve.

But first, let us stop by Fátima, Portugal in the year 1917. Mary had been appearing to three children, Jacinta, Francisco, and Lucia, asking them to make sacrifices to God as reparation for people's sins. The children started giving up food, even water, on the hottest days, and devoting much more time to prayer. The Blessed Mother, who appeared "more brilliant than the sun," instructed them to say the Rosary daily for world peace.

Mary showed them a vision of Hell, where frightful demons and deformed human forms floated in a sea of fire, shrieking and groaning. Mary told the three that "many souls go to Hell because they have no one to make sacrifices and pray for them," and that Jesus is deeply offended by sin. At one point, they saw an angel holding a flaming sword and crying out, "Penance, Penance, Penance!"

Mary transmitted messages to the children about the end of World War I, the threat of World War II, and other topics. These have been recorded and are available for perusal. But perhaps the most pivotal question she asked them was this:

"Are you willing to offer yourselves to God to bear all the sufferings He wants to send you, as an act of reparation for the sins by which He is offended, and for the conversion of sinners?"

Lucia answered yes for the three of them.

Although Mary promised to take all three children to Heaven, she said only Jacinta and Francisco would be going there soon. Our Lady then added:

"But you, Lucy, are to stay here some time longer. Jesus wishes to make use of you in order to make Me known and loved. He wishes to establish in the world devotion to My Immaculate Heart."

Francisco, who was nine years old at the time of the apparitions, fell ill and died at age ten. Jacinta, seven years old during the apparitions, died at age nine after suffering greatly from pneumonia, tuberculosis, and other ailments, which she cheerfully offered up to God for sinners. Mary appeared to her several times in the hospital.

Lucia, who was ten when Mary appeared to the children, lived almost a century, devoting her long life to her Heaven-sent assignment. Born as Lucia Dos Santos on March 22, 1907, this cloistered nun went by the name Maria Lucia of the Immaculate Heart when she died on February 13, 2005, just a month before her ninety-eighth birthday. She lived in the Carmelite convent in Coimbra, Portugal.

As a child, Lucy asked the Blessed Mother for a miracle so that all would believe in her appearances. Mary agreed, promising the children that on October 13, 1917, there would be a miracle for all to see.

Miracle of the Sun

About 70,000 people — including curious Catholics, atheists, and agnostics —showed up to see what would happen. In the early afternoon, after a long and non-eventful waiting period during which some debated going home, the sun began spinning like a disc. Then, it danced and zigzagged in the sky. Finally, it began plummeting to earth menacingly, as if it were going to crush the crowd. Just as spectators feared they were doomed, it stopped all its terrifying motion and resumed its regular position in the sky.

Meanwhile, the three children witnessed Heavenly events that the crowd could not see. Mary appeared in the sky, announcing that she was "The Lady of the Rosary. Let them continue to say the Rosary every day." The children saw in the sky three tableaux representing the Joyful, Sorrowful, and Glorious Mysteries of the Rosary. Next, the children saw St. Joseph with the Baby Jesus, who blessed the crowd three times.

The Miracle of the Sun was reported in European newspapers by Christian and non-Christian reporters alike. An article in a pro-government, anti-clerical newspaper in Lisbon, *O Seculo,* described the events in the following way:

". . . the sun trembled, made sudden incredible movements outside all cosmic laws — the sun 'danced' according to the typical expression of the people."

". . . others affirmed that they saw the face of the Blessed Virgin; others, again, swore that the sun whirled on itself like a giant Catherine wheel and that it lowered itself to the earth as if to burn it in its rays."[74]

Another secular daily newspaper in Lisbon, the *O Día,* remarked that the sun "was seen to whirl and turn in the circle of broken clouds. A cry went up from every mouth and people fell on their knees in the muddy ground. . . ."[75]

As part of his personal eyewitness account of the miracle, Dr. José Maria de Almedia Garrett, then a professor at Coimbra University, wrote:

> The sun, whirling wildly, seemed all at once to loosen itself from the firmament and, blood red, advance threateningly upon the earth as if to crush us with its huge and fiery weight. The sensation during those moments was truly terrible.[76]

And so the laws of the universe bowed down to the almighty God, who ardently desires that even children know the truth about the wages of sin, the power and necessity of penance, and the importance of honoring the Blessed Mother.

Mary's apparitions in Fátima — like her apparitions in the French town of Lourdes and the Guadalupe section of Mexico City — have been confirmed by the Church to be authentic. The degree to which Christians heed her message of conversion, penance, and prayer, including the daily recitation of the Rosary, directly determines the extent of peace on earth. As the message has been sent to us from God Himself, our response directly determines the eternal destiny of many.

Mary will always be leading people to her Son. She will always be ready to intercede for us before her Son, just as she did at the wedding feast of Cana in Galilee, when the wine ran out. On that day, Mary approached her Son with her concern; Jesus responded by ordering the servers to fill six stone water jars with water, which He then changed into wine.

Like any Christian on earth or in Heaven, Mary may intercede for us in prayer if we ask. Thanks to their special closeness to God in Heaven, the Blessed Mother and all the other saints serve as our strongest prayer warriors.

Just as Jesus is known as the "New Adam," Mary is called the "New Eve." Although both Eve and Mary were created without sin on their souls, the first Eve said yes to the evil serpent, while the Second Eve said yes to the angel Gabriel from above. As a result, the first Eve acted as a vehicle for the sin of Adam to enter into the world, while the second Eve served as a vehicle for the Savior to enter the world.

> And so the knot of Eve's disobedience received its unloosing through the obedience of Mary; for what Eve, a virgin, bound by incredulity, that Mary, a virgin, unloosed by faith.
>
> — St. Irenaeus, Bishop of Lyons
> (*Against Heresies,* Book 3: 22.34, 189 A.D.)

The parallels and contrasts between the two women and their roles in salvation history go on and on, but suffice it to say that Eve cooperated with sin, while Mary cooperated with grace.

Also prefigured in the Old Testament is the queen mother role of Mary, a role evident in ancient Israel; interestingly, it wasn't the wife of the king of Judah who sat at the king's right hand in the official post as queen, but rather the mother.

As true brothers and sisters of Jesus, we have a true and eternal mother in Mary, whose soul magnifies the Lord and whose spirit rejoices in her Savior (Lk 1:46-47). Jesus Himself honored Mary in obeying the Fourth Commandment to honor one's mother and one's father.

Need another reason to honor Mary?

From the time she was conceived in the womb of her mother Anne by the seed of her father Joachim, Mary was blessed with a soul pure as snow as part of God's wondrous saving plan. The special role God prepared for her is prophesied in the first book of the Old Testament as well as the last book of the New Testament. The Book of Genesis (3:15) prefigures her participation in the crushing of the serpent, while the Book of Revelation (12:1) depicts the Mary figure as "a woman clothed with the sun, with the moon under her feet, and on her head a crown of twelve stars." (Incidentally, the "woman clothed with the sun" is a symbolic reference not only to the Blessed Mother but, simultaneously, to the Church and to the people of Israel. The woman of Rev. 12 was to give birth to a Son who would rule all nations, one the seven-headed dragon wanted to destroy.)

Of course, the devil would never have power over the humble and obedient Mary, whose Lord and Savior willed that his mother never be infected with original sin, a sin that the rest of us inherit from Adam. While original sin is removed from our souls in Baptism, its stain continues to affect us, leaving on us a tendency to commit actual sin; Mary never suffered either the stain of sin or its lingering aftereffects.

The formation of the baby Mary's soul without original sin is the doctrine of the Immaculate Conception of Mary. Unfortunately, late-night comedians are notorious for attributing the phrase to the Baby Jesus' conception in Mary's virginal womb. (If you didn't know this already, now you know we can't depend on contemporary culture or sitcoms to accurately teach us doctrines of the faith!)

Those who do understand that the Immaculate Conception refers to Mary's soul being created without the stain of original sin often then mistakenly conclude that Catholics must think Mary did not need to be saved by Christ. Au contraire. It was only because of her Son's merits that Mary was able to be saved from the imperfect nature she would have otherwise inherited. Her soul was saved from imperfections in advance of her Son's arrival in her womb.

But, since every sin committed contributes to the agony and crucifixion of Jesus, it makes sense that God would prevent Jesus' own mother from contributing to His bloody wounds. St. Augustine said that out of honor for the Lord, we should be so confident Mary was without sin that there should be "absolutely no question" about the matter:

> We must except the holy Virgin Mary, concerning whom I wish to raise no question when it touches the subject of sin, out of honor to the Lord; for from Him we know what abundance of grace for overcoming sin in every particular was conferred upon her who had the merit to conceive and bear Him who undoubtedly had no sin.
> — St. Augustine, *Nature and Grace,* 42 [36] (415 A.D.)

Mary is not the only human being who ever benefited from Christ's work in advance. All those saints who lived before Christ's time could have been sent straight to Hell upon dying, but, instead, they were directed to a place of waiting known as the Bosom of Abraham[77] in anticipation of Christ's redemption. When the gates of Heaven were open, the Old Testament saints received their reward.

St. Ambrose, Bishop of Milan, wrote that Mary was "a Virgin not only undefiled but a Virgin whom grace has made inviolate, free of every stain of sin" (Ambrose, *Commentary on Psalm 118:22:30,* 387 A.D.).

By virtue of her Immaculate Conception, Mary was so filled with God's grace that she had the power to reject every temptation that arose during her life on earth. The rest of us will be given this same power, but we will have to wait for it until we enter Heaven, where sin does not exist.

And why is Mary continually referred to as a Virgin, even after the birth of Christ? Considering the arrival of Jesus was unique in the history of mankind, it is not surprising that the Lord was the only child to be born of Mary; nobody else could be worthy to share that womb. Understandably, God did not wish the mother of our Lord to have babies with two different fathers.

If only one human being on earth had offered up the gift of lifelong virginity to God for the sake of the Kingdom, it would have been

Mary. Yet, we know that even human beings of lesser greatness — John the Baptist, Moses, and Elijah, to name a few — had been willing to do the same for the Lord.

Some of the Reformed churches mistakenly interpret the phrase "brethren of the Lord" in the Bible to mean Mary had other children, but historical writings attest to the fact that Mary was a perpetual virgin or "ever-virgin," dedicated to the service of the Lord from the beginning.

St. Jerome (342-420 A.D.), a Doctor of the Church who was known as the Doctor and Father of Biblical Science, chided a man named Helvidius who tried to say that Mary did not remain a virgin after the birth of Jesus: "You neglected the whole range of Scripture and employed your madness in outraging the Virgin."[78] As a matter of fact, St. Jerome sweeps clean the first three centuries of Christianity from any disbelief in Our Lady's perpetual virginity. "Pray, tell me," he asks Helvidius, "who, before you appeared, was acquainted with this blasphemy? Who thought the theory worth two-pence?"[79]

According to a second-century work called the *Protoevangelium of James,* the phrase "brethren of the Lord" referred to children of Joseph by his former wife who had died. Other early writings suggest the word "brethren" refers to cousins.

Many Protestants don't realize that not only the beloved St. Augustine, but also the founders of their religions, including Martin Luther, John Calvin and Ulrich Zwingli, believed Mary was a life-long virgin, or "Ever-Virgin."

In a prayer book he wrote in 1522, Luther said Mary was "full of grace, proclaimed to be entirely without sin — something exceedingly great."[80] In a sermon in 1527, Luther also preached:

> It is a sweet and pious belief that the infusion of Mary's soul was effected without original sin; so that in the very infusion of her soul she was also purified from original sin and adorned with God's gifts, receiving a pure soul infused by God; thus from the first moment she began to live she was free from all sin.[81]

The Reformers taught that Mary should be called the "Mother of God," but nowadays, some Christians harbor suspicion of the term "Mother of God" because they mistakenly fear that the phrase implies Mary was the mother of God the Father, or of the whole Trinity. No, we simply give her this title because she is the mother of Jesus, and Jesus is God in the fullest sense possible. The phrase also reminds us of the words of Elizabeth in Scripture, who greeted Mary as "the Mother of my Lord" (Lk. 1:43). Even while in Mary's womb, Jesus was the true and living God, whose presence made St. John the Baptist leap for joy from his own womb within St. Elizabeth.

Many theologians have theorized that it was from Mary that the Lord Jesus received his full set of DNA. The Holy Spirit, who came upon Mary, is not a physical entity. And, of course, St. Joseph, Jesus' stepfather, did not contribute to the flesh or genetic material inherited by Jesus.

We do know, from Rom. 1:3, that Jesus "was descended from David according to the flesh." Yet, Jesus received no flesh from St. Joseph, a direct descendant of David, who was in turn a descendant of Abraham and Abraham's son Isaac. To prove St. Joseph's legacy leading back to Abraham, the Bible lists the names of the descendants between the Patriarch and Jesus (see Mt. 1:1-16).

But history leads us to believe that Mary, too, was a direct descendant of David. According to the *Catholic Encyclopedia,* after St. Justin Martyr and St. Ignatius of Antioch, the Church Fathers "generally agree in maintaining Mary's Davidic descent, whether they knew this from an oral tradition or inferred it from Scripture (e.g. Rom. 1:3; 2 Timothy 2:8)."

Because Mary was exempted from sin, Catholics hold she was also exempted from bodily decay. The Blessed Mother's remains are not to be found on this earth, because her body is glorified in Heaven. Each August 15, we celebrate the Assumption of Mary, which proclaims that Mary was taken up to Heaven, body and soul. The rest of us will have to wait until the Last Day of earth for our bodies to rise up from our graves to meet our souls in Heaven.

The Second Vatican Council put it this way:

> The Immaculate Virgin, preserved free from all stain of original sin, was taken up body and soul into Heavenly glory, when her earthly life was over, and exalted by the Lord as Queen over all things.

Just as Christ reigns eternally as king, Christ's Mother will eternally share in His royalty; as our queen mother, she knows all of us by name.

✝

Now . . . We Are Divided

I finally got it straight. Calvin was the bratty boy, and Hobbes was the stuffed pet tiger. If I had made that mix-up back in college, certain classmates would have lost all respect for me. I was still a bit foggy on the namesakes of the characters of the then wildly popular *Calvin and Hobbes* comic strip, though, and was worried someone might try to trip me up on them.

Alas, before I could get to the library, my greatest fear came true, and the question was posed to me: "Do you know who the real Calvin and Hobbes are, Claire?"

"Of course I know that," I replied, bluffing. "It's Hobbes, you know, as in Hobbes, Locke, and Rousseau. . . ." (Phew, that was a close one! I could barely even remember what any of those men stood for.) I was hoping my challenger would now be satisfied, and would move on to other topics. I had no such luck.

"And what about Calvin?" continued my interrogator.

I was stumped. "Well, gosh, there were so many Calvins," I started out. "There was the musician Calvin, the philosopher Calvin, the president Calvin . . ."

"There was? . . . No, I think there was a President Calhoun, not Calvin," he said, undoubtedly confused enough to throw John C. Calhoun, the seventh *Vice* President of the United States, into the mix.

"How about President Calvin Coolidge?" an eavesdropper chimed in.

"That's right," I bluffed further. "There were two presidents named Calvin. One with a first name and one with a last. You really don't know your presidents, do you? It goes Washington, Adams, Jefferson, Madison, Monroe, Adams, Jackson, Van Buren, Harrison, Tyler, Polk, Taylor, Calvin, Buchanan, Calvin Coolidge . . ."

For a moment, the guy look truly dazed, but he soon reiterated his demands for me to identify Calvin. Instead, I surrendered.

"Okay, fine," I said. "Who is he? Who is Calvin? Tell me!"

My interrogator, who happened to be Protestant, replied, "I'm not telling you. Go look it up at the library."

"No, just tell me!" I pleaded.

"No, go to the library," he said. "It's somebody you should not like. He's Protestant. What the heck did they teach you in twelve years of Catholic school?"

"Um, Catholic stuff?" I meekly replied.

I never got around to looking it up — mostly because I didn't know if Calvin was the first name or last name — until many, many years later when the name was brought to my attention again, by yet another Protestant. As it turned out, John Calvin's fame stemmed from helping to lead millions of people out of my Church!

John Calvin, Martin Luther, and Ulrich Zwingli — all former Catholics — helped spark the Protestant religions in the sixteenth century. In doing so, they broke off from the Catholic Church, and the original unity of St. Peter.

Of course, they had no right to do this. Jesus had established only one Church for us. While in the Upper Room, not long before the agony that awaited Him in the Garden of Gethsemane, Jesus somberly prayed to his Father that we would all be one. He said:

> "As thou didst send me into the world, so I have sent them into the world. And for their sake I consecrate myself, that they also may be consecrated in truth. I do not pray for these only, but also for those who believe in me through their word, that they may all be one; even as thou, Father, art in me, and I in thee, that they also may be in us, so that the world may believe that thou hast sent me. The glory which thou hast given me I have given to them, that they may be one even as we are one, I in them and thou in me, that they may become perfectly one, so that the world may know that thou hast sent me and hast loved them even as thou hast loved me."   — Jn. 17:18-23

Yes, Jesus was clear about the oneness of His Church. He built his one Church on St. Peter (Mt. 16:18). He said there should be "one flock, one shepherd" (Jn. 10:16). St. Paul not only said there should be "no dissensions" (1 Cor. 1:10), but also instructed believers to avoid "those who create dissensions" (Rom. 16:17). One cannot just break off from the historic Church that has forever been in union with the pope and bishops, who are the successors of St. Peter and the other Apostles.

But clergy abuse — which was rampant at the time — can make anyone angry enough to do things they ought not do. Although Church dogma has never contained anything but truth, many Catholic clergy members were not adhering to the dogma in Luther's time, nor were they keeping their vows. The overall state of morality had deteriorated. Many priests (although certainly not all) had, unfortunately, succumbed to the worldly pursuits of pleasure and materialism.

Nevertheless, this was no grounds for abolishing the entire priesthood, which is what these Reformer guys wound up doing. Without priests, the priestly powers that came from Christ would no longer be available to the faithful in many of the new denominations. There would no longer be a place for Confession, the Anointing of the Sick, or, in some cases, the awesome gift of Christ's Body, Blood, Soul, and Divinity under the appearance of bread and wine.

What kind of doctrine would you need in order to get rid of all these things? The new cry was "salvation by faith alone."[82]

It was a Catholic priest named Luther who triggered the initial stages of the Protestant Reformation when he posted his famous 95 Theses on a church door in Wittenberg, Germany, in 1517. As we have seen, he had a legitimate concern — clergy had been abusing their powers, especially regarding the proper use of indulgences. Motivated largely by frustration over abuses and hypocrisy within Church leadership, Luther rightly emphasized dependence on God for salvation rather than on oneself.

But what started out as more of an academic exercise later led to declarations of new teachings and denials of ancient Christian doctrines such as the importance of penance, the possibility of losing grace, and so on.

Traditionally, Church authority and Scripture had worked together, but Luther came to believe that the sole authority for Christian teaching was "scripture alone" (or *Sola Scriptura,* as this belief came to be called), wherein private interpretation of scripture, rather than the Magisterium of the Church, would be the standard for individuals.

Today, most evangelical Protestant churches adhere to the doctrine of *Sola Scriptura,* as modern-day evangelical Protestant authors Norman Geisler and Ralph E. MacKenzie write:

> Scripture alone is the primary and absolute source of authority, the final court of appeal, for all doctrine and practice (faith and morals).

The authors further explain,

> The Bible alone is sufficiently clear that no infallible teaching magisterium of the church is necessary to interpret it.[83]

A Catholic might well respond that if all salvation-related truths were "sufficiently clear," as they say, then we would not have one denomination interpreting "This is my body" literally and the other interpreting it symbolically. We would not have one denomination interpreting the "mortal" sin of 1 Jn. 5:16 as "sin causing spiritual death" and another interpreting it as "sin causing physical death." We would not see denominations clashing over the meaning of that Bible's teaching that Baptism "saves you" (1 Pet. 3:21). One could list many other examples. (It's interesting to note that, although most evangelical Protestant churches today ascribe to *Sola Scriptura* as a doctrine, they differ with Luther's Biblical interpretations in many different ways.)

Curiously enough, although a "Sola Scripturist" does not subject himself to an infallible teaching Magisterium, he has no problem turning to sources outside the Bible — such as early Christian writings, texts on early Greek, or published books of his minister — to assist him in understanding the Bible. But, in the end, the individual is the one who decides definitively what Scripture teaches.

Of course, if after all that study and prayer the individual decides Scripture contains one or two Catholic doctrines, this may cause problems for him when he tries to join the church of his choice!

But from the start of Christianity, only the Catholic Church was regarded as possessing the gift of preserving Sacred Tradition. In 360 A.D., St. Athanasius wrote:

> Let us note that the very tradition, teaching, and faith of the Catholic Church from the beginning, which the Lord gave, was preached by the Apostles, and was preserved by the Fathers. On this was the Church founded; and if anyone departs from this, he neither is nor any longer ought to be called a Christian. . . .
> — St. Athanasius, *Four Letters to Serapion of Thmuis* 1, 28

Even earlier, around 230 A.D., Origen wrote:

> The teaching of the Church has indeed been handed down through an order of succession from the Apostles, and remains in the Churches even to the present time. That alone is to be believed as the truth which is in no way at variance with ecclesiastical and apostolic tradition.
> — *Fundamental Doctrines 1*, preface 2

The New Testament warns us to "hold to the traditions which you were taught by us, either by word of mouth or by letter" (2 Thess. 2:15), and even to shun those who are not living "in accord with the tradition that you received from us" (2 Thess. 3:6).

In fact, no Church Father denied that the Church put in motion by Jesus was the one led by St. Peter's successors. Author Stephen K. Ray writes:

> The earliest records tell us that the Apostles themselves set the doctrine of apostolic succession in motion (I Clem. 44). Even William Webster, who has made a career of refuting the Papacy, admits that no father denies that Peter had a primacy or that there is Petrine succession. Denial of apostolic succession is of recent origin. If apostolic succession were a false teaching, or contrary to the teachings of Christ and his Apostles, orthodox

writers would have opposed it ferociously from the beginning, as they did all other doctrinal deviations and heresies.[84]

To his credit, Luther was certainly aware of the early doctrines and of the miraculous origin of the one true Church. Even more than a year after posting his 95 Theses, he still opposed breaking with the Catholic Church. In 1519, he wrote:

> I never approved of a schism, nor will I approve of it for all eternity. . . . That the Roman Church is more honored by God than all others is not to be doubted. St. Peter and St. Paul, forty-six Popes, some hundreds of thousands of martyrs, have laid down their lives in its communion, having overcome Hell and the world; so that the eyes of God rest on the Roman church with special favor. Though nowadays everything is in a wretched state, it is no ground for separating from the Church.[85]

But later, his attitude changed. Luther — excommunicated by the Catholic Church in 1520 — and the other Reformers would cause rifts in Christianity that would not be reversed even by the millennium's next turn.

As we have seen, Luther's most famous theory was his doctrine of justification[86] by "faith alone," which held that a saving faith did not include love or obedience, although those things would follow. To make his point, he added the word "alone" to the Bible after the word "faith" in St. Paul's letter to the Romans (Rom. 3:28) when he translated Scripture into German. When people questioned this addition, Luther responded, "Luther will have it so, and he is a doctor above all the doctors in Popedom."[87]

When taken to its logical conclusion, Luther's doctrine led to a rejection of penance, asceticism, Purgatory (although Luther personally wavered on this one), and the Church's historic emphasis on radical commitment to good works. In fact, Luther even hinted that good works could be more dangerous to a person than sin!

> Those pious souls who do good to gain the Kingdom of Heaven not only will never succeed, but they must even be reckoned among the impious; and it is more important to guard them against good works than against sin.[88]

Now, while Catholics would not try to guard a person against good works, they would agree with Luther that nobody can "do something" to get grace, since it is freely offered to us, undeservedly, by God. In fact, the Catholic Church had always universally held this teaching, despite the practices of some Church leaders who were undermining the doctrine.

Traditionally, the main ways for Christians to receive grace after Baptism would include participating in the Mass, receiving the real Jesus in Communion, and confessing sins to a priest. By the powers that Christ invested in His priests through ordinations connecting back to the Apostles, Christ's own grace was poured out through the sacraments.

Then came Calvin.

Two decades after Luther's posting on the church door, a twenty-six-year-old Frenchman named John Calvin came out with a book called the *Institutes of the Christian Religion* (or the *Institutes*), which ostensibly summarized the Christian faith — but which, curiously, left out a whole list of core doctrines that had historically been part of Christianity. Calvin instead inserted some new points of theology that had never been part of the faith. In the words of historian Hilaire Belloc, Calvin's famous work presented "a system which explained in a full and worked-out philosophy how one might be rid of the Priest."[89]

First published in 1536, the famous work also spread Calvin's formula of predestination, which holds that God does not consider one's personal choices before damning a person to Hell. According to Calvin, Christ died only for a certain group of people, dooming the others to Hell without having looked ahead at their sins, good works, or cooperation with God's grace, but rather used only His own hidden divine will. Calvin's doctrine is contained within the *Westminster Confession of Faith*[90], which is commonly used by Presbyterian and certain other churches in the Reformed tradition.

Catholics and Calvinists do agree that only works prompted by grace in us — and not works of human origin or self-interest — pave a path to God. But Catholics believe in infused grace, where God actually transforms us internally, whereas Calvinists believe in imputed grace, where God covers us legally with his righteousness without truly transforming our souls from the inside. Once a person is in grace, a Catholic would say, the more good works the person does, the better! All grace-driven works help accomplish God's work in the world and can help save souls. Catholics believe that the more we cooperate with grace, the greater number of souls will be brought to the infinite lake of saving grace won by Jesus. No work done in Christ is done in vain, as the Bible tells us: " . . . in the Lord your labor is not in vain" (1 Cor. 15:58).

On predestination, the Catholic Church holds that God did look at the states of our souls at the ends of our lives prior to making a space for each person in Heaven or Hell from the beginning.[91] Calvinists[92] believe God made salvation available only to some people. Catholics believe that by dying and rising, Christ made salvation available to all people.

According to the Bible, God "desires all men to be saved and to come to the knowledge of the truth" (1 Tim. 2:24).

Of course, God never forces people into salvation, and He knew from the start which people would reject the free gift made available to them.

The Catholic Church would also disagree with Calvin's conclusion in the *Institutes* that the first sin — the sin of Adam — was predestined by God. Our Church teaches that Adam could have avoided that sin, and that things could have turned out much differently for the future of the world.

But Calvin wrote: "For the first man fell because the Lord had judged it to be expedient; why he so judged is hidden from us."[93]

Without going into more specific detail on the particulars, then, suffice to say the theologies laid out by different Reformers were not in alignment with one another. The followers of Calvin could not completely agree with the followers of Zwingli or Luther or the other men who came on the scene, all of whom favored private interpretation of Scripture. The chaotic state of affairs that resulted was perturbing even for Luther, who wrote, in his letter against Zwingli, that to preserve the unity of the faith, it would eventually be necessary to return to the decrees of the Church Councils due to the many interpretations being given to the Scriptures.[94] (This obviously contradicts other writings in which Luther argues instead that Scripture was self-interpreting, and that no other authority was needed.)

When the dust settled, the Reformed movement resulted in the expulsion of priests, the seizing of Catholic Church property, the destruction of religious art and relics, and the closing of Catholic schools.

And, of course, not just one but numerous schisms.

In 1534, King Henry VIII declared that he was the supreme head of the church in England rather than the pope, thus breaking his country off from the unity of Rome. The action was motivated by the pope's refusal to grant a divorce to Henry, who had wanted to divorce his wife, Catherine of Aragon, and marry Ann Boleyn. Eventually, Anglicanism was established in England, and led to the Episcopalian denomination in the United States.

Additional religious communities, such as the Anabaptists, the Schwenkfeldians, the Socinians, the Mennonites, and the Congregationalists, were founded in the sixteenth century. A Scottish Protestant named John Knox started the Presbyterians in 1560; the Baptists got their start with John Smyth in the very early 1600s; and George Fox, who had been raised in the Anglican Church, triggered the Quaker movement in England in 1647. An Anglican named John Wesley formed the Methodists in 1729. Chuck Smith founded Calvary Chapel in 1965.

Because each Reformer interpreted the Bible differently than the next, the array of Protestant denominations hold a host of conflicting views. For example, Lutherans believe the Body and Blood of Jesus are truly present in the Eucharist, whereas Baptists and fundamentalists do not. Most Protestants christen their babies; Baptists reject infant baptism. Calvinists believe God does not look at a person's choices before predestining a soul to Hell, whereas Methodists (and other adherents to Arminianism) reject absolute predestination. Most Christians believe it possible to lose one's salvation; Baptists and Presbyterians regard it impossible.

Meanwhile, reacting to liberalizing trends within Protestantism, the Fundamentalist movement started to show itself in the late 1800s, and got its name in the early 1900s when men at Princeton Theological Seminary in Princeton wrote a series of books called *The Fundamentals*.[95] Later, in the twentieth century, non-denominational churches appeared, upholding similar Protestant tenets of theology.

Along with diverse religions springing up within Christianity came other ideas of worship — churches that range from slightly to glaringly off the beaten path from mainstream Christianity:

Mormons: The Mormons, whose worldwide center is Salt Lake City in Utah, are members of the Church of Jesus Christ of Latter-day Saints (LDS). Mormonism was founded in the 1820s by prophet Joseph Smith, who claimed to have been visited by an angel who led him to golden plates engraved in a strange language, which Smith translated into what became the Book of Mormon. Mormons believe that the true Christian faith had disappeared — they often mention the "Great Apostasy" — and Smith was chosen to restore it. Mormons, known for their practice of baptizing the dead, reject the Trinity and a number of other Christian doctrines. Among the more obscure teachings of the religion are: God, who they call the Heavenly Father, has a physical body and lives on a planet near the star Kolob; God had a wife with whom he procreated Jesus Christ; and faithful Mormons can transform into a God in the next world.

Unitarians: Unitarianism is not technically a religion, since it adheres to no formal creed; nor is it technically Christian, since members generally deny that Jesus is God. Unitarians, who have their roots in liberal Protestantism, reject the Trinity, worshipping instead a Uni-personal God. (The title *Unitarian* may have tipped you off that the group distances itself from *Trinitarianism*). Members of Unitarian churches read from the Bible, but do not regard Scripture to be of divine origin. Jesus is regarded as a moral teacher, service to humanity is emphasized, and varying theological views are permitted. There is no specific belief in an afterlife, but one is free to believe in one. According to the official Unitarian Universalist Association, "Classically, Unitarian Universalist Christians have understood Jesus as a savior because he was a God-filled human being, not a supernatural being." The official web site also states that at a Unitarian Universalist worship meeting, "you are likely to find members whose positions on faith may be derived from a variety of religious beliefs: Jewish, Christian, Buddhist, naturist, atheist, or agnostic."

Unitarians often cite a sixteenth-century Spaniard named Miguel Servetus as one of the first Unitarians. Servetus, a Catholic physician and heretic who denied the Christian doctrine of the Trinity, was burned at the stake in Geneva after Protestant Reformer John Calvin charged him with numerous counts of heresy.

Christian Scientists: Often in the news for its members' refusal of traditional medical care, Christian Science is a prayer-based system of healing developed by Mary Baker Eddy, who founded this anti-Trinitarian religion in 1879. The religion, whose pillar church is located in Boston, is known for its many "Reading Rooms" where members go to study the works of Eddy, and to develop their spirituality. The author of Science and Health with Key to the Scriptures, Eddy believed that bodily perfection increased as people drew closer to God, and that illnesses were due to separation from and misperceptions of God. In 2002, the church opened a $50 million building called the Mary Baker Eddy Library for the Betterment of Humanity. Eddy, who believed that illness and death were more of an illusion than anything based in reality, died in 1910.

Jehovah's Witnesses: These members of the Watch Tower Bible and Tract Society reject the divinity of Christ, believing instead that Jesus was Michael the Archangel, became a human being on earth, and did not rise physically, but rather only as a spirit. Founded in the late 1800s, they oppose blood transfusions and the celebration of birthdays and many other holidays. They believe only 144,000 people are going to heaven, and that upon death, our souls are destroyed and will not materialize again until the end of the world. Jehovah's Witnesses are expected to spend long hours in door-to-door evangelizing and distributing literature. The sweetest old woman accompanied by a most polite man in a suit from the local Kingdom Hall came to my own door. Hearing that I was Catholic, the man told me that the term "Roman Catholic" did not appear until some late century. I told him that my church, officially called the "Catholic Church," had its name even around the turn of the first century, and that Roman just means it's based in Rome. He looked at his watch, and suddenly realized he and the woman were late for something. I offered the woman some literature for the road, but she smiled and replied I would have to come to her house for that sort of thing.

Scientologists: The Church of Scientology has no connection to Christianity at all, but it has gotten its share of press recently. Founded in the 1950s by science fiction writer L. Ron Hubbard, Scientology is the religion of Tom Cruise, John Travolta, and Kirstie Alley. The religion affirms the existence of a Supreme Being and opposes many psychiatric drugs, and, generally, the medical field of psychiatry. In 2005, movie star Tom Cruise came under fire for publicly criticizing the use of anti-depressant drugs used by Brooke Shields, who had suffered from postpartum depression.

Scientology is known for its intense counseling sessions and emphasis on self-help and career success. Hubbard, the founder, developed a self-help technique called Dianetics, which was designed to relieve physical, mental, and emotional problems. Machines he invented called E-meters, or electropsychometers, continue to be used on new Scientologists to test stress levels and identify problem points by sending tiny electrical charges through people. "Auditing" sessions are designed to erase or "clear" packets of negativity called "engrams," supposedly generated in the mind by past traumatic events. Critics say newcomers to Scientology get hooked by taking inexpensive sessions, but later face more exorbitant costs as they progress through the various levels of Scientology and its accompanying therapy sessions.

One of the religion's more unique beliefs is one that a galactic warlord named Xenu transported frozen people by spaceships to volcanoes on earth to help alleviate overpopulation problems on other planets. Xenu then dropped a hydrogen bomb, killing the people, whose troubled souls still invade people's bodies today.

The official Scientology web site (www.scientology.org) specifically states that the religion is not a cult. Many other organizations (such as www.xenu.net) vehemently disagree, saying the group is a dangerous, mind-controlling organization designed to drain its members' bank accounts while harassing and intimidating its critics. I had planned to see what the Cult Awareness Network had to say about

Scientology, but then I learned that followers of Scientology had taken over the once-neutral network.

Scientology keeps many of its teachings secret, claiming that use of its religious texts would amount to copyright or trademark infringements, and has aggressively pursued legal action against newspapers and former Scientology members who have published excerpts from the church's texts.

The Moonies. These members of the Unification Church — widely regarded as a cult — get their name from their Korean-born leader, Rev. Sun Myung Moon, a controversial figure who has claimed he is the new Messiah. The aging Moon is perhaps best known for presiding at mass weddings in which hundreds of couples are married after being personally matched by Moon, with the help of photographs and biographical forms.

Born in 1920, Moon was an ousted Presbyterian minister when he founded the group in Korea in 1954 and came to the United States in 1971. According to the church's theology, Jesus died not because He came into the world with that precise mission, but because he failed to unite the Jews to follow Him.

Here are two of the more bizarre incidents involving Moon this decade.

- In July of 2002, Moon published full-page ads in the *Los Angeles Times, Philadelphia Inquirer,* and other major city newspapers throughout the country, publicizing a meeting in the spirit world that had taken place, during which a long line of historical figures had hailed Moon as the Messiah and the "Second Coming." The meeting's guest list included U.S. presidents, Jesus, Mohammed, Confucius, Buddha, Martin Luther, and John Harvard, who was the founder of Harvard University (the alma mater of the religious leader's son, Justin Moon). According to the ad, those who attended the meeting unanimously proclaimed Moon "the Savior, Messiah, and King of Kings of all of humanity."
- On March 23, 2004, Moon declared himself Savior and Messiah of humanity and was crowned at a ceremony attended by

at least a dozen Congress members at a federal office building in Washington D.C. After Rep. Danny K. Davis of Illinois placed an ornate crown on Moon's head, the maroon-robed Moon declared himself to be "God's ambassador, sent to earth with his full authority. I am sent to accomplish his command to save the world's six billion people, restoring them to heaven. . . ."

The event took place at the Dirksen Senate Office Building, where Moon also announced that he had helped Hitler, Stalin, Marx, and Lenin mend their ways in order to be "reborn as new persons." The event had been advertised as a dinner to honor world peace activists. Moon, whose son Justin launched a gun company, promotes peace and family values as missions of his church. The story of the "coronation," first broken by Salon.com writer John Gorenfeld, later appeared in the *Washington Post* and other major publications.

As head of the Unification Church, Moon ultimately aims to unite all the religions of the world into one unified entity under him; he once went on a traveling campaign to urge the removal of crosses from Christian churches. As part of his strategy to control public opinion and policy, Moon, a billionaire, has acquired numerous media outlets around the globe and has handed over large sums of money to influential people.

Over the years, Moon's generous donations have funded causes ranging from Jerry Falwell's Liberty University to former president George H.W. Bush's presidential library. Moon and his publishing company, New World Communications, Inc., own the conservative-leaning *Washington Times, Insight* magazine, *World Peace Herald* and UPI wire service, acquired by New World in 2000. The owner of countless properties and businesses around the world, Moon purchased 138,000 acres in southern Brazil in the late 1990s to form a community of followers called "New Hope," according to a report by Reuters.

Meanwhile, back in sixteenth-century mainstream Christianity . . .

The Catholic Reformers, who had been just as concerned as the Protestant Reformers about clergy abuses in the Church, worked hard to cleanse and reinvigorate the Catholic Church. They succeeded. The Church remained intact, as Jesus promised it would.

Although efforts to reform the Church in some regions had emerged even before the Protestant Reformation, historians often designate the period of Catholic renewal between 1560 and 1648 as the "Counter-Reformation." During this time, virtuous Catholic reformers such as St. Ignatius of Loyola, St. Philip Neri, and St. Vincent de Paul set out to imitate Christ as closely as possible. Saintly men and women such as St. Peter of Alcántara, St. Teresa of Ávila, St. Robert Bellarmine, St. John of the Cross, and Abbott García de Cisneros restored the true spirit of Christ to religious orders such as the Franciscans, Carmelites, and Benedictines. Wonderful reform-minded popes, such as St. Pius V, Gregory XIII, and Sixtus V helped restore the glory of apostolic Church and its true mission.

Today, 1.07 billion of the world's 2 billion Christians are Catholic. As Europe was suffering tragic divisions, the Blessed Mother appeared in Mexico in 1531, assuring the growth of the Church on two continents. Today, between the northern boundaries of Canada and the southern tips of Chile and Argentina, about 63 percent of the human population is Catholic, according to the pontifical yearbook *Annuario Pontificio,* released in 2003.

And what about prospects for future Christian unity? Many are working hard to iron out misunderstandings and ancient feuds. In 1999, the Catholic Church and the Lutheran World Federation signed a historic agreement called the Joint Declaration of Justification, highlighting their common beliefs. Although differences remain, the gap between the two views on salvation turned out to be smaller than many had believed. The document cleared up misunderstandings stemming from the two groups' emphasis on different aspects of justification and use of the same words to convey different meanings.

Pope John Paul II, who took great joy in the reaching of the agreement, has even called Luther a "man of profound religiousness" and had high regard for Luther's "original intention" of reform. According to the late pope:

Luther's thinking was characterized by considerable emphasis on the individual, which meant that the awareness of the requirements of society became weaker. Luther's original intention in his call for reform in the Church was a call to repentance and renewal to begin in the life of every individual. There are many reasons why these beginnings nevertheless led to division. One is the failure of the Catholic Church . . . and the intrusion of political and economic interest, as well as Luther's own passion, which drove him far beyond what he originally intended into radical criticism of the Catholic Church, of its way of teaching. We all bear the guilt. That is why we are called upon to repent and must all allow the Lord to cleanse us over and over.[96]

In heeding Christ's cry for us to be one (Jn. 17:11, 21-22), Pope John Paul II urged Catholic, Orthodox, and Protestant Christians to charitably question each other, explain to each other, and genuinely try to understand where the other is coming from.

Upon the death of Pope John Paul II on April 2, 2005, the Lutheran World Federation immediately released a statement saying that his demise marked "the end not only of a truly remarkable human life but also of a highly significant pontificate of the Roman Catholic Church at a crucial stage of human history."

Even the Church of England, which has not been in union with Rome since 1534, has been making news of interest. In 2004, the General Synod of the Anglican Church put on the table a discussion over whether to again recognize the pope as "universal primate," as part of an arrangement that would have still allowed England certain legislative freedoms. Although that particular discussion has not yet led to tangible results, in 2005, Catholics and Anglicans reached an agreement on the Blessed Mother; both acknowledged that honoring the Virgin Mary and seeking her help were worthy practices. According to the 2005 statement by Anglican-Roman Catholic International Commission, "We believe there is no continuing theological reason for ecclesial division on these matters."

A reunion with the Eastern Orthodox Churches (which have always honored Mary) seems to hold much promise, as these churches are so doctrinally similar to the Catholic Church. Since breaking off from union with Rome in the eleventh century, the Orthodox Churches have laudably maintained the ancient apostolic teachings not only of the Sacrifice of the Mass, but of all seven sacraments. The sacraments of these Orthodox churches are valid because — like the Catholic Church — they have also maintained the apostolic lines of ordination for their bishops and priests. In other words, they share in the powers of the universal priesthood because the ordinations of their priests have always been in an unbroken succession going back to the College of Apostles, and thus to Christ.

Many of God's truths, and much of God's saving work, can be found in Christian chapels outside the Catholic Church. But only when one takes the leap into the Catholic Church, which contains the fullness of Christian truth, has one gone all the way. Many non-Catholic Christians don't even realize that one of their favorite Christians in history — St. Augustine — was horrified at the very thought of leaving the Catholic Church.

> Whoever is separated from this Catholic Church, by this single sin of being separated from the unity of Christ, no matter how estimable a life he may imagine he is living, shall not have life, but the wrath of God rests upon him.
> — St. Augustine, *Letters,* 141:5 (412 A.D.)

Many of these same Christians do not realize that St. Augustine — whom they regard as perhaps the greatest figure in Christianity after the Apostles — considered membership in the Catholic Church to be the most basic doctrine of Christianity.

> A man cannot have salvation, except in the Catholic Church. Outside the Catholic Church he can have everything except salvation. He can have honor, he can have Sacraments, he can sing alleluia, he can answer amen, he can possess the gospel, he can have and preach faith in the name of the Father and of the Son and of the Holy Spirit; but never except in the Catholic Church will he be able to find salvation.
> — St. Augustine, *Discourse to the People of the Church at Caesarea,* Chapter 6 (418 A.D.)

It comes as a surprise to some Christians that St. Augustine considered the Catholic Church to possess "the crown of teaching authority" (*The Advantage of Believing* 35, 392 A.D.).

Some do not realize that the Church was founded on the Chair of Peter, much less that their own churches have deserted this Chair. In 251 A.D., St. Cyprian wrote:

> If someone does not hold fast to this unity of Peter, can he imagine that he still holds the faith? If he [should] desert the chair of Peter upon whom the Church was built, can he still be confident that he is in the Church?
> — St. Cyprian of Carthage, *The Unity of the Catholic Church 4*; 1st edition (251 A.D.)

The Catholic Church's ecumenism decree, *Unitatis Redintegratio*, reminds us: "The restoration of unity among all Christians is one of the principal concerns of the Second Vatican Council. Christ the Lord founded one Church and one Church only."

This unity is celebrated in its full glory at the Catholic Mass. It is that same Sacrifice on Calvary that becomes present to us as an eternal source of grace and salvation, no matter where we are. It is the same whether we worship at a Mass in Paris or Prague, in the Western Sahara or Baghdad.

As a matter of fact, in Iraq, it is a mind-boggling fact that some Catholic Masses are still said in Aramaic, the native language of Jesus. Present-day Iraq was home not only to some of the first Christians (and now, to descendants of the first Christians), but also to Mesopotamia, the region that contained the ancient city of Ur, where Abraham was born 4,000 years ago.

Today, the same prayers, and even the same Scripture passages, are read at most Catholic Churches around the world on the same day. It is the same Christ that comes into us when we receive Communion. We become one with Christ's Body and, therefore, one with all other receivers of Christ around the globe. The Mass of all ages also unites us to our brethren in Heaven.

In his first few days of being pope, Pope Benedict XVI said he was prepared to give everything he has to reach out to other religious communities. He said his "primary task" would be "that of working

"So there shall be one flock, one shepherd."
— Jn. 10:16

"The glory which thou hast given me I have given to them, that they may be one even as we are one, I in them and thou in me, that they may become perfectly one."
— Jn. 17:20-23

St. Paul urged disciples to ". . . maintain the unity of the Spirit in the bond of peace. There is one body and one Spirit, just as you were called to the one hope that belongs to your call, one Lord, one faith, one baptism."
— Eph. 4:3-5

St. Paul also urged ". . . that all of you agree and that there be no dissensions among you, but that you be united in the same mind and the same judgment" (1 Cor. 1:10), advised his disciples to avoid "those who create dissensions" (Rom. 16:17), and requested that his followers "complete my joy by being of the same mind, having the same love, being in full accord and of one mind."
— Phil. 2:2

Also see: Rom. 15:5, 1 Cor. 12:13, Jn. 17:17-23, and Col. 3:15.

— sparing no energies — to reconstitute the full and visible unity of all Christ's followers."

Fr. Thomas Richstatter, a priest and Franciscan friar in Indiana, envisions the day when the beauty and diversity of all the world's Christians will shine through at the Eucharistic table.

The transcendent splendor of Orthodox liturgies; the reverence and ecumenical zeal of the Churches of the Anglican Communion; the gratitude for God's free grace and the

Lutheran Church's contributions to liturgy through music; the missionary spirit of the Baptist Churches; the Disciples of Christ's dedication to Church unity; the call to social responsibility proclaimed by the United Methodist Church; the confidence in God's faithfulness as witnessed to by the Presbyterian and Reform Churches — these rich gifts which God has given to each of the Churches are to be preserved and developed until the day we weave them together in a wonderful tapestry to be placed on the table when "many will come from the east and the west, and will recline with Abraham, Isaac and Jacob at the banquet in the kingdom of heaven" (Mt. 8:1).[97]

SELECTED BIBLIOGRAPHY

✝

Akin, James. *The Salvation Controversy.* El Cajon, CA.: Catholic Answers, 2001.

———. "The Successors of the Apostles." *This Rock.* El Cajon, CA.: Catholic Answers, July-August 2001.

St. Ambrose of Milan. *Commentary on Psalm 118.* 387 A.D.

———. *The Mysteries.* 390 A.D.

———. *de Poenit.*

Aquilina, Mike. *The Mass of the Early Christians.* Huntington, IN: Our Sunday Visitor Books, 2001.

Aquinas, St. Thomas. *Summa Theologica.*

Armstrong, Dave. "Luther vs. the Canon of the Bible." Oct. 5, 1998. (http://ic.net/~erasmus/RAZ325.HTM)

St. Athanasius. *Four Letters to Serapion of Thmuis.* 360 A.D

St. Augustine. *The Advantage of Believing.* 392 A.D.

———. *Against the Letter of Mani Called "The Foundation."* 397 A.D.

———. *Baptism.* 400 A.D.

———. *The Care to Be Had for the Dead.* 421 A.D.

———. *The City of God.* 413-426 A.D.

———. Bishop of Hippo. *Confessions.* 397 A.D.

———. *De agon. Christ.* 430 A.D.

———. *Discourse to the People of the Church at Caesarea.* 418 A.D.

———. *Explanations of the Psalms.* 405 A.D.

———. *The Gift of Perseverance.* 428 A.D.

———. *Letters.* 412 A.D.

———. *Nature and Grace.* 415 A.D.

———. *Sermon to Catechumens on the Creed.* 395 A.D.

———. *Sermons,* 227. 411 A.D.

———. *Sermons,* 352. 411 A.D.

Baldwin, Lou. *Saint Katharine Drexel: Apostle of the Oppressed.* Philadelphia, PA: Catholic Standard & Times, 2000.

St. Barnabas. *Epistle of St. Barnabas.* C. 70-130 A.D.

St. Basil the Great. *Rules Briefly Treated*, 288. 374 A.D.

Belloc, Hilaire. *How the Reformation Happened*. Rockford, IL: Tan Books and Publishers, Inc., c. 1929.

Bennett, Rod. *Four Witnesses: The Early Church in Her Own Words*. San Francisco, CA: Ignatius Press, 2000.

Butler, Scott, Norman Dahlgren, and David Hess. *Jesus, Peter & the Keys*. Santa Barbara, CA: Queenship Publishing Co., 1996.

Calvin, John. *Institutes of the Christian Religion*, ed. John T. McNeill, trans. F.L. Battles. Philadelphia: Westminster Press, 4th printing, 1967.

Catechism of the Catholic Church. New York, NY: Doubleday, 1995.

St. Catherine of Genoa. *Treatise on Purgatory*.

Cates, JR, Herndon, NL, Schulz, SL, & Darroch, JE. "Our Voices, Our Lives, Our Futures: Youth and Sexually Transmitted Diseases." Chapel Hill, NC: School of Journalism and Mass Communication, University of North Carolina at Chapel Hill, 2004.

Catholic Answers, Inc. (www.catholic.com)

Catholic Encyclopedia, The. New York, NY: Robert Appleton Company, 1907.

Carty, Rev. Charles Mortimer. *Padre Pio: The Stigmatist*. Rockford, IL: TAN Books, 1999.

Chacon, Fr. Frank and Jim Burnham. *Beginning Apologetics 6: How to Explain and Defend Mary*. Farmington, NM: San Juan Catholic Seminars, 2001.

———. *Beginning Apologetics 5: How to Answer Tough Moral Questions — Abortion, Contraception, Euthanasia, Test-Tube Babies, Cloning, & Sexual Ethics*. Farmington. NM: San Juan Catholic Seminars, 2000.

———. *Beginning Apologetics 3: How to Explain and Defend the Real Presence of Christ in the Eucharist*. Farmington, NM: San Juan Catholic Seminars, 1999.

———. *Beginning Apologetics: How to Explain and Defend the Catholic Faith*. Farmington, NM: San Juan Catholic Seminars, 1993-1996.

Chapin, John, ed. *A Treasury of Catholic Reading*. New York: Farrar, Straus & Cudahy, 1957.

Chesterton, G. K. *The Catholic Church and Conversion.* New York: MacMillan & Co., 1926 (www.dur.ac.uk/martin.ward/gkc/books/conversion.txt).

———. *Orthodoxy.* New York: Doubleday, 2001 (orig. 1908).

St. John Chrysostom. *Homilies on 1 Corinthians.* 392 A.D.

———. Homily "On Frequent Assembly" in *P.G.,* LXIII, 463 A.D.

———. *The Priesthood.* 387 A.D.

St. Clement of Alexandria. *The Instructor of Children.* 195 A.D.

———. *Miscellanies.* 208 A.D.

St. Clement of Rome. *Letter to the Corinthians.* 80 A.D.

St. Cyprian of Carthage. *Catechetical Lectures.* 350 A.D.

———. *The Lapsed, 28.* 251 A.D.

———. *Letters 1-69.* 253 A.D.

———. *The Unity of the Catholic Church.* 251 A.D.

St. Francis de Sales. *The Catholic Controversy.* Trans. Henry B. Mackey. Rockford, IL.: TAN Books. 1989 printing (orig. 1596).

Doherty, Msgr. John T. "A New York Story." *The Catholic New York* (April 7, 1998).

The *Didache.* 70 A.D.

Eusebius. *The History of the Church from Christ to Constantine.* Trans. G.A. Williamson. London: Penguin Books, 1988.

Geisler, Norman L. and Ralph E. MacKenzie. *Roman Catholics and Evangelicals: Agreements and Differences.* Grand Rapids, MI: Baker Books, 1995.

Graham, Henry G. *Where We Got the Bible: Our Debt to the Catholic Church.* El Cajon, CA: Catholic Answers Inc., 1997.

Hahn, Scott. *The Lamb's Supper: The Mass as Heaven on earth.* New York, NY: Doubleday, 1999.

Hebert, Rev. Albert J. *Raised from the Dead: True Stories of 400 Resurrection Miracles.* Rockford, IL: TAN Books, 1986.

Hippolytus of Rome. *Refutation of All Heresies.* 255 A.D.

Howell, Kenneth J. "The Crisis of Authority in the Reformation." *Coming Home Journal* (www.chnetwork.org/journals/authority/authority_4.htm).

St. Ignatius of Antioch. *Letter to the Romans.* 110 A.D.

———. *Letter to the Ephesians.* 110 A.D.

———. *Letter of Ignatius to the Trallians.* 107 A.D.

————. *Letter to the Smyraeans*. 110 A.D.

St. Irenaeus. *Against Heresies*. 189 A.D.

Jaki, The Rev. Stanley L. "Two Lourdes Miracles and a Nobel Laureate: What Really Happened?" Catholic Medical Association, Sept. 13, 1998.

St. Jerome. *Against Jovinian*. C. 393 A.D.

————. *Letter to Pammachius* (Letter XLVIII). 393 or 394 A.D.

Joint Declaration on the Doctrine of Justification, by the Lutheran World Federation and the Catholic Church (www.ewtn.com/library/CURIA/pccujnt4.htm).

Jurgens, William A. *The Faith of the Fathers*. Collegeville, MN: The Liturgical Press, 1979.

St. Justin Martyr. *First Apology*. c. 150 A.D.

Keating, Karl. *Catholicism and Fundamentalism*. San Francisco, CA: Ignatius Press, 1997.

Kelly, J.N.D. *Early Christian Doctrines*. San Francisco, CA: HarperCollins, 1978.

Lewis, C.S. *Mere Christianity*. HarperCollins Edition, Harper Collins Publishers, New York, NY, 2001 (First copyright 1952).

Liguori, St. Alphonsus. *What Will Hell Be Like?* Rockford, IL: Tan Books & Publishers Inc., 1988.

Luther, Martin. *Epistle against Zwingli*.

————. *On the Day of the Conception of the Mother of God*. 1527 A.D.

Madrid, Patrick. *Where is That in the Bible?* Huntington, IN: Our Sunday Visitor, 2001.

Martino, Archbishop Renato, *Address to the U.N. International Convention Against the Reproductive Cloning of Human Beings,* Nov. 19, 2001(www.vatican.va/roman_curia/secretariat_state/documents/rc_segst_doc_20011119_martino-vi-comm_en.html).

Fr. Mateo. *Refuting the Attack on Mary*. San Diego, CA: Catholic Answers, 1999.

Most, Rev. William G. *Catholic Apologetics Today*. Rockford, IL: TAN Books, 1986.

O'Hare, Patrick. *The Facts About Luther*. Rockford, IL: TAN Books, 1987.

Origen. *Fundamental Doctrines 1*. 230 A.D.

Orlando, José. *A Short History of the Catholic Church*. Dublin, Ireland: Four Courts Press, 1993.

Pillar of Fire, Pillar of Truth. San Diego, CA: Catholic Answers, 1996.

Ray, Stephen K. *Upon This Rock: St. Peter and the Primacy of Rome in Scripture and the Early Church*. San Francisco, CA: Ignatius Press, 1999.

Rengers, Rev. Christopher, O.F.M. Cap. *The 33 Doctors of the Church*. Rockford, IL: TAN Books, 2000.

Ruffin, C. Bernard. *Padre Pio: The True Story*. Huntington, IN: Our Sunday Visitor, 1991.

Fr. F.X. Schouppe S.J. *The Dogma of Hell*. Rockford, IL: Tan Books and Publishers, 1989.

The Shepherd of Hermas. 140-155 A.D.

Stravinskas, Rev. Peter. "The Place of Mary in Classical Fundamentalism." *Faith & Reason*; Summer, 1994 www.ewtn.com/library/ANSWERS/FR94101.htm (Date of access: 6 April 2005).

Strobel, Lee. *The Case for a Creator*. Grand Rapids, MI: Zondervan, 2004.

The *Summa Theologica* of St. Thomas Aquinas; Second and Revised Edition, 1920, Literally translated by Fathers of the English Dominican Province. Online Edition, Copyright © 2003 by Kevin Knight.

Sungenis, Robert. *"Have you not Read?" The Authority Behind Biblical Interpretation* (www.chnetwork.org/journals/authority/authority_5.htm).

Tertullian. *The Crown*. 211 A.D.

Theophilus of Antioch. *To Autolycus*. 181 A.D.

Thompson, Bard. *Humanists and Reformers: A History of the Renaissance and Reformation*. Grand Rapids, MI: William B. Eerdmans Publishing Co., 1996.

Unitatis Redintegratio (Decree on Ecumenism), Second Vatican Council.

Van Zeller, Dom Hubert. *Suffering: The Catholic Answer: The Cross of Christ and Its Meaning for You*. Manchester, NH: Sophia Institute Press, 2002 edition.

West, Christopher. *Theology of the Body for Beginners*. West Chester, PA: Ascension Press, 2004.

Whitehead, Kenneth D. *One Holy Catholic and Apostolic*. San Francisco, CA: Ignatius Press 2000.

The Westminster Confession of Faith.

Works of Martin Luther. Philadelphia: Muhlenberg Press, copyrighted by the United Lutheran Church in America, translation C.M. Jacobs, 1932.

World Christian Encyclopedia. Oxford, England: Oxford University Press, 2001.

Quotes from the Early Church Fathers were taken from *The Faith of the Early Fathers* (William A. Jurgens), *Catholic Encyclopedia*, the *Catechism of the Catholic Church* and the Web site of Catholic Answers, Inc. (www.catholic.com).

WANT MORE?

✝

For the convenience of parish education classes and group Bible studies, a chapter-by-chapter study guide has been provided at *www.stillcatholic.com/GUIDE.htm.* The online guide includes Scriptural citations, quotes from Church Fathers, review questions, lists of related resources for further reading, and topics for reflection.

NOTES

✝

[1] The *Seven Storey Mountain* is the 1948 autobiography and spiritual conversion story of Thomas Merton, who abandoned his promising literary career to become a Trappist monk. Matthew Lickona's *Swimming with Scapulars* (2005) contains the reflections and confessions of one Catholic soul in modern-day southern California.

[2] In John 1:42, Jesus said to him "So you are Simon the son of John? You shall be called Cephas." Later, as recorded in Mt 16:18, Jesus said to Peter "I tell you, you are Peter, and on this rock I shall build my church." Of course, in Jesus' native language of Aramaic, the word for Peter and rock was the same: ("Cephas," also transliterated "Kepha"). In the Greek translation of Matthew, the feminine noun "petra" was used for the object "rock" while the masculine noun "Petros" was used for the Apostle's name. A few recent critics of the papacy have used this play on words to suggest Jesus was contrasting Peter with, rather than identifying him as, the rock on which the church would be built. Suggestions that Jesus was really trying to call Peter a "little stone" rather than a rock are erroneous. Although "Petros" could have referred to a small stone in some ancient Greek poetry long before Christ's time, the word was a synonym of "petra" in the first century in the particular dialect of Greek (Koyne Greek) used in the New Testament. For more information on this topic, read chapter 2 of Patrick Madrid's *Pope Fiction* or p. 368 of *The Expositor's Bible Commentary* (Vol. 8) by Protestant scholar D.A. Carson. For almost 2,000 years, the Catholic Church has been led by a successor of St. Peter.

[3] Michael M. Winter. *Saint Peter and the Popes* (Baltimore, MD: Helicon, 1960): as quoted in *Jesus, Peter & the Keys: A Scriptural Handbook on the Papacy,* pp. 3-4.

[4] Catholic Answers, Inc. *Pillar of Fire, Pillar of Truth.* San Diego: Catholic Answers, 1996.

[5] Letters of Augustine 53, 2 in *The Nicene and Post-Nicene Fathers* 1st series, 1:298.

[6] Kenneth D. Whitehead, *One Holy Catholic and Apostolic* (San Francisco, CA: Ignatius Press, 2000) p. 168.

[7] James Akin, "The Successors of the Apostles." *This Rock*, July-August, 2001.

[8] *Ibid.,* Akin.

[9] Lee Strobel, *The Case for a Creator* (Grand Rapids, MI: Zondervan, 2004), p. 225

[10] Strobel, 134 .

[11] Strobel, 134.

[12] Writing in 200 A.D., Tertullian wrote: ". . .you have Rome, from which there comes even into our own hands the very authority (of Apostles themselves). How happy is its church, on which Apostles poured forth all their doctrine along with their blood! where Peter endures a passion like his Lord's! where Paul wins his crown in a death like John's where the Apostle John was first plunged, unhurt, into boiling oil, and thence remitted to his island-exile!" (Tertullian, *The Prescription Against Heretics*, Chapter 36, 14-16 [200 A.D.])

[13] Fr. William G. Most, *Catholic Apologetics Today* (Rockford, IL: Tan Books and Publishers, 1986), p.57.

[14] *Ibid.* Here, Most is echoing observations once made by St. Augustine.

[15] Jose Orlandis: *A Short History of the Catholic Church* (Dublin: Four Courts Press 1993) p. 51.

[16] The hospital extension was located on Edgecomb Ave. around 164th Street.

[17] A 1925 Church-approved miracle attributed to Mother Cabrini's intercession was the cure of a young nun known as Sister Delfina Graziola in Seattle. The dying nun had already received Last Rites, and the children had already been practicing for her requiem (funeral) Mass, when Mother Cabrini appeared to the nun in a dream and told her she was "needed for more work." The following day, the nun's health was fully restored. She lived to the age of 76. Today, Mother Cabrini's body is behind glass at a chapel in the Washington Heights section of northern Manhattan on a property overlooking the Hudson River. The property had once been purchased by Mother Cabrini to build a boarding school for girls. I was surprised to learn recently that the official medical and other documentation for the priest's miraculous cure are preserved on the campus of Cabrini College in Radnor, Pa., a college where I had taught Spanish courses for nine years. Mother Cabrini, who became a U.S. citizen in 1909 in Seattle, was the first American saint to be canonized by the Church. She is not to be confused with St. Elizabeth Ann Seton (1774-1821), who was the first *American-born* saint when she was canonized in 1975. St. Elizabeth Ann Seton was instrumental in the launching of the first Catholic girls' school in the United States.

Special thanks to Sister Mary Louise Sullivan, MSC, Ph.D., former president of Cabrini College, who graciously allowed me to look at the Vatican documentation related to the Peter Smith miracle.

[18] *The Catholic Encyclopedia*, online edition. Robert Appleton Co., 1907.www.newadvent.org/cathen/07790a.htm.

[19] The Church teaches the Old and New Testaments "are sacred and canonical because written under the inspiration of the Holy Spirit, they have God as their author and have been handed on as such to the Church herself. In composing the sacred books, God chose men and while employed by Him they made use of their powers and abilities, so that with Him acting in them and through them, they, as true authors, consigned to writing everything and only those things which He wanted." (Second Vatican Council, Dogmatic Constitution on Divine Revelation, *Dei Verbum*, Chap. 3, #11, Nov. 18, 1965) www.vatican.va/archive/hist_councils/ii_vatican_council/documents/vat-ii_const_19651118_dei-verbum_en.html.

[20] To be clear, it is Christ's Sacrifice that saved, or redeemed, us. Baptism has a saving role in that it washes away our sin and applies us to Christ's saving work.

[21] Catholic apologist Jimmy Akin writes: "The canon of Scripture, Old and New Testament, was finally settled at the Council of Rome in 382, under the authority of Pope Damasus I . . . The same canon was affirmed at the Council of Hippo in 393 and at the Council of Carthage in 397. In 405 Pope Innocent I reaffirmed the canon in a letter to Bishop Exuperius of Toulouse. Another council at Carthage, this one in the year 419, reaffirmed the canon of its predecessors and asked Pope Boniface to 'confirm this canon, for these are the things which we have received from our fathers to be read in church.' All of these canons were identical to the modern Catholic Bible, and all of them included the deuterocanonical." (Jimmy Akin, "Defending the Deuterocanonicals," www.ewtn.com/library/ANSWERS/DEUTEROS.HTM).

[22] Although this canon was universally accepted since the fourth century, the Catholic Church did not solemnly define the canon until 1546 at the Council of Trent. The pronouncement was a response to the Reformers, who were subtracting from the contents of Scripture.

[23] Printed in 1450s, the first Gutenberg Bible was, of course, a Catholic Bible, in that it contained the Deuterocanonical books of the Old Testament. In the 1500s, Reformer Martin Luther, who was not particularly happy with Catholic doctrines taught by these books (for example, the book of Maccabees encouraged prayer for the dead), relegated the seven books to an appendix in the Bible. That is how the Protestant Old Testament remained

for centuries. In the early 1800s, the Deuterocanonical books were completely removed from most Protestant Bibles when the British and Foreign Bible Society stopped printing them. Protestants now call these omitted books the "Apocrypha."

[24] J.N.D. Kelly, *Early Christian Doctrines* (San Francisco, CA: Harper & Row, 1978) p.440.

[25] Fr. Frank Chacon and Jim Burnham, *Beginning Apologetics 3: How to Explain and Defend the Real Presence of Christ in the Eucharist* (Farmington, NM: San Juan Catholic Seminars, 1999) p. 23.

[26] St. Alphonsus Liguori. *The Holy Eucharist* (New York: Alba House, 1994) edited and abridged by Msgr. Charles Dollen, p.7.

[27] Jason Evert, "Is the Mass a Sacrifice?" *This Rock*, Sept. 2001.

[28] Scott Hahn. *The Lamb's Supper: The Mass As Heaven on Earth* (New York: Doubleday, 1999), p. 9.

[29] Hahn, p. 10.

[30] J.N.D. Kelly, *Early Christian Doctrines* (San Francisco, CA: Harper & Rowe, 1978) p.447.

[31] Mike Aquilina, *The Mass of the Early Christians* (Huntington, IN: Our Sunday Visitor, 2001) p. 21.

[32] Pope John Paul II, Aug. 15, 1993, speech in Denver.

[33] "Confirmation," *Catholic Encyclopedia, The*. New York, NY: Robert Appleton Company, 1907.

[34] Pope John Paul II, General Audience of July 21, 1999, as quoted *in L'Osservatore Romano* (English ed., July 28, 1999.

[35] Rev. William G. Most, *Catholic Apologetics Today*, (Rockford, IL.: Tan Books and Publishers, 1986) p. 159. . . .comment on St. Thomas comes from St. Thomas, *Summa,* Suppla. 92.1

[36] The *Summa Theologica* of St. Thomas Aquinas Second and Revised Edition, 1920, Literally translated by Fathers of the English Dominican Province, Online Edition Copyright © 2003 by Kevin Knight.

[37] Council of Trent, Canon 1.

[38] The old *Catholic Encyclopedia* defines justification as "the transforming of the sinner from the state of unrighteousness to the state of holiness and sonship of God" and adds that justification is "the work of God alone."

[39] "A standard Protestant reference work on Scripture, the *Interpreter's Dictionary of the Bible*, Supplement Volume, tells us "Paul uses *pistis/pisteuein* [Greek words for faith and believe] to mean, above all, belief in the Christ *kerygma* [proclamation or preaching], knowledge, obedience, trust in the Lord Jesus. Note the word obedience. The Interpreter's Dictionary admits St. Paul includes it in an important place in his idea of faith." Rev. William

G. Most, *Catholic Apologetics Today* (Rockford, IL: Tan Books and Publishers, 1986) p. 108-109.

[40] Most, p. 108-109.

[41] Bard Thompson, *Humanists and Reformers: A History of the Renaissance and Reformation* (Grand Rapids, MI: William B. Eerdmans Publishing Co., 1996], pp. 403-404.

[42] Here, Pope John Paul II quotes the Second Vatican Council.

[43] Fr. Albert J. Hebert, S.M. *Raised from the Dead: True Stories of 400 Resurrection Miracles.* (Rockford IL.: Tan Books, 1986) p. 99.

[44] Hebert, p. 99.

[45] Hebert, p. 100.

[46] *Catholic Encyclopedia.*

[47] C. S. Lewis, *Letters To Malcolm: Chiefly on Prayer*, chapter 20, paragraphs 7-10, pages 108-109.

[48] For some fundamentalist and Protestant denominations, the "Rapture" does not refer to this gathering on the Last Day, but rather to an event in end times which entails the true Christians being silently taken up from the Earth before a seven-year period of Tribulation, during which the remaining unbelievers have the chance to repent. The Catholic Church rejects this notion, widely publicized in recent years by the *Left Behind* series of books, which have sold more than 60 million copies. Books that clarify the Catholic position on End Times include *Will Catholics Be Left Behind?* by Carl E. Olsen and *The Rapture Trap* by Paul Thigpen.

[49] Even though the Church would regard such visions as valid and divinely sent, the Church would add that such visions have limitations, as the supernatural world contains realities that human beings on Earth do not yet have the power to perceive with their existing senses. Thus, although it could be said that the souls of the children were touched by something real, we cannot view the children's vision simply as the equivalent of a videotape capturing the full reality of Hell. With interior visions, "we do not see the pure object, but it comes to us through the filter of our senses, which carry out a work of translation," according to *The Message of Fátima* by the Congregation for the Doctrine of the Faith. The document also states that such interior visions involve "true" objects, "which touch the soul even if these 'objects' do not belong to our habitual sensory world." (*The Message of Fátima*, CDF, July 6, 2000) p. 122.

[50] "Pope defends rights of persons in 'vegetative' state, questions term 'vegetative'" (Catholic News Agency, March 22, 2004) (www.catholic-newsagency.com/new.php?n=827).

[51] Nat Hentoff, "Terri Schiavo: Judicial Murder" (*The Village Voice*, March 29, 2005).

[52] Fr. Frank Chacon and Jim Burnham, *Beginning Apologetics #5: How to Answer Tough Moral Questions* (Farmington, NM.: San Juan Catholic Seminars, 2000) p. 7.

[53] This paragraph is based on John T. Noonan, Jr, *Contraception: A History of Its Treatment by the Catholic Theologians and Canonists* (Cambridge: Cambridge University Press, 1966) pp. 9-11, as mentioned in Fr. Frank Chacon and Jim Burnham: *Beginning Apologetics 5: How to Answer Tough Moral Questions* (Farmington, N.M.: San Juan Catholic Seminars, 200) p.23.

[54] Christopher West, *Theology of the Body for Beginners* (West Chester, PA: Ascension Press, 2004) p. 97.

[55] Archbishop Renato Martino, *Address to the U.N. International Convention Against the Reproductive Cloning of Human Beings,* Nov. 19, 2001.

[56] Rev. Tadeusz Pacholczyk, Ph.D., testimony at the Hearing on Ban on Human Cloning, Wisconsin State Assembly, Public Health Committee, May 20, 2003.

[57] The one out of two figure comes from a report by the University of North Carolina (named below), which derived the statistic from the Center of Disease Control and Prevention's STD prevalence estimates (~14 million) in the US sexually active youth population (~25-27 million). Cates, JR, Herndon, NL, Schulz, SL, & Darroch, JE (2004). *Our Voices, Our Lives, Our Futures: Youth and Sexually Transmitted Diseases.* Chapel Hill, NC: School of Journalism and Mass Communication, University of North Carolina at Chapel Hill.

[58] According to a study done by the John Jay College of Criminal Justice in New York, 81 percent of the victims of abusive priests between 1950 and 2002 in the United States were male. Most of the abused victims had reached puberty.

[59] Thomas E. Woods, Jr., *How the Catholic Church Built Western Civilization* (Washington, DC: Regnery Publishing, 2005), p. 112.

[60] Woods, p. 47.

[61] John Gerard, "Galileo Galilei," *(The Catholic Encyclopedia, Volume VI,* Copyright © 1909 by Robert Appleton Company; Online Edition Copyright © 2003 by Kevin Knight; Nihil Obstat, Sept. 1, 1909. Remy Lafort, Censor Imprimatur. +John M. Farley, Archbishop of New York). www.newadvent.org/cathen/06342b.htm

[62] Rizzi's comments were derived from a ZENIT International News Agency interview with Rizzi that was published Sept. 17, 2003 at www.zenit.org/english/visualizza.phtml?sid=41084.

[63] G.K. Chesterton, *The Catholic Church and Conversion* (New York: MacMillan Co., 1926) (www.dur.ac.uk/martin.ward/gkc/books/conversion.txt).

[64] Chesterton.

[65] St. Francis de Sales, *The Catholic Controversy* (Rockford, IL: TAN Books), p. 329.

[66] *The Catholic Church and Conversion.* New York: MacMillan Co. 1926. (www.dur.ac.uk/martin.ward/gkc/books/conversion.txt)

[67] Chesterton.

[68] Dom Hubert van Zeller, *Suffering: The Catholic Answer; The Cross of Christ and Its Meaning For You* (Manchester, N.H.: Sophia Institute Press, 2002) p. 18.

[69] The Barna Group, a Christian research group in Ventura, Calif.

[70] *World Christian Encyclopedia*, Oxford University Press, 2001.

[71] "Most interesting of all, perhaps, is the realization that his burial chamber in the Wittenberg church, on whose door he had posted his 95 Theses, was adorned with the 1521 Peter Vischer sculpture of the Coronation of the Virgin, with the inscription containing these lines: *Ad summum Regina thronum defertur in altum: Angelicis praelata choris, cui festus et ipse Filius occurrens Matrem super aethera ponit.* Rev. Peter Stravinskas, "The Place of Mary in Classical Fundamentalism," *Faith & Reason*, Summer 1994, p. 8.

[72] Pope Pius XII gave Mary the designation of patroness of the Americas in 1946. In 1961 Pope John XXIII called her Mother of the Americas.

[73] Oct 12 is the feast of Our Lady of the Pillar in Spain.

[74] www.ewtn.com The web site of the Eternal World Television Network.

[75] www.ewtn.com.

[76] (Source: the above account can be found at www.ewtn.com and www.Fátima.org The Fátima web site tell us that Professor Almeida Garrett's full account may be found in *Novos Documentos de Fátima* (Loyala editions, San Paulo, 1984).

[77] The Bosom of Abraham, also known as the "Limbo of the Fathers," was the place where the souls of the righteous dead from Old Testament times were kept in waiting before Jesus ascended into Heaven, opening the gates once and for all. The Gospel of Luke tells the story of the rich man who dressed in fine linen and ate sumptuously each day went to Hell, but

Lazarus, a poor man who was covered with sores, "was carried away by angels to the bosom of Abraham." The *Catholic Encyclopedia* states: "According to Jewish conceptions of that day, the souls of the dead were gathered into a general tarrying-place: the *Sheol* of Old Testament literature, and the *Hades* of New Testament writings (cf. Lk. 16, 22 in the Gr. 16:23). A local discrimination, however, existed among them, according to their deeds during their mortal life. In the unseen world of the dead the souls of the righteous occupied an abode or compartment of their own which was distinctly separated by a wall or a chasm from the abode or compartment to which the souls of the wicked were consigned. The latter was a place of torments usually spoken of as Gehenna (cf. Mt. 5:29, 30: 18:9; Mk. 9:42, Latin Vulgate) — the other, a place of bliss and security known under the names of "Paradise" (cf. Lk. 28:43) and "the Bosom of Abraham" (Lk.16:22-23). And it is in harmony with these Jewish conceptions that Our Lord pictured the terrible fate of the selfish rich man and, on the contrary, the glorious reward of the patient Lazarus. In the next life, Dives found himself in *Gehenna*, condemned to the most excruciating torments, whereas Lazarus was carried by the angels in the "Bosom of Abraham," where the righteous dead shared in the repose and felicity of Abraham "the father of the faithful." (*Catholic Encyclopedia*, "The Bosom of Abraham").

[78] Fr. Christopher Rengers, O.F.M. Cap., *The 33 Doctors of the Church* (Rockford, IL.: TAN Books 2000) p.97.

[79] Rengers, p.97.

[80] Martin Luther, *Personal {"Little"} Prayer Book*, 1522) quote from Dave Armstrong, "Martin Luther's Devotion to Mary," *Coming Home Journal*, Zanesville, OH.

[81] Martin Luther, *On the Day of the Conception of the Mother of God*, 1527.

[82] The phrase "faith alone" (or faith "only") only appears once in the Bible. According to James 2:24, ". . . a man is justified by works and *not* by faith alone." Many Protestants consider Luther's doctrine of "justification by faith alone" one of the "great discoveries" of the Protestant Reformation, and further regard Luther as having reclaimed Gospel truth for Christians. Despite the fact that Luther's doctrine of "faith alone" (as defined by Luther) contradicted all teaching from the early Church, Luther declared this doctrine was the article on which the Church "stands or falls." Luther based his teachings on "Scripture Alone," yet at the same time questioned whether certain books of the Bible were inspired Scripture or not. He took his four least favorite New Testament books – Revelation, James, Jude, and Hebrews – and demoted them to an appendix in the Bible. Luther declared St. Paul's letter

to the Romans to be "the purest gospel." Referring to the Book of Revelation, Luther wrote, "I feel an aversion to it" and "there are many things objectionable in this book" (*Sammtliche Werke*, 63, pp. 169-170, as quoted in *The Facts About Luther,* Msgr. Patrick F. O'Hare, Rockford, IL: TAN Books, 1987, p. 203). In prefaces to New Testament books, Luther called the Epistle of James in the New Testament "an epistle of straw" compared to other books, and wrote that the author of James "mangles the Scriptures and thereby opposes Paul and all Scripture." Regarding the Book of Revelation, Luther wrote in 1522 that he could "nohow detect that the Holy Spirit produced it." Some of the harsher statements contained in Luther's 1522 prefaces to New Testament books were omitted in later prefaces. But it is evident that Luther had been formulating teachings, ostensibly from the Bible alone, while somewhat undecided as to which books counted as inspired Scripture.

[83] Norman L. Geisler and Ralph E. MacKenzie. *Roman Catholics and Evangelicals: Agreements and Differences.* (Grand Rapids, MI: Baker Books, 1995) pp. 178-180.

[84] Stephen K. Ray, *Upon This Rock* (San Francisco, CA: Ignatius Press, 1999) p. 158.

[85] Patrick O'Hare, *The Facts About Luther* (Rockford, IL: TAN Books, 1987) p. 356.

[86] Adherents to faith-alone theory object to the Catholic view of justification on the basis that it requires a person's cooperation with God's grace, which they say is impossible. Catholics would answer that human cooperation is not independent of God's grace, but rather, is possible only because of God's awesome gift of grace. Once we are in grace, we truly participate in the life of God as "partakers of the divine nature" (2 Pet. 1:4).

[87] O'Hare, p.201, citing *Amic. Discussion*, I, 127.

[88] O'Hare, p. 122., citing *Wittenberg*, VI, 160.

[89] Hilaire Belloc, *How the Reformation Happened* (Rockford, IL.:Tan Books, 1992) p. 81.

[90] The Westminster Confession states: "Those of mankind that are predestinated unto life, God, before the foundation of the world was laid, according to His eternal and immutable purpose, and the secret counsel and good pleasure of His will, hath chosen, in Christ, unto everlasting glory, out of His mere free grace and love, without any foresight of faith, or good works, or perseverance in either of them, or any other thing in the creature, as conditions, or causes moving Him thereunto: and all to the praise of His glorious grace" (*Westminster Confession of Faith* 3, 5).

[91] My now-retired parish priest, Monsignor James Meehan, offered this metaphor for the two views of predestination: a guy on a motorcycle speeds faster and faster down a straightaway that has a brick wall at the end, the brick wall being Hell. A Catholic would say that God knew from the beginning of time that the guy would crash into the wall, and offered to him the grace he could have used to reject the wall, but did not stop him. A Calvinist would say that God steered him into the wall, i.e. God created the guy to crash into the wall.

[92] For a thorough treatment of the Calvinist and Catholic views of justification, read Jimmy Akin's book, *Salvation Controversy,* and the *Catholic Encyclopedia* article "Calvinism" (www.newadvent.org/cathen/03198a.htm).

[93] John Calvin. *The Institutes of the Christian Religion.* ed. John T. McNeill, trans. F.L. Battles. (Philadelphia: Westminster Press, 4th printing, 1967) 3, xxiii, 11, p. 957.

[94] Luther wrote: "If the world lasts for a long time, it will again be necessary, on account of the many interpretations which are now given to the Scriptures, to receive the decrees of the councils, and take refuge in them, in order to preserve the unity of the faith" (Martin Luther, *Epistle to Zwingli*).

[95] Karl Keating, *Catholicism and Fundamentalism* (San Francisco, CA: Ignatius Press, 1988) p.13, 16.

[96] Pope John Paul II's encyclical *Ut unum sint*, 1995.

[97] Fr. Thomas Richstatter, O.F.M., S.T.D., "Eucharist: Sign and Source of Christian Unity" (www.americancatholic.org/Newsletters/CU/ac0500.asp).

Our Sunday Visitor ...
Your Source for Discovering the Riches of the Catholic Faith

Our Sunday Visitor has an extensive line of materials for young children, teens, and adults. Our books, Bibles, pamphlets, CD-ROMs, audios, and videos are available in bookstores worldwide.

To receive a FREE full-line catalog or for more information, call **Our Sunday Visitor** at **1-800-348-2440, ext. 3**. Or write **Our Sunday Visitor** / 200 Noll Plaza / Huntington, IN 46750.

Please send me ___ A catalog
Please send me materials on:
___ Apologetics and catechetics
___ Prayer books
___ The family
___ Reference works
___ Heritage and the saints
___ The parish

Name _____
Address _____ Apt._____
City _____ State _____ Zip_____
Telephone ( ) _____

A63BBBBP

Please send a friend ___ A catalog
Please send a friend materials on:
___ Apologetics and catechetics
___ Prayer books
___ The family
___ Reference works
___ Heritage and the saints
___ The parish

Name _____
Address _____ Apt._____
City _____ State _____ Zip_____
Telephone ( ) _____

A63BBBBP

OurSundayVisitor

200 Noll Plaza, Huntington, IN 46750
Toll free: **1-800-348-2440**
Website: www.osv.com